A World of Images

Stanton MacDonald-Wright, *Conception Synchromy*, 1914. Oil on canvas, 36 $\frac{1}{4}$" x 30 $\frac{1}{4}$" (93 x 77 cm). Hirshhorn Museum and Sculpture Garden, Washington, DC.

**A
Discover
Art
Book**

A World of Images

Laura H. Chapman

Davis Publications, Inc.   Worcester, Massachusetts

Managing Editor: Wyatt Wade
Production Editor: Nancy Dutting
Photo Acquisition: Victoria Hughes and
    Dawn Reddy
Graphic Design: Douglass Scott
Illustrator: Susan Christy-Pallo

Set in Minion and Frutiger types by
Mary Jane Walsh at WGBH Design

Printed in the United States of America
ISBN: 0-87192-230-4
SE 7

10 9 8 7 6

Front cover:
Alfred Pellan, *Mascarade*,
1942. Oil on canvas,
51" x 64" (130 x 162 cm).
Museé d'art contemporain
de Montreal.

Back cover:
Faith Ringgold, *Mrs. Jones
and Family*, 1973. Sewn
fabric and embroidery.
Courtesy Bernice Steinbaum
Gallery, New York City.

Contents

Introduction

You don't have to be an artist to care about art.

When you doodle with a pencil, putting ideas or feelings on paper, you are creating art. When you see a sculpture in a gallery or a painting by a classmate, you are looking at and thinking about art. When you watch the purple clouds of a sunset creep across the sky, you are noticing the beauty that can be found all around you.

This book will help you learn to create your own art and express your ideas visually. It will help you understand artists of the past and present. You will learn to study artworks the way art experts do. Whether you plan to become an artist or not, this book will show you how to look for beauty and design in everyday life.

This book will also help you find out about careers in art and places in your community to learn about and enjoy art.

Photograph by Barbara Caldwell.

Photograph by Barbara Caldwell.

Temple Guardian, ca. 1300 (detail). Kamakura period. Wood, fully painted. Toshogu Shrine, Kyoto, Japan.

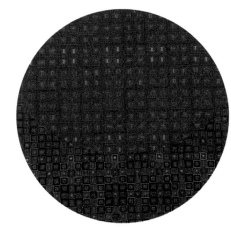

Toshinobu Onosato, *Painting A,* 1961-1962 (detail). Oil on canvas, 76 1/4" x 51 3/8" (194 x 130 cm). Solomon R. Guggenheim Museum, New York. Photograph by David Heald.

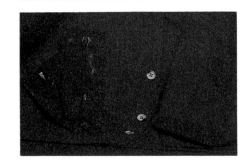

Photograph by Verna E. Beach.

Photograph by Verna E. Beach.

Creating Art

Could a lump of clay become a space alien? Could you turn angry words into a painting with dark, streaky brushstrokes?

When you create art, you express your feelings and ideas in ways people can see. You use your eyes, your mind, your imagination. You think about and shape materials.

Creating art begins with an idea. As you learn about design, you learn to express your ideas through the "language" of lines, colors, shapes and textures. With practice, you can learn to use art materials to show what you think and feel. That is what artists do.

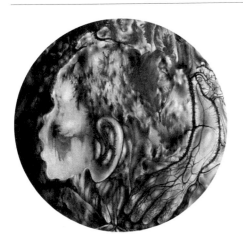

Pavel Tchelitchew, *Hide-and-Seek*, 1940-1942 (detail). Oil on canvas, 6' 6 1/2" x 7' 3/4" (199 x 215 cm). Collection, The Museum of Modern Art. Mrs. Simon R. Guggenheim Fund.

Looking at Art

People create art so other people will look at it and appreciate it. Learning about art will help you appreciate it more.

Looking at artworks can be as enjoyable and as interesting as creating artworks. Many photographs of artworks are in this book. It is best to see original artworks, but these photographs will help you appreciate many kinds of art. They will also help you learn about the importance of art in history, in your everyday life and in the lives of people in other cultures.

Living with Art

Look for beauty in nature and in things people make. Look for buildings and products that you think are interesting or well-designed. Learn about the variety of art forms and careers in art. If you do these things, art will be part of your life.

Sa'di, Bustan *(Garden of Perfume): Darius and the Herdsmen.* This lively Persian painting is a miniature. A miniature painting is very small. How large is the original painting in relation to the size you see here? Ink-colors and gold on paper, 11 ½" x 7 ¾" (29 x 20 cm). The Metropolitan Museum of Art. Frederick C. Hewitt Fund.

Chapter 1

Basic Art Concepts

Chapter Vocabulary

functions of art
varieties of art forms
media for art
subjects and themes in art
design elements and principles
styles of art

Sa'di, Bustan *(Garden of Perfume): Darius and the Herdsmen* (detail).

Sa'di, Bustan *(Garden of Perfume): Darius and the Herdsmen* (detail).

If you ask your friends to say what art is, they will probably give different answers. Throughout history, art has meant different things to different people. That is true today, too.

For example, most art museums display beautiful objects from different cultures. We call these objects *works of art.* Some of the objects may not have been thought of as art by the people who made them. In fact, many cultures have no word for art. People in these cultures do create pottery, jewelry, masks and other carefully made objects, but these things have many purposes and meanings in their lives.

As you can see, the question "What is art?" can be answered in different ways. To answer this question, you must learn how experts think about art. You must understand the basic art concepts, or ideas, they use. Art concepts tell you how experts think about art, what they observe, and why.

After you have completed this chapter you will be better able to:

Creating Art	• understand the purposes of art and kinds of art people have created.
Art History	• use your knowledge of basic art concepts to study art history.
Aesthetics	• recognize important features of art.
Art Criticism	• use your knowledge of basic art concepts to describe, analyze and interpret art.

Functions of Art

People create art for four main reasons, or *functions:* practical, social-cultural, personal and educational.

Practical Functions

Much of the world's art has been created to help meet day-to-day needs. For example, the art of architecture came from the need for shelter.

People also need useful things such as clothing, containers for food, tools and utensils. Years ago these needs were met by artists who made practical and beautiful objects by hand. These objects were often used in ceremonies. Ceremonial objects are practical, but they also have other meanings for the people who make them.

In our industrial society, only a few people make objects by hand. Most people buy ready-made clothing, utensils and the like. But most factory-made things such as kitchenware, appliances and automobiles are first planned by designers – people trained in art.

Think about the practical functions of art in your life. How are they different from other times and cultures? What products are skillfully made today? What things also add beauty or special meaning to everyday life? Why?

Cultural Functions

Much of what we know about other cultures and times comes from artwork.

Architecture, painting and other kinds of art have been created to honor leaders and to teach religious beliefs. People have created art to celebrate their victories and remember their defeats.

In our own culture today, many artworks are created for social, civic, political and economic purposes. One example is sculpture honoring leaders. Can you think of other examples?

Temple Guardian, ca. 1300, Kamakura period, Japan. Art is one way people express their cultural traditions and beliefs. Wood, fully painted. Toshogu Shrine, Kyoto.

David Melior, *Chinese Black Cutlery Range.* Art includes the design of many items you use every day. Photograph by Phillipe Garner.

Daniel Chester French, *Lincoln.* Art can be an important record of people and events in history. Courtesy of The Library of Congress.

Personal Functions

The personal function of art – using art to express a person's thoughts and feelings – is also important.

This purpose of art goes back to a period called the Renaissance in Europe (1400-1600), a time when individual achievement in art was truly honored. The Renaissance gave us the idea that art should be original and a unique expression of the artist.

Art as a form of personal expression is still respected in our culture. Artists are free to create art based on their ideas and experiences. This freedom of expression is one of the benefits of living in a democracy. Why is freedom of expression important in a democracy?

Educational Functions

When you learn about art, you are filling an important function in human history: Knowledge about art is being passed along to you.

Every original work of art you see in a museum is part of your art heritage. All the art that you see and discuss helps you understand how and why art is created. What would happen to the heritage of art if there were no art museums or other places to see original art?

With every studio activity you complete, you try out your own skills in creating art. What would happen to artistic activity if you and other young people did not learn to appreciate and create art?

Patricia Renick at work in her studio. Art is an important way for people to express their individuality. Photograph courtesy of the artist.

Jean Dubuffet, *Le Vociferant.* Art is a subject for study and a heritage for each new generation. Photograph copyright Patricia Layman Bazelon.

Marsden Hartley, *The Aero*, ca. 1914. Artists approach painting in many ways. This artist's work is in a style known as Abstract Expressionism. Canvas, 39 ¹/₂" x 32" (100 x 81 cm). Courtesy of the National Gallery of Art, Washington, DC. Andrew W. Mellon Fund.

Pablo Picasso, *Man with a Hat*, 1912. Pablo Picasso and Georges Braque first explored the possibilities of collage. Charcoal ink-pasted paper. 24 ¹/₂" x 18" (63 x 48 cm). Collection, The Museum of Modern Art, New York. Purchase.

Varieties of Art Forms

Art comes in many forms. You already know some of them. Read about the art forms listed here. Have you seen examples of each type?

Drawing and Painting

Drawings and paintings are two-dimensional images. That means that they have height and width but they are flat. Artists draw and paint on different surfaces, such as paper, wood and canvas.

Pencil, crayon, charcoal, chalk, pen and ink are often used for drawing. Paintings can be created with types of paint such as oil, tempera, watercolor and encaustic (colored wax). A *fresco* is a tempera painting created on a fresh plaster surface.

Collage

Collage is a French word for pasted paper. In a collage, flat materials such as paper or fabrics are pasted on a background. Collages are sometimes combined with drawing and painting too. A *montage* is a collage made from photographs. Mosaics, a related art form, are made from colored glass, stones and the like. What kinds of drawings, paintings, and collages have you made?

Jomo-o Inagaki, *Pumpkins*, 1949. How does the process of creating this woodcut print differ from the process used to create the printed stamp below? Color woodcut, 18" x 23 ⁷/₈" (46 x 61 cm). Collection, The Museum of Modern Art, New York. Gift of Mrs. John D. Rockefeller III.

Margaret Bourke-White, *Contour Plowing*. Photography is one of the newer forms of art in the long, long history of art. Photograph. LIFE Magazine copyright 1954 Time Inc.

Printmaking and Graphic Design

In these art forms, an image is created so it can be printed many times. In Chapter 10 you can learn about ways to make prints. Perhaps you have created relief prints using a carved block of wood or linoleum. Have you made stencil prints using cutout paper? What other kinds of printing have you tried?

Graphic designers prepare the artwork for mass-produced posters, signs, advertisements and other images. Mechanical printing processes are used to reproduce the designs. *Graphic* is a general term for many ways to picture and record ideas. What examples of graphic design do you see around you right now?

Photography, Film, Television

Many artists today use cameras to create photographs, motion pictures and television programs. These are all fairly new art forms in history. The "art" in photographing or filming comes from the artist's careful choice of images and how he or she puts those images together.

Motion pictures and television programs are created by a team of artists in music, drama, theater and the visual arts. Motion pictures and television programs are often called time and motion arts. Have you ever created art using a still camera or a video or motion picture camera?

Architecture and Related Fields

Architects are artists who plan the spaces in which we live, work and play. They consider the function of a building, its beauty and the way the space inside relates to the space outside. Interior designers plan the arrangement of furniture and other details for the inside spaces.

Environmental designers plan the relationship of natural spaces and the spaces for the buildings and streets in a community. Today, there are specialists who plan landscapes as well as whole communities. What might happen if architects were no longer trained to plan buildings and communities?

Sculpture

Sculpture is a three-dimensional art form, which means that it has height, width and depth. A *relief sculpture* has surfaces raised up from a flat background. A *statue* is a freestanding sculpture that sits on a base and can be seen from all sides. A *mobile* is a sculpture with moving parts.

In a carved sculpture, the artist cuts away wood, stone or other solid material. Materials can also be constructed or assembled to create a sculpture.

In a cast sculpture, the artist first creates a model and then makes a mold of the model. A liquid such as molten metal is poured into the mold. When the liquid turns hard, the mold is removed. The final sculpture is similar to the model. Where have you seen sculpture in your community? Why was it created? Have you created sculpture? What kinds?

Philip Johnson and John Burgee, Penzoil Place, Houston, Texas, 1976. Architecture is one of the major art forms you encounter every day. Photograph by Richard W. Payne.

Elizabeth Catlett, *Mother with Child*, 1972. Sculpture is a three-dimensional art form. What does "three-dimensional" mean? Pecan wood. Museum of African Art, Los Angeles.

Crafts and Product Design

Crafts are called art when they are carefully designed and skillfully made by hand.

Among the many crafts are *ceramics* – clay objects fired in a kiln to make them hard – and *fiber arts* such as weaving, stitching and knotting. Other crafts are made from metal, glass and stained glass, paper, leather and wood.

People who design products plan things such as furniture, appliances, tools, containers and automobiles. Product designers care especially about the appearance of the object as well as what the things are used for. What are some of the main differences between handcrafted and mass-produced products?

Arts of Celebration

Many artworks are created as part of a ceremony or celebration such as an anniversary, birthday or holiday. Examples include masks, clothing, hair styling and face makeup. Other examples are kites, banners, flags and trophies.

Items like these can become art when they are created, chosen or arranged to help make an event special. What is one of the most important ceremonies or celebrations you have attended? What visual forms helped make it a special event?

China, Sung dynasty, White jar with flowers in gray, 960-1280. Ceramic, 3 ½" (9 cm) high. The Metropolitan Museum of Art. Bequest of Robert West.

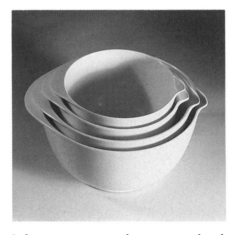

In how many ways are these mass-produced bowls different from the Chinese bowl? What similarities can you identify?

The image being created in sand is part of a healing ceremony of the Navaho people. Courtesy Department of Library Services. American Museum of Natural History. Neg. #2A3634. Photograph by Boltin.

Henry Moore, *Reclining Figure*, 1945. The material for this sculpture is bronze. The artist's technique reflects an interest in smooth forms. Bronze, 3 ¼" x 7 ⅞" x 3 ⅞" (8 x 20 x 8 cm). Hirshhorn Museum and Sculpture Garden, Smithsonian Institution. Gift of Joseph H. Hirshhorn, 1966.

Michael Erhart, *Young woman in the costume of the Burgundian court,* 1475-1480. What materials, forming process and techniques were used by this sculptor? Polychromed linden wood, 21" x 12" x 9" (53 x 30 x 22 cm). Courtesy Ulm Museum.

Media for Art

Every day, you use words to say what you think and feel. Your voice is a *medium* of expression. Dancers use body movements as a medium of expression. Musicians put together sounds for their medium of expression.

Visual artists use materials as media for expression. Their materials include paint, clay, wood and metal. The way an artist uses these materials is usually called a forming process. For example, wood can be given form by carving it or by putting pieces of wood together.

Many materials can also be shaped using special techniques. Wood can be carved with chisels, or saws or rough files called rasps.

Artists use materials, forming processes and techniques to express ideas visually. The artist's materials, processes and techniques are *media,* or means, for expression. What media for creating art do you enjoy using most? Why?

Heide Fashacht, *Pell Mell II*, 1985. Wood and India ink, 58 ⅝" x 20 ¼" x 50" (71 x 51 x 128 cm). Collection of the Columbus Museum of Art. Purchased with funds made available from the Awards in the Visual Arts program, 1986.

12

Patti Warashina Bauer, *Customized Car Kiln.* Ceramic with wood and leather base, 30" (76 cm) long. Courtesy of the artist and Foster/White Gallery.

Steve Geddes, *Rooster,* 1984. Imaginary creatures are the inspiration for many artworks. Carved, painted wood, 18" (46 cm). Courtesy of the artist.

Subjects and Themes in Art

Artists find subjects and themes for their work in everything they see and do. As you create and study art, you will discover many kinds of subjects, visual symbols and themes.

Subject Matter

Subject matter refers to things you can recognize in an artwork such as people, animals or clouds. Some familiar subjects in art are:

- people – groups, portraits, self-portraits
- the natural world – plants, animals, landscapes, seascapes
- the constructed world – cityscapes, streets, machinery
- still life – arrangements of objects that are not alive
- genre (say JAHN-rah) – everyday activities of people
- fantasy – imaginary places, events, objects
- history – people, events, political, military, social change
- religion – leaders, symbols, events
- literature – myths, legends, stories, parables

What other subjects for art can you name? What are some favorite subjects for your artwork?

Subject Matter in Your Own Art

If you find yourself saying "I don't know what to draw" or using a subject over and over in the same way, it is time to explore other subjects for art.

Keep a sketchbook. Make drawings that help you recall details, textures, colors and other qualities in things you see. Let your imagination play with combinations of ideas, strange creatures, fantastic landscapes.

Try drawing just the gestures of moving things you see, such as a gliding, swooping bird. Record the gestures without drawing the bird. Observe your world as artists do, noting colors, lines, shapes and other qualities. How could you use your sketches as ideas for artwork?

Emily Carr, *Reforestation*, 1936. Does this painting seem to be as perky as the one below? Is it as mysterious as the one by Tchelitchew? Why or why not? Do you see how the same basic subject can be interpreted in different ways? Oil on canvas, 43" x 26" (110 x 67 cm). The McMichael Canadian Collection. Anonymous donor.

Kason, *Birds in Bamboo Tree*. Complex artworks often have many "wordless messages." This means they can be interpreted in more than one way. Japanese, from an original woodblock print.

Symbols and Themes

In some works of art, the subject of the work is used as a *symbol* for a broader idea or theme.

A familiar symbol is the hourglass, which is often used to show passing time, growing older or human mortality – the idea that people live and die. Strong animals may be visual symbols for human strength. What are some common visual symbols for our nation? What other symbols can you think of?

A *theme* in art is a broad idea or feeling such as peace, love or sadness. Other examples are work, play or faith. Many themes are about human life: birth, the family, childhood, youth, old age, death, wisdom and dreams. Others focus on the beauty of nature. Themes like these are found in the art of many cultures.

Different artists in different cultures choose their own special subjects to express a theme. Suppose, for example, that every person in your class made drawings on the theme of work. The drawings from your class might show ideas about work that are very different from the ideas shown by students in Bolivia or in Tibet. Why might people in other cultures interpret a theme like work in different ways?

Cultural Meanings of Subjects

The meaning of a subject, theme or symbol often says something about the culture the artwork is from.

For example, in Japan, the bamboo plant has many uses and special meanings. It has long been used to weave baskets, construct homes and make furniture. It can be shaped into weapons as well as tools for making art. When a Japanese artist shows bamboo in a painting, he or she may want you to think of its strength, beauty and many uses.

You can understand the meaning of subjects, symbols and themes in art by learning about the culture the art is from.

Personal Meanings of Subjects

Many artists create art about subjects such as the city, flowers or people. The artworks are not alike. They differ because each artist has unique experiences with the subject.

If you study a work carefully, you can often discover what the artist thinks and feels about the subject. It will show up in the design of the work, in the medium that was used and in other features.

In the same way, everyone in your class can create original artworks even if they choose the same subject. In art class, you will often be asked to create an original artwork of a subject such as a still life, portrait or landscape.

Your response to the subject should be unique. It should show how *you* see, feel or think about the subject or theme. Hundreds of other artists may have created art on the same subject or theme. Do you understand why your creative art should express what no other person has seen, felt or known in exactly the same way?

Absence of Subject Matter

Many people expect to find a familiar subject or theme in artworks. This is a bit like wanting all music to have words that we can understand.

But in many works of art, the artist is only interested in creating a design with lines, colors, shapes or forms. In some ways, appreciating these artworks is like appreciating music without words.

When paintings, sculptures and other artworks have no recognizable subject, they are called *nonobjective*. This means that no familiar subjects are shown. We respond just to the way the artwork is designed and made. You might imagine a gentle sweeping feeling when you look at long curving lines. You might sense the "quiet" mood of a work done in light pastel colors shaded together.

When you look at nonobjective or abstract artwork, make gestures or motions to show how the artist may have created the visual qualities. This will help you to discover the mood, feeling or expression.

Use this same approach when you look at useful or decorative art such as architecture, vases, furniture or fabric designs. In these art forms, there is often no obvious subject. Look around your room. What objects give you a feeling or idea just from the lines, colors and other visual elements?

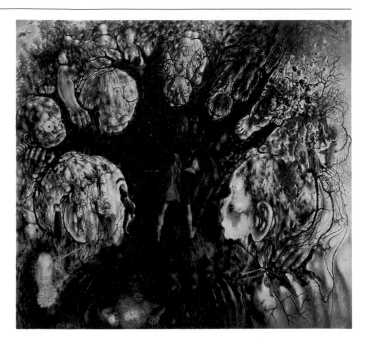

Pavel Tchelitchew, *Hide-and-Seek*, 1940-1942. Works of art can express thoughts and feelings through their design. Oil on canvas, 6' 6 ¹/₂" x 7' ³/₄" (199 x 215 cm). Collection, The Museum of Modern Art, New York. Mrs. Simon Guggenheim Fund.

Morris Louis, *Point of Tranquility*, 1958. Synthetic polymer oil on canvas, 102" x 135" (259 x 342 cm). Hirshhorn Museum and Sculpture Garden, Washington, DC.

Design in Art

An artist organizes lines, colors, shapes and other sensory qualities for you to experience. These qualities are often called *elements of design.* Artists carefully plan their use of these elements. *Principles of design* help us describe the plan that is used for the elements. In almost every art lesson, you will need to understand how elements and principles work together. They are reviewed here. Study Chapter 3 to learn more about them.

Elements of Design

The elements of design are qualities that we can learn to see, describe and create.

Lines are made by moving a point, such as when you draw with a pencil or pen. Lines may be three-dimensional too, like a wire or a rope.

The direction lines go and where they are placed can suggest actions, moods or space. Lines can be used to create shapes, textures, patterns and forms. Artists plan their use of lines to express feelings and ideas. What kinds of lines do you see around you right now?

Stuart Davis, *Composition No. 5*, 1932. Thick even lines unify this work. Brush and ink, 22" x 29 3/8" (56 x 74 cm). Collection, The Museum of Modern Art, New York. Gift of Abby Aldrich Rockefeller.

Shapes are flat areas and surfaces. They may have "hard" edges or "soft" fuzzy outlines. Shapes can be shown by areas of color or texture. Even a group of dots in a circle can make an implied shape.

Organic shapes are shapes that look like things in nature, such as fish or tree limbs. *Geometric shapes* such as circles, squares and triangles are based on numbers and measurements. Artists call the shapes that you notice *positive shapes.* The background or part around the positive shape is called *negative space.* What shapes do you see around you? Describe them in several ways.

Nell Blaine, *Lester Leaps*, 1944. Irregular puzzle-like shapes dominate this painting. Oil on canvas, 24" x 13" (61 x 33 cm). The Metropolitan Museum of Art, New York.

Forms are three-dimensional, with height, width and depth. Forms can be solid or have *voids* – open spaces or holes. Like shapes, forms may have straight or curved surfaces and edges. They can have organic or geometric qualities. What are the main shapes and forms in an automobile? In your shoe?

Nancy Graves, *Tarot*, 1984. Interesting lines and irregular shapes make up this lively sculpture. Bronze with polychrome and enamel. 88" x 49" x 20" (224 x 124 x 51 cm). Courtesy M. Knoedler and Co., New York.

Colors come in different hues. A hue is the name of a color, such as red. Hues differ in *intensity* (purity or brightness). Colors cans also be symbolic meaning (such as warm or cool), and *value* (the lightness or darkness of a color). Shading is a gradual shift from light to dark values. Contrast is a noticeable difference between light and dark. Choose an object in your room. Describe its color as fully as you can.

Toshinobu Onosato, *Painting A*, 1961-1962. Why do the colors in this work seem to push, pull and vibrate? Oil on canvas, 76 1/4" x 51 3/8" (194 x 130 cm). Solomon R. Guggenheim Museum, New York. Photograph by David Heald.

René Magritte, *The Thought Which Sees*, 1965. Textures of wood, clouds and other surfaces are an illusion in this drawing. Graphite, 15 3/4" x 11 5/8" (40 x 29 cm). Collection, The Museum of Modern Art, New York. Gift of Mr. and Mrs. Charles B. Benenson.

Textures are differences in the surfaces of a material – whether it feels rough, smooth, pebbly, prickly or slick. Artists can use different media to create textures and the *illusion* of textures in artworks. How might you create the illusion of cat's fur, bark or glass with a pencil?

Space is the feeling created by the way shapes or objects are placed, such as near or far away. Space is created by the way shapes or objects are placed.

In two-dimensional artwork, artists create the illusion of space in many ways. For example, they may overlap shapes. They may show objects smaller than normal to suggest they are far away.

In three-dimensional artwork, space is organized by the placement of positive shapes or solid forms. Artists plan the "air," or negative spaces, between and around the forms, too.

You can look at spaces from many points of view. For example, you can look at your school from different places and angles. You can study spaces inside and outside. Can you think of other ways to describe space?

Jane Sauer, *Implications*, 1985. Waxed linen, paint, knotted, 14" x 6" (36 x 15 cm) diameter; 8 1/2" x 5" (22 x 13 cm) diameter; 3 1/2" x 3 1/2" (9 x 9 cm) diameter. Courtesy of the artist.

Attributed to Li Ch'eng, *A Solitary Temple Amid Clearing Peaks* (Ch'ing-luan hsiao-ssu), Northern Sung Dynasty. A vast space with towering mountains is suggested by this artist's fine use of values and overlapping shapes. Hanging scroll. Ink and color on silk. 44" x 22" (112 x 56 cm). The Nelson-Atkins Museum of Art, Kansas City, Missouri. Nelson Fund.

Principles of Design

The principles of design are guides to think about – not strict rules – for planning artwork. The principles also help you analyze artworks. Artists use the principles of design to fit their ideas or purposes.

Pattern is a repeated arrangement of lines, colors, shapes or forms. When the elements of a pattern are repeated in a regular way, they are like a rhythmic beat.

Like patterns in music, patterns in art can have regular or irregular parts or be put together with gradual changes in color, shape and the like. Large patterned areas tend to unify a work, or hold it together. Smaller patterns in only a few areas tend to add interest. What patterns can you see in buildings? In fabrics? In a leaf?

Valerie Jaudon, *Yazoo*, 1975. The intricate pattern in this painting includes circular and straight bands of color. Oil on canvas, 72" x 72" (183 x 183 cm). The Aldrich Museum of Contemporary Art, Ridgefield, Connecticut.

Rhythm refers to the way an artist puts visual elements together to create a feeling of movement. Visual patterns can create rhythms. Rhythms can also be created by flowing lines or gradual changes in the spacing of shapes or colors.

Rhythms tend to unify an artwork, just as they do in music or dance. They lead us from one point to another in a planned way. What rhythms do you experience every day?

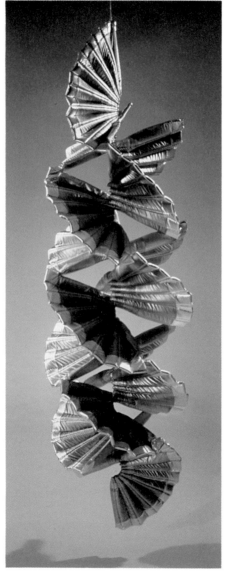

Priscilla K. Sage, *Triune Helix I*, 1984. Do you see the spiral-like rhythm in the overall form? Can you also see an alternating (up-down) rhythm? Where? Mylar fabric dyed, 6' x 2' (183 x 61 cm). Courtesy Artworks, Ames, Iowa.

Balance refers to the way things are arranged. Formal or *symmetrical* balance is often used to suggest a feeling of stability or quietness. *Radial* balance is a type of formal balance with parts leading away from or toward a center point.

Informal or *asymmetrical* balance is often used to express a feeling of motion or action. How might an artist arrange visual elements to create a feeling that everything is out of balance and in motion?

Mask (spirit of brown bear), Tlingit, Alaska, 1875. Wood, 7" x 11 ¹/₂" (18 x 29 cm). Museum of the American Indian.

Seneca Iroquois, *Clown Mask.* What forms of balance do you see in this mask and the Tlingit mask? Unpainted pine, string, 6 ¹/₂" x 9 ¹/₂" (17 x 24 cm). The Denver Art Museum.

Proportion refers to the sizes of things compared to each other. We usually judge proportions in relation to our own human size and proportions. Artists often make one part of an artwork bigger – or exaggerate its proportions – to show that it is important.

A *caricature* is an artwork that changes the normal proportions of a person to capture the unusual features of that person. Humor is often the aim in caricatures. Have you heard people refer to "ideal proportions?" What do they mean?

Amedeo Modigliani, *Head*, 1912. Are the proportions in this sculpture normal or exaggerated? Limestone, 25" (63 cm) high. Solomon R. Guggenheim Museum, New York. Photograph by David Heald.

Emphasis is achieved by planning a work so that some features are more dominant, or stronger, than others. People usually notice the dominant feature first. A bright patch of color in a painting with many dull colors may hold your attention. Can you think of other ways to achieve emphasis?

Troy Allen Gerth, *Waking the Witch*, 1989. How is emphasis achieved in this work? What has the artist emphasized? Mixed media, 36" x 24" (91 x 61 cm). Courtesy of the artist.

Unity and variety are qualities that most people appreciate in all parts of life, including artwork. Artists achieve unity in a work by using related or repeated elements, by creating a center of interest, or by setting up a path of movement that draws the eye along it. Variety is achieved by adding visual surprises. These may be unexpected contrasts, exaggerations, bright colors in a subdued area and the like.

By planning for unity and variety – the process of design – artists can express their ideas and help us respond to their work. Can you explain why unity and variety are qualities most people appreciate in art and in life?

Albert Gleizes, *Les Quatres Personnages Légendaires du Ciel-Aladin*, 1939-1940. Oil on canvas, 121 ⅝" 73 ⅜" (309 x 189 cm). Marion Koogler McNay Art Museum, San Antonio, Texas. Gift of Robert L. B. Tobin, 1973.

John Marin, *Lower Manhattan*, 1922. Watercolor and charcoal with paper cutout attached with thread on paper, 22" x 27" (55 x 68 cm). Collection, The Museum of Modern Art, New York. Acquired through the Lillie P. Bliss Bequest.

Charles Sheeler, *City Interior*, 1936. Oil on fiberboard, 22" x 27" (56 x 69 cm). Worcester Art Museum, Massachusetts.

Styles of Art

A style is a similarity you can see in a group of artworks. You can figure out an artist's *individual* style by looking for things that are the same in a group of his or her artworks.

Cultural or *historical* styles are identified by features that come from the art and culture of a certain time and place.

There are also four *general* style categories often used by art experts. These style terms help us remember that artists have different reasons for creating art. These general styles can be seen in artworks from very different times and cultures.

Expressionism

In expressionist works, the artist wants to show a mood or feeling. This aim is more important than trying to portray how something really looks.

The artist may exaggerate some details and leave out others. The artist may use intense colors, strong lines or unusual shapes. When you take time to look at expressionist art, you get a definite feeling about the subject or theme.

John Marin's painting has many of these style qualities. The buildings seem to be pulling upward. The train platform seems to rush through the city and cover the people below. His work captures the feeling of energy and movement in a big city. Analyze the work. In what other ways has the artist expressed action and a feeling of movement?

Realism

In realistic art, artists look at the world selectively, choosing the things they want to put in or leave out of their work. They want to show familiar subjects in a way that is fresh and memorable to us. They often set up a mood by the details they create. The design can also make an ordinary subject seem extraordinary.

Charles Sheeler's painting also has some of these stylistic qualities. Study the way color, light, shadow and detail work together. Sheeler used paint to make you feel that you are looking at a real scene. See if you can figure out why the scene seems so quiet and still. What might have been present that the artist did not put in the painting? How else can you tell that the artist was using a selective "eye" when he designed the painting?

Abstraction

Artists often create arrangements of lines, shapes and colors in ways that are just meant to be fascinating in their own right. *Abstract* means the artist has invented a new way to show common things or ideas. Experts often use the word *nonobjective* when there is no subject you can recognize in art.

Abstract artwork appeals to your mind and your senses. For example, most people see and feel that flowing curved lines are graceful. Jagged lines remind most people of sharp objects or sudden unexpected events like lightning. Do you see how lines, shapes and colors can refer to experiences like these?

Some of these qualities are present in Piet Mondrian's painting. The title refers to the end of World War II. Winning the war made people very excited. "Boogie-Woogie" is as fast, jazzy way of playing a piano. How has Mondrian shown excitement in his painting? Study the way the space is divided. Look for "jazzy" shifts in colors and sizes of shapes. What other interesting qualities do you see?

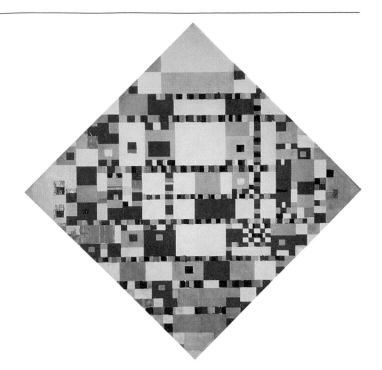

Piet Mondrian, *Victory Boogie Woogie*. Private Collection.

Fantasy

In fantasy art, artists put together familiar subjects or scenes in ways that may remind you of the strange images that come to you in dreams. The work is filled with details that don't seem to make sense, which make the scenes seem even more unreal. It would be impossible to find events in real life like the ones in these artworks.

Peter Blume's painting shows an eerie dreamlike landscape with some elements you can recognize. This work is about the dictatorship of Benito Mussolini in Italy during World War II.

Mussolini's portrait head pops up from a jack-in-the-box. He is shown as hating the Italian culture, especially ancient Rome – often called "the eternal city." Why might the artist have portrayed the dictator the way he did?

Peter Blume, *The Eternal City*, 1937. Oil on composition board. 34" x 47 ⅞" (86 x 122 cm). Collection. The Museum of Modern Art, New York. Mrs. Simon R. Guggenheim Fund.

Basic Concepts in Art

The following categories and terms have been illustrated and defined in this chapter. You may want to use this list to discuss art and to get ideas for your own artwork.

Functions of Art
Practical
Cultural
Personal
Educational

Art Forms
Drawing
Painting
Collage
Printmaking
Graphic Design
Photography
Film
Television
Sculpture
Architecture (Related Fields)
Crafts
Product Design
Arts of Celebration

Media for Art
Materials
Forming Processes
Techniques

Subjects/Themes in Art
Subject Matter
  People
  Natural World
  Constructed World
  Still Life
  Genre
  Fantasy
  History
  Religion
  Literature
Visual Symbols
Broad Themes
  Peace
  Love
  Sadness
  Work
  Play
  Faith
  Birth
  Family
  Childhood
  Youth
  Old age
  Death
  Wisdom
  Dreams
Meanings of Subjects/Themes
  Cultural Meanings
  Personal Meanings
  Nonobjective Meanings

Design in Art
Elements of Design
  Line
  Shape
  Form
  Color
  Space
  Texture
Principles of Design
  Pattern
  Rhythm
  Balance
  Proportion
  Emphasis
  Unity
  Variety
See Chapter 3 for a detailed vocabulary for the elements and principles of design.

Styles of Art
Individual
Cultural
Historical
General
  Expressionism (Feelings)
  Realism (Observations)
  Abstraction (Ideas)
  Fantasy (Imagination)

Summary

Communication about art is based on ideas that art experts agree are important. Even though experts do not always agree on answers to the question "What is art?" they do agree on basic concepts – tools for thinking about this question and other features of art.

The basic art concepts introduced in this chapter will help you think about functions of art, varieties of art forms, media, subjects and themes in art, design elements and principles and styles of art.

These concepts will be explained further as you study this book and try activities. The concepts are important in your own artwork, in looking at art and in understanding art in your daily life.

Using What You Learned

Art History

1 Look through Chapter 2. Identify* at least one example of artwork that was created for each of the four functions of art described in this chapter.

2 Eight varieties of art were identified in this chapter. List them on paper. Look through other chapters. Identify* at least one example for each type of art form.

3 Look through other chapters in the book. Identify* three examples of nonobjective art.

4 Four general styles of art were named in this chapter. Look through other chapters. Identify* at least one additional example of each general style.

Identify means: List the title, artist, date and page on which the artwork can be found.

Aesthetics and Art Criticism

1 Briefly define and give an example of:
- *a subject matter in artwork.*
- *a theme in artwork.*
- *a visual symbol.*
- *a medium used to create an artwork.*
- *a cultural meaning of a subject.*

2 Look at the painting by Sa'di on page 4. On a sheet of paper, write six sentences about it that demonstrate your knowledge of the elements and principles of design.

3 Explain why art experts do not always agree on answers to the question "What is art?"

Creating Art

1 As directed by your teacher, choose a medium and create an original work of art. Choose one of the four general style categories to use. An original work of art is not copied or traced.

2 Create an artwork that includes as many visual symbols for our nation as you can. Organize your visual symbols to demonstrate your understanding of at least two principles of design.

3 Create a nonobjective artwork that communicates a definite mood or feeling. Demonstrate your present knowledge of the elements and principles of design.

Sally Bishop's studio. Courtesy of the artist.

Chapter 2
Careers in Art

Chapter Vocabulary

environment
architecture
design
fine art
craft
form follows function
classic
stylist
layout
visual identity
logo
avant-garde
portfolio
resumé

Art and design touch your life in a thousand ways. Look around your classroom. Think of all the images you have seen today and all the products you have used. Almost all of them were designed or influenced by people with training in art.

Fashion designers plan the clothes sold in stores. Graphic designers create the plans for almost all the posters, books and signs you have seen today. The important buildings in your community are designed by architects and interior designers. Product designers for industry plan many of the things you have already used today: lights, furniture, cars, telephones and the like.

All these forms of art, and many more, are part of today's art world. Learning about art careers is one way to become aware of this larger world of art. For example, fine artists and craftsworkers, museum workers, art teachers and many other people are also part of this art world.

Maybe you are considering a career in art. Maybe not. In either case, this chapter will help you learn more about careers in art as well as how art is part of your everyday life. After you study this chapter you should be better able to:

Aesthetics and Art Criticism
- understand the work of art scholars such as aestheticians and art critics.
- appreciate the variety of art forms and activities in the art world.

Art History
- understand why knowing art history is important in art careers.
- understand how history has influenced present-day careers in art.

Creating Art
- evaluate your interest in an art career and find out what you would need to do to enter it.

These students are learning to create and interpret architectural plans.

Michael Graves, Public Services Building, Portland, Oregon. Graves is one of many architects who believes color is an important element in architecture. What other design elements do you see in this building? Photograph courtesy of Tom Clark, Architectural Associates.

Environmental Design

Our *environment* includes nature – land, water, plants and animals. It also includes everything people have created – the human-made environment.

The human-made environment includes everything that has been constructed or assembled by people: roads, automobiles, buildings and whole cities. Some artists specialize in planning the human-made environment and how it relates to nature.

Architecture

Architects are artists who design buildings. They often work with other specialists – engineers, community officials and builders. They consult with clients – people who commission the building.

Since the Renaissance, architects have tried to plan for the use, construction, appearance and symbolism of buildings. *Use* refers to the purpose or function of buildings. Homes, theaters, factories, offices and schools all have different functions. One of the first steps in planning is to analyze all of the activities and needs a building must meet.

Construction refers to the materials and systems that make up a building: heaters or air conditioners, lights, walls, bricks, windows and the like. These things must be planned so the building will be useful and pleasing to look at.

The *appearance* of the building is also important to the design. Today, most architects think about how new buildings fit into the places they will be built. They consider what their clients want. They put these ideas together with what they know about design.

Symbolism refers to what a building means to the community, owners or people who will use it. Symbolism is especially important in public buildings. For example, a courthouse should probably not look like a fast-food restaurant.

Today, some architects specialize in saving historic buildings. Sometimes a whole section of town is saved and fixed up again. In these projects, the architect must follow rules for safe buildings and save the most important architectural features of the buildings.

Urban and community planning are also careers in architecture. These artists work on designs for entire areas of a city, such as fixing up a downtown. Some planners design big new communities – suburbs with houses, apartments, parks, shops and the like.

Big architectural firms employ many specialists such as engineers, interior designers and landscape architects. They also hire specialists in *drafting* (drawing the plans an architect creates), model building, illustration and graphic design.

If you are interested in research and writing, you might want to learn more about architectural history, theory and criticism. If you like mathematics, try working out some scale models or floor plans of buildings.

Related Careers Jobs in the building trades – electrical service, carpentry, plumbing, etc. – architectural photography and building management.

This model maker works for an architectural firm. Models help a client visualize the plan for a building. Photograph courtesy of Meyers and D'Aleo, Architects, Baltimore, Maryland.

Paseo Del Rio – The Downtown River Walk. This urban renewal project in San Antonio, Texas transformed the waterfront area into a people-oriented space. Courtesy San Antonio Convention and Visitors Bureau.

Interior Design

Interior designers plan the indoor spaces of businesses, public buildings and buildings people live in. Many interior designers are specialists. They work as designers for homes, or offices, or stores or hotels. Interior designers often work closely with architects. This kind of teamwork helps make sure that indoor and outdoor spaces in buildings meet the needs of their clients.

Interior designers choose and arrange furnishings, partitions, and many other details – carpets, wall coverings, lights, fabrics for furnishings and other accessories. They coordinate the colors, textures, patterns and proportions of these to give their clients what they need and want.

Interior designers use presentation boards to show clients their ideas. The presentation boards often include floor plans to show where people will walk as well as drawings to suggest how the spaces will look when finished. Samples of carpets and fabrics, and photographs of furnishings and accessories are also presented.

Interior designers often work for large architectural firms or design studios. Some have their own freelance businesses. Most interior designers are trained in colleges. They study architecture as well as how to plan interior spaces.

Related Careers Interior decorators are people who offer ideas on how to improve the design of a place that is already built. College is not usually needed for this kind of work. Other related jobs include illustrating or photographing interiors; drafting plans; and computer-aided design, which often uses animation to show how spaces look as you move through them.

Collier Campbell textiles: Havanna and Cote d'Azur, 1984. Susan Collier's fabrics show her interest in painting. Interior designers must learn about new and traditional designs for fabrics, furniture, lighting and many other items.

Archizoom Plastic Laminate Screens, 1970's.

Landscape Architecture

Landscape architects plan the natural outdoor spaces in parks and around buildings and highways. Some design waterfront parks, golf courses or campsites. Others specialize in landscapes for homes, public gardens or big housing projects.

Landscape architects decide where to put grass, trees, shrubs, flowers, water and other natural elements. Often, some natural features, like big trees, are preserved. Other features may be changed, such as making a grassy area bigger. Sometimes new features, like shrubs and flowers, may be added.

The overall plan must pay attention to climate, seasonal changes, the way the land is shaped, drainage and patterns of sunlight and shade. The way the land will be used and cared for is also considered. Changes in plant and animal habitats are studied, too.

The design for large projects is almost always based on discussions with engineers, architects and clients. Good designs are attractive and well-suited to their purposes and locations. They are beautiful in different seasons and over periods of time.

You might want to do research on the pioneering work of landscape architect Frederick Olmsted. He designed Central Park in New York City. Other topics for research might be the traditions of garden design in Japan and England, and labyrinth (maze-like) gardens in France. You might find out about the people who helped set up major national, state or local parks.

Related Careers Horticulture, recreational facilities planning, ecological planning, geographic research and mapping and photography (still, video or film recording of landscapes before, during and after changes).

Sanzen-in Garden, Kyoto. Photograph courtesy of George Barford.

Frederick Law Olmsted, Jr., Senate Park Commission Plan for Washington, DC, 1901. The plan for parks in Washington, DC. was developed in 1901. It helps to make the city an attractive place to visit.

Design for Business

Three major branches of art have developed since the Industrial Revolution and growth of manufacturing: industrial design, graphic design and fashion design. There are many career opportunities in each branch.

Industrial Design

Industrial designers plan the forms of products you use everyday. Examples of industrial design can be seen in appliances like stoves and telephones, tools and machines, furniture, cars and other forms of transportation. Industrial designers are sometimes called the "sculptors" of industry. Many product designers work with engineers and experts in marketing, or selling, their products.

Industrial design began around 1870. At that time, people in business discovered that the design of a product could help to sell it. The first designers for industry were often trained as painters, sculptors or architects.

Professionals in industrial design are especially interested in the idea that *"form follows function."* This means that a chair, for example, must first be designed so it is comfortable to sit on. The form, or way the chair looks, can then be designed to fit this function.

Classic industrial designs are designs that stay useful and popular for many years. One of these is Michael Thonet's bentwood chair design. These chairs are made by bending wood into a variety of patterns. Thonet's chairs were first manufactured in 1840. They are still being produced.

Many of the ideas industrial designers use today can be traced to the leading teachers at the Bauhaus, a German art school (1919-1933). The Bauhaus taught artists to think about design as the combination of art, craft, architecture and industry. Artists were encouraged to experiment with materials and try out ideas for use in industry.

Some designers are called *stylists*. Stylists create new designs for products so that people will want to have the latest models.

Michel Boué works on a clay model for an automobile. At the right is the artist's drawing of the automobile and a later model based on Boué's design. Prototype Renault 5, 1972; designer's rendering of the first production Renault 5, 1972 and Renault 5, 1984.

Daniel Sturges designed this "platform vehicle." Copyright, Caleb Incorporated.

Some special kinds of product design include prefabricated houses, instruments and special tools, toys (mechanical, electronic), containers (packages, boxes), athletic equipment, furniture (chairs, desks, lamps, cabinets), communications equipment (telephones, television sets, radios, computers), transportation vehicles (automobiles, boats, airplanes, space capsules), appliances (refrigerators, stoves, can openers) and utensils (kitchenware, dinnerware).

Related Careers Model making, drafting, engineering, photography, teaching and consulting.

Fashion Design

Clothing is a basic human need. Fashion designers plan the clothes, jewelry, shoes and other items you wear. Most fashion designers are trained in all aspects of clothing. They learn to design clothes and create patterns so the designs can be mass-produced. They learn about fabrics, weights, colors, and textures. They also learn how people respond to different types of clothing.

Some fashion designers try to create new clothing designs each year. Some of these trend-setting designs are widely copied.

Costume designers work in the theater as well as in motion pictures and television.

Many people like to wear up-to-date fashions. Clothes also help people show their individuality. For these reasons, fashionable clothing is now one of the biggest industries in the world.

Leading fashion designers often use their names on the products they design. This trend began in the early 1900's when fashions, especially for wealthy women, were shown in popular magazines and newspapers.

Classic fashion designs, like other forms of design, stay popular a long time. Denim blue jeans are one example. Rubber-soled shoes are another. Both came from the idea of creating useful clothing.

Related Careers Illustration, photography, consulting, publicity, art direction, custom tailoring, pattern making, manufacturing, sales, buying, model, research. Specializations include dealing with costumes, accessories (shoes, hats, belts), fabric design, store display and apparel for a special purpose or group (sports, formal wear, informal wear, uniforms, children's clothing).

Running Shoe for Kappa by ItalDesign, early 1980's.

Kenzo Takada's fashions are admired for their innovative shapes and silhouettes. Photography courtesy of John Senzer for Fashion Institute of Technology.

Graphic Design

Graphic designers specialize in planning the layout of printed materials such as newspapers, magazines and books. They also design advertisements, posters, record covers, labels, packages and stationery. Good graphic design attracts attention, gives information and, in some cases, changes how you think, feel or act.

A *layout* is a sketch that shows the size, placement and style of all written text and illustrations. The designer chooses the style of lettering and illustrations such as drawings or photographs.

Layouts are shown to clients for approval. The final design, called camera-ready artwork, is then put together. This artwork includes the *type* (lettering), artwork and instructions for printing it.

Corporate *visual identity* programs are also developed by graphic designers. A corporate identity program includes the designs for a *logo* and other things such as stationery, packages, labels and the like. A logo is a visual symbol for the company.

Graphic design began as a specialty in the 1800's when businesses began to think that their products needed a special brand name and identity to compete with other similar products. At about the same time, the growing publishing business began to use graphic design in books, magazines and newspapers. Both of these changes created a need for skills in designing type and logos, and in combining these with illustrations.

Some graphic designers create the titles, credits and advertisements for television and films. The layouts are usually small sketches arranged in a sequence called a storyboard.

Related Careers Art Direction – managing a group of designers. Design – type, outdoor advertising, record jackets, greeting cards, titles, sign, magazines. Illustration – cartoons, comic strips, greeting cards, books, technical or medical manuals. Illustrators – specializing in photographs, computer graphics or calligraphy, which is the art of beautiful handwriting.

Milton Glaser and Seymour Chwast, *Dylan Poster*. Courtesy Milton Glaser, Inc., New York.

Computers are being used for many kinds of graphic and product design. Photograph by John Senzer for the Fashion Institute of Technology.

Fine Art

Fine artists are painters, sculptors, printmakers, photographers and others who create art mainly as a personal challenge or to please themselves. Professional artists usually show their work in galleries or museums. They value what other artists and critics think about their work.

Amateur artists, like amateurs in sports and other activities, are still learning skills. Some amateurs hope to become professionals. Many create art just to please themselves or friends.

During the Renaissance, fine artists tried to show how their work differed from crafts work. Renaissance artists set up the difference this way: Fine artists have original ideas and use these in creating art. Craftsworkers care mostly about using materials and techniques skillfully.

These same ideas explain why critics, historians and other art experts today expect artists to be original or part of the *avant-garde* – leaders of new ways to create art. Fine artists and crafts artists who work in traditional ways using ideas or methods from the past also have large audiences.

Fine artists who want to exhibit in galleries and museums develop *portfolios* of their work. The portfolio contains their best examples of original art or photographs of the artwork. A *resumé* is an outline telling about the artist's education, exhibitions and related information.

Related Careers Gallery owning, art materials sales, art law, teaching art, art representation or dealing.

Crafts

Craftsworkers usually specialize in creating unique (one-of-a-kind) objects by hand. Most prefer to work in one major medium such as ceramics, glass, fiber, metal or paper. Some specialize in a certain kind of craft such as pottery, furniture, jewelry or the like.

The differences between crafts and fine art are beginning to fade. This is happening because fine artists are exploring traditional craft media, such as paper-making, and because craftsworkers are creating non-functional items such as woven sculpture.

Some craftsworkers today want to keep using traditional techniques and materials. Others are exploring new combinations of materials and techniques. Because handcrafted things are now more rare than mass-produced things, many people buy craft objects mainly for their beauty and uniqueness.

Related Careers Gallery owning, crafts materials sales, teaching crafts.

Artist Betye Saar works in a variety of media. Photograph by Barbara DuMetz.

Fiber artist Lenore Tawney in her studio working on *Dove*, 1974. Copyright 1990. Photograph by Clayton Price.

33

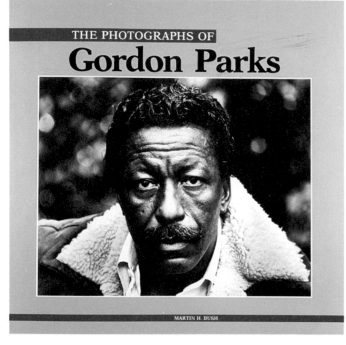

Gordon Parks, *Self-portrait.* Cover of "The Photographs of Gordon Parks" by Martin H. Bush. Edwin A. Ulrich Museum of Art, Wichita State University, Wichita, Kansas.

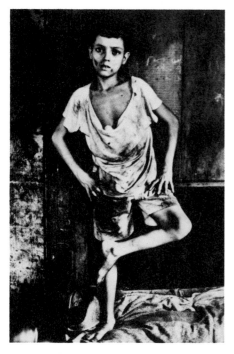

Gordon Parks, *Flavio,* 1961. Parks created these powerful photographs as part of a photo-essay on poverty in a Brazilian slum. Photograph, 28 7/8" x 19" (73 x 48 cm). Edwin A. Ulrich Museum of Art, The Wichita State University, Wichita, Kansas.

Entertainment, Journalism and Advertising

Many art-related careers can be found in film, television, theater and in businesses that gather news and information.

Photography is often used for advertising, entertainment and journalism. Photojournalists are people who use cameras to report news. Some specialize in still photography. Motion pictures and television companies hire artists who are skilled in using cameras and in editing film or tape.

Film animations are created from many separate drawings or illustrations – about 24 for each second of motion picture film. The films are planned around storyboards – sketches that look like comic strips. The final artwork is done by artists who specialize in drawing animations. Animated puppet-like figures can also be shaped from materials such as clay or foam rubber. Computers can also be used for film animation. Computers make this slow, hard process quicker and easier.

All major advertising companies have art directors. The art director works with a team of writers, salespeople, and experts in visual communication. Together, they work out plans for advertising in different media such as television, magazines and billboards. Art directors do rough visual layouts for the ads. Then they arrange for specialists to help finish making the ads.

Art directors also work in films, television dramas and stage plays. They coordinate all of the elements you see in a program or production. They work with people who design sets and costumes, with lighting specialists, makeup artists and hair stylists. They also work with the artists who create special effects. *Special-effects artists* work on a variety of projects. They may be asked to create fog on a stage or a model of an alien creature for a film.

Most publishers of books, magazines and newspapers have art directors who coordinate the work of other graphic designers and illustrators.

Graphic designers enjoy working with page layouts, type and other elements of a design. Their works are usually printed and seen by many people. Photograph by John Senzer for Fashion Institute of Technology.

Animation by Scott Baldwin.

Computer graphics and animations are widely used in advertising and entertainment.

Art teachers enjoy communicating with others about art.

Museums employ many people who have special skills in studying, displaying and teaching art.

Art Research and Service

Many careers in art involve research, writing and working with people.

Scholars and writers in art do research. They usually write about art and often teach about art in advanced schools or in museums.

Art historians study works of art, artists and the cultures that shaped the artists' works. Some scholars are psychologists. They study how and why people create art and respond to it.

Aestheticians are philosophers. They specialize in logical thinking and writing about art. They help people understand theories about art. Most aestheticians teach in universities.

Art critics are writers who describe, analyze, interpret, and judge art. Some art critics are scholars who write for art magazines. Many are journalists who write for newspapers.

Art museums employ many art specialists. Museum *curators* do historical research on artworks in their collections. Preservation experts save art works from decay. Restorers clean and repair damaged work. Exhibition designers plan displays of artworks in museums. Education curators and *docents* (teacher-guides), teach about museums and their collections.

Art teachers help people learn about art. Teachers in schools have a broad knowledge of art and enjoy teaching full-time. Art therapists help disabled or troubled people understand themselves. Most art therapists work in hospitals and other centers.

Many people are involved in buying and selling art. Gallery owners sell art. Art consultants or dealers help buyers find artwork to purchase. Collectors are people who buy art. Art auctioneers sell art to the highest bidders.

In many ways, the audience for art is the most important group in the art world. The art audience includes you and all people who appreciate art. The ability of many people to appreciate and support art is essential for artists in a democratic society. All art is created to be seen and understood.

Critical Thinking Suppose you were appointed to an art council in your town. This group would get government money from taxes to spend on art programs and activities for citizens in the community. What art programs and activities would you like to see this tax money used for? Why?

Computer-Aided Design

Computer-aided design (CAD) is now widely used in many fields of art, architecture and design. The CAD programs can be tools for drafting plans, creating drawings that look three-dimensional, and trying out ideas. For example, some programs create animations that show how a building will look as you move around and through it.

Graphic designers can use computers to design posters, magazines and illustrations for publications. Computers are also being used to create animated films and advertisements on television. Architects, interior designers, product designers and fashion designers all may use computers to draw their plans.

Self-chilling can design created by PictureMaker, a 3-D design program. Copyright 1987, Ian Jaffray Design.

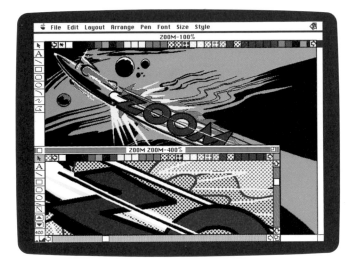

This software program allows an artist to work on an enlarged section of an image. Courtesy Apple Computer, Inc.

Courtesy Apple Computer, Inc.

Thinking About Careers in Art

Answer the questions listed below on a separate sheet of paper. Answer them with a yes, or a no. You may want to consider a career in art if you have many yes answers.

1. Do you enjoy seeing colors, lines, shapes and other visual elements around you?

2. Do you like to draw, sculpt or create other kinds of art?

3. Do you often create or study art on your own, outside of school?

4. Do you enjoy experimenting with ideas and materials in art?

5. Do you work on complex art projects until they are completed?

6. Do you enjoy finding out about unusual styles or kinds of art?

7. Is it easy for you to find original ideas or designs for your artwork?

8. If you don't like your artwork do you try again?

9. Do you like to talk about art with other people?

10. Do you sometimes find yourself teaching friends or classmates about art?

11. Is art one of your favorite subjects or hobbies?

12. Maybe you would like to go into a career outside of art. On a separate sheet of paper, write the name of a career that is not directly related to art. Then list all the ways people in that career can use skills or products from people who are trained in art.

Noel Mayo, designer. Photograph by Jeffrey A. Rycus.

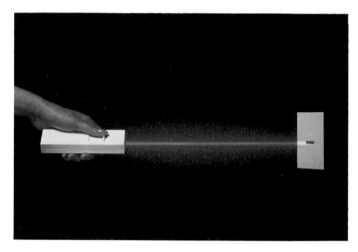

Lutron remote control dimmer. Design by Noel Mayo.

The Gallery. Complete signage system for 4-block-long, 4-level mall. Design by Noel Mayo.

Computer-driven telephone product. Design by Noel Mayo.

Summary

There are many careers in art. Environmental design includes architecture, urban planning, interior design and landscape architecture. Industrial, fashion and graphic designers plan many of the images and products you use in everyday life.

Fine artists and craftsworkers create work mainly for personal expression. Some work in traditional artistic ways. Others try to begin new directions in art.

Art research and service also offer many different careers. These include jobs in museums, galleries, schools and other places where art is displayed, studied or exchanged. Computer technology is used in many branches of art as a tool for creative work and research.

All art is created to be seen and appreciated. The audience for art has an important role in the art world. The art audience includes all people who want to learn about and support artistic activity.

Using What You Learned

Art History

1 What are three art careers that people need a knowledge of art history to work in?

2 What difference between fine art and crafts work was set up during the Renaissance? Why is this difference no longer as strong as it used to be?

3 What are four ideas for planning architecture that came from the Renaissance?

Aesthetics and Art Criticism

1 What do aestheticans do? Why is their work important?

2 What are the main responsibilities of a good art critic?

Creating Art

1 Gather pictures from old magazines or newspapers. Create a collage that illustrates one of the following careers: architecture, interior design, urban planning, landscape architecture, fashion design, graphic design, product design.

2 Every day you see images and use forms created by people trained in art. Create a funny artwork that shows how miserable your life might be if all the things created by art-trained people were not in your life.

3 Choose one art career that is the most interesting to you. Find out more about it. Write a one-page report stating: (A) The name of the career, (B) related careers, (C) typical jobs and tasks, (D) abilities and traits needed for success in the field, (E) education needed and (F) possible summer jobs to learn more about the career.

39

Stuart Davis, *Owh! in San Paõ*, 1951. The design of this lively painting is just as important as the theme. You will learn more about design in this chapter. Oil on canvas, 52 ¼" x 41 ¾" (133 x 106 cm). Collection of Whitney Museum of American Art, New York. Purchase. Photograph by Geoffrey Clements.

Chapter 3
Design: The Language of Art

If you wanted to create a painting of a lively, loud concert, you would plan colors and lines to make people "feel" the action of that scene when they looked at your work. If you wanted to create a painting of a still, calm lake, you would make a different plan.

The purpose of an artist's plan, or *design*, is to share an experience with people who look at a work. Design is the process of organizing visual parts into a whole artwork. This process is sometimes called *composition* – bringing ideas together so they work as a team.

Artists use materials, tools and techniques to create the qualities you see in artworks. These qualities are called the elements and principles of design. The elements of design include ***line, shape, form, texture, value, color*** and ***space***. The principles of design are ***balance, rhythm, movement, proportion, emphasis, pattern, unity*** and ***variety***.

When you learn about design elements and principles, you can communicate your ideas better. You can also analyze and appreciate art more.

How should elements be created and put together? That depends on your idea or purpose. The design process is really like putting a puzzle together, or solving a problem.

After you study this chapter and do some of the activities, you will be better able to:

Creating Art
- use the elements and principles of design in creating art.

Aesthetics
- use the vocabulary of design to describe artworks.

Art Criticism
- use what you know about design to describe, analyze and interpret art.

Art History
- use what you know about design when you study art history.

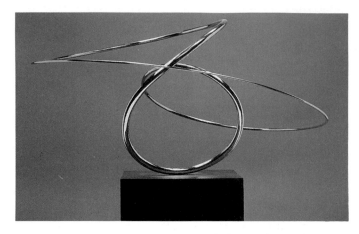

Jose de Rivera, *Construction #107*, 1969. Three-dimensional lines can bend and twist in space. Stainless steel forged rod, 21 ¹/₂" x 41" x 41" (55 x 104 x 104 cm). Hirshhorn Museum and Sculpture Garden, Smithsonian Institution. Gift of the artist through the Joseph H. Hirshhorn Foundation, 1972.

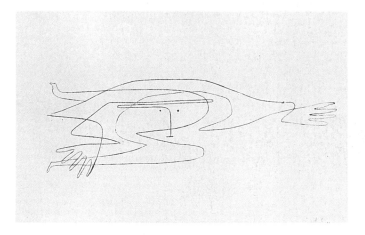

Paul Klee, *Lying as Snow, 10*, 1931. Lines can cross over each other to create shapes. Ink on paper, 12 ³/₈" x 18 ³/₄" (194 x 130 cm). Solomon R. Guggenheim Museum, New York. Photograph by David Heald.

I. Rice Pereira, *Black and White*, 1940. What kinds of lines do you not see in this work? Ink on scratchboard, 18 ⁷/₈" x 12 ⁵/₈" (48 x 32 cm). Solomon R. Guggenheim Museum, New York. Photograph by Robert E. Mates.

Elements of Design

Line

Artists often see and talk about lines as paths of movement. Lines can have qualities that suggest motion – jagged or wavy, straight or curved, thick or thin.

Artists know that qualities of line such as dark or light, and continuous or broken, can show ideas and feelings. They often speak of lines as active or passive, bold or delicate, flowing or tight.

Artists see and think about lines in many ways. Lines can be outlines or edges of shapes and forms. The contours, or edges, may be *geometric*, which means measured or precise. The outlines may be *organic* – like irregular or curved forms you see in nature. In two-dimensional (2-D) art, lines can be used to create the illusion of shadows, textures or forms in space.

Implied lines are not actually seen. They can seem to be present in the way edges of shapes line up. In architecture, sculpture and other three-dimensional (3-D) forms, lines can twist, turn or move up or down in space.

In the art of *calligraphy* (beautiful handwriting) you enjoy the flow of curved lines and spaces between them. In many cartoons, artists use just a few lines to capture the personality of a person or situation.

M. C. Escher, *Lucht en Water I (Sky and Water I)*, 1938. Positive and negative shapes and forms are a very important part of this work. Can you explain why? Woodcut, 17 3/8" x 17 3/8" (44 x 44 cm). Collection Haags Gemeente-museum,   The Hague.

David Smith, *Cubi XII*, 1963. The shapes and forms in this work were created by welding together flat shapes of metal. Stainless steel, 9' 1/2" x 4' 1/2" x 2' 2" (278 x 125 x 82 cm). Hirshhorn Museum and Sculpture Garden, Smithsonian Institution. Gift of Joseph H. Hirshhorn, 1972.

Jaune Quick-To-See Smith, *Jumper*, 1986. What are the dominant shapes in this work? How are they varied? Pastel on paper, 30" x 22" (76 x 56 cm). Courtesy Bernice Steinbaum Gallery, New York City.

Shape and Form

Shapes are two-dimensional surfaces such as circles, squares or triangles. Forms are three-dimensional, like spheres (round balls), cubes or pyramids.

Organic shapes and forms remind you of curves in plants, clouds, people and other natural forms. Geometric shapes and forms are usually precise and regular. Artists often use geometric shapes and forms to suggest machine-made things or parts of the environment created by people.

A *free-form* can be found in nature. It often has organic qualities and may be either two- or three-dimensional.

A *concave* form has a pushed-in surface that goes down like the inside of a crater or bowl. A *convex* form has a raised surface that goes up like a mound or the outside of a bowl.

Your eyes and mind work together when you see shapes and forms. The shape you see first is called a figure or *positive* shape. The surrounding area is called the ground or *negative* shape. Artists often plan their work so that you shift your eyes back and forth between positive and negative shapes.

Light, Value and Color

Without light you cannot experience the wonderful world of color. The wavelengths of light that people can see are called the visible color spectrum. You see this spectrum in a rainbow or when a prism splits sunlight – white light – into colors. A *prism* is a clear wedge-shaped form.

A color wheel shows the spectrum of colors in a circle. In order to use color expressively, artists learn some of the following basic facts and terms about color. Many are easiest to remember by using a color wheel diagram.

Color Facts and Terms

A *hue* is a common name for a color such as red, orange, yellow, green, blue and violet. A *pigment* is a coloring agent, such as paint or dye, that reflects certain wavelengths and absorbs others.

Primary hues in pigments are red, yellow and blue. *Primary* means first or basic. The primary hues cannot be mixed from others. With the primary hues, along with black and white, you can mix almost every color.

Secondary hues – orange, green and violet – are mixed from primary hues. Mix red and yellow for orange, red and blue for violet, yellow and blue for green.

To create *intermediate* colors, you mix a primary hue and a secondary hue that is next to it on the color wheel. For example, you mix yellow and orange for yellow-orange, blue and green for blue-green and so on.

red
orange
yellow
green
blue
indigo
violet

prism

When a ray of white light shines through a prism, the wavelengths separate into the visible spectrum—hues of the rainbow.

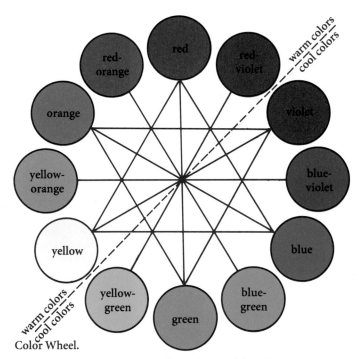

Color Wheel.

The color wheel arranges the colors of the visible color spectrum into a circle.

Value refers to how light or dark a hue is. *Shading* is a very gradual change in values to make a smooth transition between dark and light. Gradual changes in value can give the feeling of shadows on a form, or a misty atmosphere or a calm, quiet mood.

Values can also be used to create a strong *contrast*, or difference, between very light areas and areas of deep shadow. A light value of a hue is called a *tint*. It is made by adding white to a hue. Artworks dominated by tints are called *high key* works. They are usually seen as cheerful, bright and sunny.

To darken a color, add black. A dark value of a hue is called a *shade*. A *low key* artwork is dominated by dark values. They are often seen as dark, mysterious or gloomy.

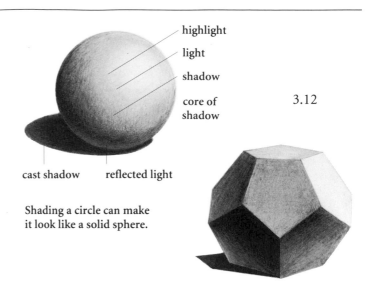

highlight
light
shadow
core of shadow

3.12

cast shadow   reflected light

Shading a circle can make it look like a solid sphere.

When shaded, lines can look like a solid geometric form.

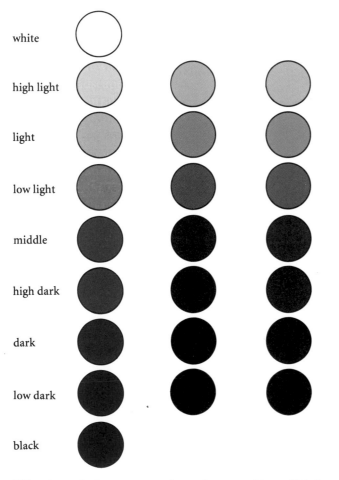

white
high light
light
low light
middle
high dark
dark
low dark
black

This value scale shows a range of grays between white and black. Hues can also be arranged by their values.

Georgia O'Keeffe, *Light Iris*, 1924. This painting is dominated by tints – light values. That means it is a high key painting. Oil on canvas, 40" x 30" (102 x 76 cm). The Virginia Museum of Art. Gift of Mr. and Mrs. Bruce C. Gottwald.

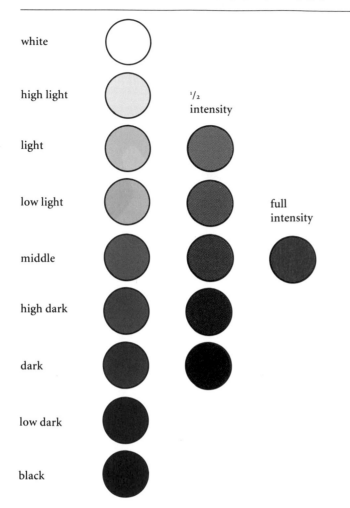

white

high light

½ intensity

light

low light

full intensity

middle

high dark

dark

low dark

black

This intensity scale shows how a pure color – bright, full intensity – can be changed to duller tints and shades.

Simultaneous contrast means that your perception of one color (the inside box) is affected by the colors around it.

The *intensity* of a color refers to how bright or dull it is. Bright, or high-intensity, colors are similar to those in the spectrum. Dull, or low-intensity, colors are created by mixing *complementary* colors – colors that are opposite each other on the color wheel. For example, if you mix a small amount of blue with orange, the orange looks duller. Many grays, browns and other muted colors can be mixed from complements.

Color interactions can be planned by choosing color combinations. For example, when complementary hues such as blue and orange are placed side by side, they tend to "vibrate" and create visual excitement. A yellow-green circle in the middle of a green square will look more green than if it is in the middle of a yellow square. A dull or muted red will look brighter on a gray background.

Color Schemes

A color scheme is a plan for selecting colors. Some of the most common schemes, or plans, are discussed below:

WARM. Reds, oranges and yellows remind you of warm things and feelings such as fire, sun or people with "sunny" personalities.

COOL. Blues, greens and violets remind you of cool things such as water, or moods of people such as "feeling blue."

NEUTRAL. Artists and designers often refer to varieties of gray, brown, white and black as neutral colors. Neutral colors are often chosen for backgrounds in rooms or for quiet, somber effects. Bright colors may be used for accents or centers of interest.

Neutral colors can be slightly warm – yellowish-white, reddish-brown, yellowish-brown. These colors are often used to suggest the idea of warm, earthy nature.

Neutral colors can also be slightly cool – bluish-white, light gray-violet, light gray-blue. These colors may remind you of very business-like, industrial or "cool," impersonal things.

MONOCHROMATIC. *Monochrome* means "one color." A monochromatic color scheme has several values of one hue. In this kind of plan, one hue unifies a work. Artists and designers often add color accents or related hues to monochromatic schemes to make them more interesting.

ANALOGOUS. Analogous hues are next to each other on the color wheel. The colors have a common hue. Red, red-orange and orange are an example. Analogous hues are generally pleasing to look at. You tend to see them as related or part of a unit.

Piet Mondrian, *Composition (Blue, Red & Yellow)*, 1930. Oil on canvas, 28 ⁵/₈" x 21 ¹/₄" (73 x 54 cm). Private Collection, New York.

Follot, *Leaves Fabric*, 1925 Paris Exposition. Definite color schemes are often used in fabrics designed for furniture and window drapes. Can you explain why? Rayon and cotton, 26" x 37 ¹/₂" (66 x 95 cm). Courtesy Schumacher, New York.

Seguy, *Butterflies*, 1925. Rayon and cotton, 26" x 56" (66 x 142 cm). Courtesy Schumacher, New York.

Claude Monet, *Rouen Cathedral, West Façade, Sunlight*, 1894. Monet created many paintings of this cathedral at different times of day. He was fascinated by atmospheric color. Oil on canvas, 39 ¹/₂" x 26" (100 x 66 cm). National Gallery of Art, Washington, DC. Chester Dale Collection.

Texture

Texture refers to the way a surface feels when you touch it, such as rough or smooth. *Actual* or *tactual* textures are what you feel when you touch things. Actual textures are important in three-dimensional artworks.

In some two-dimensional arts – such as weaving, painting and collage – actual textures are created by the way a material is used. For example, thick layers of paint can be used to create textures. This technique is called *impasto*.

Visual textures are the illusion of actual textures. They can be simulated or invented.

Simulated textures are seen in two-dimensional art such as photographs, paintings or drawings where they look like actual textures of fur, velvet, grass and the like. A painting or other art form that imitates actual textures is called a *trompe l'oeil* (say tromp LOY), which is French for "fool the eye." You see many simulated textures in daily life. Plastic may be spray-painted to look like cloth. Smooth plastic tables may look like wood.

Invented textures are arrangements of lines, values and shapes that you perceive as visual textures. Very small repeated patterns can be seen as invented textures.

There are many techniques for inventing texture with paint and other media. For example, in *frottage* you apply a layer of fresh paint to a canvas or paper. Then you place the canvas or paper paint-side-up over a textured surface. When you scrape the paint with a flat tool, you see a textured pattern like the surface. In *grottage*, you scratch into wet paint with a comb, a stiff cardboard or other tools. In *decalcomania,* you place blobs of paint on two papers or canvases, then place the painted surfaces face to face and rub them. When you pull them apart, the random textures often resemble a fantasy landscape.

Textures can also be described by the way they reflect light. A *matte* surface absorbs light, so it looks dull. A *glossy* surface is shiny – it reflects light and glistens. Photographs can be printed with glossy or matte surfaces. The paper itself may be smooth or have a subtle texture. A semi-gloss paint is halfway between a very shiny and a dull, or flat, paint.

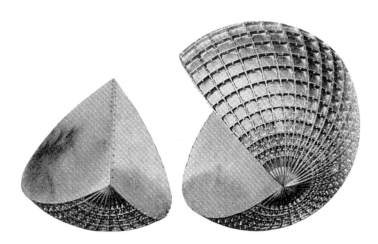

Robert Bart, *Untitled*, 1965. Cast aluminum, 12 ³/₄" x 17 ³/₄" x 17 ¹/₂" (32 x 45 x 44 cm).

Lucas Samaras, *Untitled Box Number 3*, 1963. Do the textures on this box-like form make you curious about opening the lid? What textural qualities might lead you to open it very carefully? Pins, rope, stuffed bird, wood, 24 ¹/₂" x 11 ¹/₂" x 10 ¹/₄" (62 x 29 x 26 cm). Collection of Whitney Museum of American Art. Gift of the Howard and Jean Lipman Foundation, Inc.

Max Ernst, *The Eye of Silence*, 1943-1944. Some of the textures in this painting come from a technique called decalcomania. Oil on canvas, 42 ¹/₂" x 55 ¹/₂" (108 x 141 cm). Washington University Gallery of Art, St. Louis.

Tactual textures are those you experience through touch. Courtesy of Nancy Belfer.

Anonymous, *The Ideal City*, 15th century. Palazzo Ducale, Urbino.

The linear perspective in *The Ideal City* is based on one vanishing point in the center of the rotunda doorway. The artist used a one-point perspective system.

M.C. Escher, *Convex and Concave*, 1955. Escher often uses perspective in a way that seems logical until you study the work carefully. Lithograph, 10 ¼" x 13 ⅛" (26 x 33 cm). Collection Haags Gemeentemuseum, The Hague.

Space

You usually think of space as empty. It seems to be the "air" around and between things you see. Artists think about space as a two-dimensional flat area or as a three-dimensional volume.

Artists refer to spaces as *positive* (occupied by something) or *negative* (the surrounding area). They see spaces as filled or empty. They think about *actual* space, which is measurable in some way. *Implied* space is the illusion of space on a flat surface. Space can also be defined by its *orientation* (vertical, horizontal) and *scale* (large or small).

In two-dimensional art, the illusion of space and distance can be created in many ways (see diagram on right hand page). Most of these techniques were developed by Renaissance artists. The techniques are called systems of *perspective* – systems to show the way things relate to each other in space. Perspective can also suggest the importance of certain parts of a painting.

Architects are careful about how interior and exterior spaces relate to each other in buildings. Sculptors and architects work with open spaces and enclosed spaces. In sculpture and other three-dimensional art, the idea of space includes the height, width and depth of artworks.

Graphic designers work with the spacing of things such as blocks of type and borders on pages. They notice spaces between lines of sentences, between words and between the letters within words. Comic strips are presented in series of spaces to show events over a periods of time.

Ideas of space, time and motion mix together in television and film-making. For example, films are often edited so that you seem to be in several spaces at one time.

Giorgio de Chirico, *The Mystery and the Melancholy of a Street*, 1914. Several vanishing points that don't seem to make sense help give his painting a strange, dream-like quality. Oil on canvas, 34 ¼" x 28 ½" (87 x 72 cm). Private Collection, Europe. Photograph courtesy Acquavella Galleries, Inc., New York.

Ways to create the illusion of space.

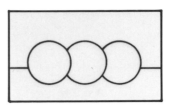

Overlap. One object appears to be behind the other.

Shading. Light and shadow create the illusion of form and space.

Placement. Objects higher in a picture appear to be in the distance.

Size. If objects are the same size, the distant ones look smaller than the closer ones.

Value and focus. Lighter values and less detail suggest distant objects.

Linear perspective. Parallel lines and edges seem to go toward one or more vanishing points.

Le Corbusier, *Notre Dame du Haut,* Ronchamp, France, 1950-1955. The way spaces relate to each other is important in architecture. In this church, the large interior space receives light from window spaces of different heights, sizes and depths from the wall. Photograph courtesy of G.E. Kidder Smith from "The New Churches of Europe."

Christian Schwizgebel, Cut paper silhouette from Gstaad, Switzerland, ca. 1950. Symmetrical balance is dominant in this work. Paper, 11 ¹/₂" x 7 ²/₃" (29 x 20 cm). Schweizerisches Museum fur Volkskund, Basel.

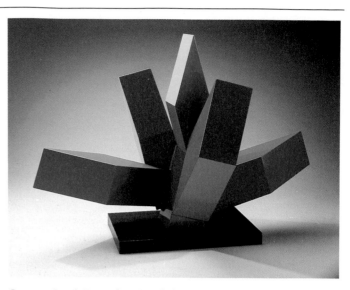

Gregory Curci, *Peacock*. Painted aluminum, 48" x 32" x 18"(122 x 81 x 46 cm). Courtesy David Bernstein Gallery.

Principles of Design

The principles of design are guides to help you plan your artwork. They are also guides for analyzing how artworks are planned. The principles most artists talk about and use today are balance, rhythm, movement, proportion, emphasis, pattern, unity and variety. These principles can help you understand beauty in nature – in the land, sea, sky, plant and animal life. The principles also fit in with ideas about living in harmony with others and balancing work and play.

Balance

Balance in things you see can be symmetrical, asymmetrical, or radial. *Symmetrical* balance is used to express ideas such as stability, uniformity and formality. In symmetrical, or formal, balance, both halves of a work are like mirror images of each other. They are exactly alike or so similar that you see them as matched.

In *asymmetrical*, or informal, balance, the halves of a work are balanced like a seesaw. For example, a large shape on the left side might be balanced by two smaller ones on the right side. A small area with bright colors can have as much visual "weight" and interest as a large area with a dull color. Asymmetrical balance is often used to express action, variety and informality.

In *radial* balance, parts of a design seem to move toward or away from a central point. Radial balance is often symmetrical. The petals on flowers and wheels of bicycles are examples of radial balance. Can you think of other examples of radial balance?

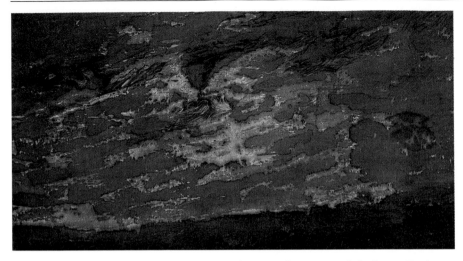

Morris Graves, *Bird Depressed by the Length of Winter of 1944.* Several rhythms – flowing, alternating, and progressive – are evident in this work. Courtesy of the Oregon Art Institute, Portland.

Ernst Barlach, *Avenger,* 1914. One dominant path of movement is seen in the overall form. Its direction is repeated by the flowing edges and surfaces of the robe. Bronze, 17 1/8" x 23 1/2" x 9" (43 x 60 x 23 cm). Hirshhorn Museum and Sculpture Garden, Smithsonian Institution. Gift of Joseph H. Hirshhorn, 1966.

Velino Shije Herrera, *Buffalo Hunt.* Curved shapes are repeated, often in groups of three, to suggest the leftward movement of the animals. Above and below are symmetrical designs suggesting the sky and earth. Tempera. University of Arizona Museum of Art, Gift of R. Vernon Hunter.

Rhythm and Movement

Many rhythms you can see are based on rhythms in nature, everyday life, music or dance. Visual rhythms are created by repeating things in a regular beat or order.

Visual rhythms can be *regular.* In a one-beat repetition of a circle, the same circle is repeated over and over. In an *alternating* rhythm, you repeat a set of visual elements – a circle, a square, a circle, and so on. A *progressive* rhythm has a repeated element with regular changes. An example would be a series of circles, each slightly bigger than the next. In a *flowing* rhythm, there is a graceful path of repeated movements with no sudden changes. In a *jazzy* rhythm, the repeated elements are used in complicated ways with unexpected elements.

Not all visual movements in an artwork are rhythmic. Sometimes a work has a *dominant path of movement* that adds to a mood. Sometimes there is a path of motion leading to a center of interest. The sense of movement may come from a tall, vertical form reaching upward. It may come from a diagonal or twisting or spiraling motion. A quiet, calm feeling may come from the use of many horizontal lines or forms.

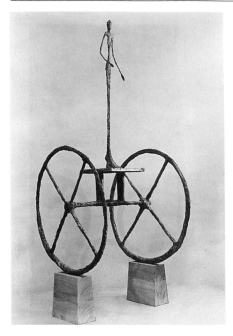

Alberto Giacometti, *Chariot*, 1950. How would you describe the proportions in this sculpture? What is the scale of the figure in relation to the height of the chariot's wheels? Bronze, 57" x 26" x 26 ¹/₈" (145 x 66 x 66 cm). Collection, The Museum of Modern Art, New York. Purchase.

Amedeo Modigliani, *Head*, 1915. Modigliani has exaggerated the proportions of this head. He was more interested in design qualities than creating a portrait. Limestone, 22 ¹/₄" x 5" x 14 ³/₄" (57 x 13 x 37 cm). Collection, The Museum of Modern Art, New York. Gift of Abby Aldrich Rockefeller in memory of Mrs. Cornelius J. Sullivan.

In ancient Greece, artists created sculptures based on an ideal ratio. The height of the figure was eight times the length of the head.

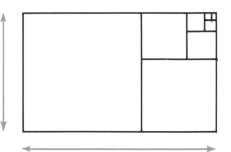

The "Golden Rectangle" is a shape divided into two other shapes. One of the two shapes is always a square. The second shape is always another Golden Rectangle that can be divided again and again.

Proportion

Proportion refers to how a part of something relates to the whole. Our sense of proportion in art comes from the human body. For example, we say artworks are life-size, *monumental* (much larger than life-size) or *miniature* (very small).

Proportions are often normal and expected. They can also be exaggerated and distorted. *Caricature* is the use of exaggerated proportions, usually to make fun of something.

Sometimes proportions are *idealized* – more perfect than you might see in nature. Ancient Greek sculptors used a mathematical formula for idealized sculptures of athletes. The height of the body was eight times the length of the head.

Scale is the size of something compared to what you would expect it to be. You do not expect to see a toothbrush bigger than a bed. Artists often change the normal size, scale or proportion of things to show their importance in artworks.

Elizabeth C. King, *Portrait of M*, 1983. What is the center of interest in this work? Porcelain and glass, 5" x 4" x 4" (13 x 10 x 10 cm). Allan Stone Gallery, New York.

Charles White, *The Mother*, 1952. The hands are the focal point or center of interest in this work. Sepia ink on paper, 30 ⁶/₁₆" x 22 ⁵/₁₆" (77 x 37 cm). Hirshhorn Museum and Sculpture Garden, Smithsonian Institution. Gift of Joseph H. Hirshhorn, 1966.

Emphasis

Emphasis refers to what you notice first about a work. The principle of emphasis can be applied in several ways. One common way is to make one element the strongest, or most *dominant*, in the whole work. The dominance of an element might come by repeating a certain kind of brushstroke, color or shape.

Another way to create emphasis is to set up a *focal point* or *center of interest*. A contrasting element – one bright element in a dark area – can create that effect. An arrangement of lines or paths coming together can seem to flow toward one main point in the work. The most important element might be larger than others or be placed near the center of a work.

Kay Sage, *I Saw Three Cities*, 1944. Oil on canvas, 36" x 27 ⁷/₈" (91 x 71 cm). The Art Museum, Princeton, New Jersey, Gift of the estate of Kay Sage Tanguy.

Pattern

A pattern is a repeated use of lines, colors or other visual elements. Patterns tend to hold a work of art together.

Two-dimensional patterns are created by using a motif over and over again. A *motif* is one complete unit in a larger design. A motif might be a simple flower-like design or a geometric shape used in a wallpaper pattern.

In three-dimensional art, a *module* is one complete unit. A brick is one kind of module. Each brick in a wall is part of a pattern. Other modules might be cylinders made of clay in a sculpture. When the motifs or modules are arranged in a regular pattern, the design is often called an *all-over pattern*.

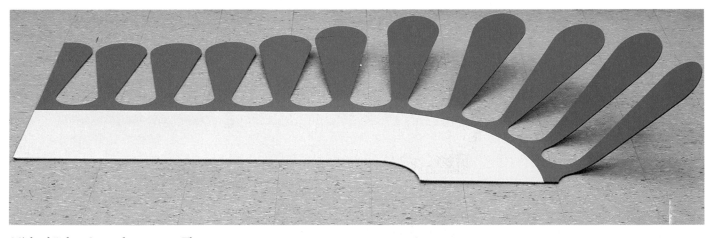

Michael Bolus, *September 64,* 1964. The smaller curved shapes form one pattern. The negative spaces between those shapes also form a pattern. Painted aluminum, 16 ¹/₈" x 7' 4 ⁵/₈" x 48 ¹/₄" (41 x 225 x 122 cm). Collection, The Museum of Modern Art, New York. Purchase.

Amish, *Double Wedding Ring,* ca. 1920. This complex pattern of interlocking circles seems to "spin" with movement. Quilt, cotton, 85" x 66 ¹/₂" (216 x 169 cm). Collection of the Museum of American Folk Art, New York. Gift of Cyril I. Nelson.

Unity and Variety

Unity is the feeling that everything fits together or works like a team. The opposite of unity is *disunity*, a feeling of disorder. In art, unity is often achieved in one of the following ways:

Repetition – using a shape, color or other visual element over and over.

Simplicity – using one major color, kind of shape or element to unify a work.

Harmony – using related colors, textures or materials.

Theme and variation – using one major element, like a circle, for a theme, and many variations on the circle, like half circles and circles in different sizes and colors.

Proximity – placing parts so they are grouped together, enclosed or clustered into sets.

Continuity – aligning edges of forms so your eye moves from one part to another in a definite order.

A totally unified work is probably boring. Just as we appreciate unity and variety in nature, we seem to want unity and variety in our lives – and in our art.

Variety is the use of contrasting elements to make something interesting. The contrast, or difference, may be subtle, such as a slight change in texture or color within an area. It may be more obvious, such as a sharp difference in the materials, colors or the size of shapes.

Wassily Kandinsky, *Study for Composition No.2*, 1909-1910. Oil on canvas, 51 5/8" x 38 3/8" (131 x 97 cm). The Solomon R. Guggenheim Museum, New York. Photograph by Robert E. Mates.

Design Vocabulary

Elements of Design

Line
path of movement
active – passive
bold – delicate
flowing – light
straight – curved
thick – thin
dark – light
broken – continuous
geometric – organic
implied – actual
precise – irregular
contour (outline, edge)
calligraphy
caricature

Shape/Form
2D – 3D
solid – void
concave – convex
positive – negative
figure – ground
ambiguous – complete
organic – geometric – free-form
circle – sphere
square – cube
triangle – pyramid – cone

Space
2D – 3D
positive – negative
open – closed
filled – empty
actual – implied
interior – exterior
scale
orientation
spacing
illusion of space
systems of perspective

Light/Color/Value
visible color spectrum
color wheel
value
  shading
  contrast
  tint
  shade
hue
  pigment
  primary
  secondary
  intermediate
  neutral
  color interactions
  simultaneous contrast
color schemes
  warm
  cool
  neutral
  monochromatic
  analogous
  complementary
  split complementary
  triad
intensity
  bright – dull
  high key – low key
local
optical (or atmospheric)
symbolic

Texture
actual (tactual) – visual
simulated – invented
matte – semi-gloss – glossy
techniques
  impasto
  rubbings
  frottage
  grottage
  decalcomania
  trompe l'oeil

Principles of Design

Balance
symmetrical
asymmetrical
radial

Rhythm, Movement
types
  regular
  alternating
  progressive
  flowing
  jazzy
dominant path of movement
  vertical
  horizontal
  diagonal
  curving

Proportion
life-size
monumental
miniature
normal – exaggerated – idealized
scale
caricature

Emphasis
by dominance
by focal point
by center of interest
by isolation
by size
by contrast
by converging lines

Pattern
repetition
motif (2D)
module (3D)
all-over

Unity and Variety
by repetition
by simplicity
by harmony
by theme and variation
by proximity
by continuity
by contrast

Summary

In order to see, describe and plan artworks, it helps to have a vocabulary for design. The most common vocabulary used in the art world is based on a system of ideas called the elements and principles of design.

A design is a plan or composition that brings parts together into a unified whole for a purpose. This system of thinking about design elements and principles is used in almost every branch of art.

The elements of design include qualities of line, shape, form, texture, value, color and space. The principles of design are balance, rhythm, movement, proportion, emphasis, pattern, unity and variety. These principles are guides for planning and analyzing artworks.

Using What You Learned

Art History

1 Choose one work of art in this chapter. Imagine you are an art historian. Part of your job is to describe and analyze the artwork. Refer to the elements of design first. Describe all of the visual elements you see. Next, analyze the work. Refer to all the principles of art that apply to the work.

2 Select two works of art in this chapter that are reproduced in color. Use as many color terms as you can to describe each work. Explain why it is important to understand color terms in studying art history.

Creating Art

1 Use six 3" x 5" plain index cards. Choose three art elements. On separate cards, create a border-to-border illustration of one art element. Neatly letter the name of the art element on the back. Select three principles of art to illustrate on your remaining cards. When you have finished, shuffle the cards and ask classmates to guess the elements and principles you illustrated. Contribute your best cards to a bulletin board display or to a flash-card game that everyone can use for review.

2 Plan two artworks based on the same subject or theme. Complete each artwork in a different color scheme and with other obvious differences in design elements. Describe the differences in mood created by your choices of design elements.

Aesthetics and Art Criticism

1 Look through the Gallery sections in your book. (Check the Table of Contents for page numbers of these sections.) Find at least three works of art that have different color schemes. Write down the number, title and artist for each work. Name the color scheme. Then describe the mood or feeling created by the use of each scheme.

2 Choose one element of art and one principle of art. Write at least three sentences. In each sentence, combine a term for one element of art with one principle of art. Examples: The thick, curved *lines* are separated for *emphasis*. The analogous *hues* create a progressive rhythm. The geometric *shapes* have exaggerated *proportions*.

Rachel Ruysch, *Flower Still Life*, after 1700 (detail). What features of this work might appeal to many people? Why do you think so? Do people always agree on what is appealing or beautiful? Oil on canvas, 29 ³/₄" x 23 ⁷/₈" (76 x 61 cm). The Toledo Museum of Art, Toledo, Ohio. Gift of Edward Drummond Libbey.

Chapter 4
Seeing and Discussing Art

Chapter Vocabulary

aesthetic perception
art criticism
natural environment
constructed environment
expressive qualities
sensory qualities
technical qualities
formal qualities
criteria for judging art
theories of art
    art as imitation
    art as formal order
    art as expression
    art as functional
masterpiece

Rachel Ruysch, *Flower Still Life,* after 1700. Oil on canvas, 29 ¹/₄" x 23 ⁷/₈" (131 x 97 cm). The Toledo Museum of Art, Gift of Edward Drummond Libbey.

You can learn to see your world in the special ways artists do – with wonder and delight. This special way of seeing is called *aesthetic perception.* A common example of aesthetic perception is seeing a glorious sunset and not wanting to do anything else but watch it. Watching a glowing campfire is another familiar example.

In aesthetic perception, you use your senses as fully as possible. Your eyes don't just glance at things but really study their lines, colors and other visual qualities.

Aesthetic is a Greek word. It means being aware of things through feeling and thought. It means using your senses, your mind and your feelings – all at the same time.

Aesthetic perception is the first step in appreciating art you see in museums and galleries. It is the beginning point for understanding art in your environment – the products you use, all kinds of packages, posters and the like.

Aesthetic perception is important in all ways of seeing and creating art. It is especially important in art criticism. *Art criticism* is the process of carefully looking at and thoughtfully discussing art – your own and others'. Art criticism helps you improve your own art. It can help you understand art in history. It can help you understand exhibits of art and what you read about them.

After completing this chapter and the activities, you will:

Aesthetics and Art Criticism	• be able to develop your aesthetic perception • understand and be able to use appropriate guidelines for perceiving, interpreting and judging art.
Art History and Aesthetics	• understand and be able to apply standards for judging art based on historically important art theories.
Creating Art and Art Criticism	• be able to use your knowledge of aesthetic perception and art criticism while creating art.

Most people are fascinated with beautiful or unusual sunsets. Why do you think this is so? Photograph by Verna E. Beach.

What forms of natural beauty have you seen today? Photograph by Verna E. Beach.

What shapes, colors, lines and textures do you see here? Photograph by Verna E. Beach.

Aesthetic Awareness

Aesthetic perception is a special kind of pleasure that comes from using your senses and your mind. Aesthetic perception is an image and a feeling you can't forget. It is a source of pleasure because you clearly recall details of an object or event.

Perceiving Your Environment

Develop your aesthetic perception of the world around you. Aesthetic perception is a feeling that ordinary things have extraordinary, poetic qualities.

You can find aesthetic qualities in the *natural environment.* Look for beauty in:
- the tiny detail and orderly repetition of large and small forms in a stalk of wheat.
- the delicate lines and radial pattern of a spider web.
- the diamond-like sparkle of dew on the grass.
- the darting movement of swallows in flight.
- the ever-changing forms and colors of the land from morning to night and with changes in season or weather.

Where else can you find beauty in the natural world?

Develop your aesthetic perception of the *constructed environment* – the buildings, streets and products people have created and added to the natural world. Look for beauty in:
- the angular lines of television antennae silhouetted against the evening sky.
- the shifting reflections of sky and clouds on tall, glass-covered skyscrapers.
- the patterns formed by bricks, their textures, their uniformity or variety in color.
- the sleek, shiny surfaces of chrome and paint on new cars.
- the dusky grays and browns in weathered lumber or soot-covered buildings.

Where else can you find beauty in the constructed environment?

What art terms can you use to describe the items in this photograph? If each object had a personality, how would you describe it?

James M. Load, *Cornelius*, 1975. What is unusual about this view of a street? From what point of view did the photographer take this picture? Photograph, 7 1/2" x 9 3/8" (19 x 24 cm). Courtesy of Neil Forsythe.

Using More Than Your Eyes

All of your senses can be important in aesthetic perception. Combine your sense of sight with your senses of touch, movement and sound.

Find a work of art in this chapter. Without using words, make sounds and movements that echo the feeling of the work. For example, you might whisper and use gentle movements to suggest leaves fluttering. You might combine the sound of a low roar and fast rhythmic motions to suggest the crash of waves on a rocky shoreline. See if your classmates can identify the artwork you chose.

VISUAL MEMORY. Remembering what you see is another feature of aesthetic perception. Practice using your visual memory. Here is one way: Distribute an object of the same type to everyone. There should be very subtle differences in each object. The objects might be old pencils, acorns, leaves or pebbles from a stream.

Ask everyone to look at his or her object for several minutes. The idea is to remember all the special features of the object. Collect the objects and place them on a counter. Now everyone must try to find his or her own unique object. Try the same experiment, but draw the object as a way to remember its special visual features.

IMAGINATIVE SEEING. In aesthetic perception, you can imagine that one thing looks like something else. You might look at the forms of puddles and imagine them as animals, faces or landscapes. Cracks in a sidewalk may look like profiles or branching rivers. Think of other examples. Make sketches of the actual forms, then change the sketch into an imaginative artwork.

SHIFTING YOUR POINT OF VIEW. The ability to shift your point of view is another feature of aesthetic perception. Imagine how the world might look from a bird's-eye view – or an ant's-eye view.

Try observing a common scene in more than one way. For example, study only the *foreground* – the parts nearest you. Then look just at the background elements. Notice gradual shifts in color. Then focus on line qualities. What do you see when you focus on textures?

DISCOVERING EXPRESSIVE QUALITIES. In aesthetic perception, we often use words for human qualities and experiences to describe what we see. We may say that dark clouds look "threatening" or "angry." We may say that the downward curves of a tree make it look "droopy" or "forlorn."

Practice this way of thinking and seeing. Search for words and phrases (especially adjectives and adverbs) to describe the human feelings that seem to go with visual qualities.

Seeing Art and Design in Everyday Life

Many of the products you use every day are designed by people who are trained in art. Have you stopped to see and study them as art?

Architecture – the design of houses and apartments, schools, hospitals and other buildings – is one of the major forms of art you see in daily life. Other examples are the design of parks, playgrounds and communities.

Study the design of automobiles and other forms of transportation. Compare the designs of appliances such as telephones, radios, television sets, household goods and furnishings. Look at the design of signs, packages, labels and related graphic images.

Think about the difference between well- and poorly-designed buildings. For example, a well-designed library will have spaces that make it easy and pleasant to borrow books. A poorly designed library might make it very difficult to borrow books. Can you think of other criteria for a well-designed library?

Look for qualities of well-designed products. Three standards are useful for judging them.
- *Careful crafting* – The item shows attention to details in its design, manufacture or assembly.
- *Attention to human needs* – The product meets your needs for comfort, efficiency and ease of use.
- *Beauty* – The item gives you pleasure while you use it. It is designed so you can find meaning in it.

Here are some other ways to increase your awareness of art and design in everyday life:

Draw pictures of parts of your town you think are beautiful and ugly. Discuss the reasons for your judgments. Then draw a picture of an imaginary town with beautiful features.

Use collections of ordinary objects for art study. Practice sorting the items using your knowledge of art concepts. For example, in a collection of forks or knives, notice the different proportions of the handles. Compare the smooth and patterned surfaces, the angular and the curved forms.

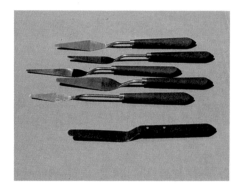

How many differences in these knives can you identify?

How do the images on these packages go with the names of the products?

Both bowls have the same function. When might the top bowl be a good choice for a table? When might the bottom bowl be used?

Looking At Works of Art

Works of art are created to be seen and appreciated. This is true for your own art and artwork by your classmates, as well as well-known artworks. Appreciating art means that you take time to look at artworks and think about what you see.

Art criticism is a method for looking at art and a method for judging art. These methods are often used by artists, art historians, art critics and other art experts.

Art Criticism

Art criticism is more than saying "I like it" or "I don't like it." It is a step-by-step process of logical thinking. Similar steps are used by scientists, lawyers, and others who present ideas clearly.

The major steps in art criticism are describing what you see, analyzing relationships, interpreting meanings and judging.

Step 1 – Describe what you see Take time to look at the work. Describe it in detail using facts, not opinions. In this step you are an art "detective." You are gathering visual evidence or clues. You will use these clues to interpret the artwork.

Step 2 – Analyze relationships Analyze the evidence. In this step, you look for similarities, differences or repeated patterns in what you have observed. You look for the most important features. These will help you interpret the artwork.

Step 3 – Interpret the meaning Interpret the evidence. In this step, you develop a hypothesis (a good guess) about the meaning of the work. A good interpretation explains what you have observed and analyzed. You will use all of your knowledge about art and life to interpret the artwork.

Step 4 – Judgment A critical judgment can be made after you have interpreted an artwork. Judging art is always a matter of being fair and logical.

George Tooker, *Government Bureau*, 1956. Egg tempera on gesso panel, 19 ⁵/₈" x 29 ⁵/₈" (50 x 75 cm). The Metropolitan Museum of Art. George A. Hearn Fund.

Thomas Hart Benton, *Cradling Wheat*, 1938. Tempera and oil on board, 30 ¹¹/₁₆" x 37 ⁵/₈" (78 x 96 cm). The St. Louis Art Museum, St. Louis, Missouri.

Step 1 – Description: What Do You See?

Take time to look at the work. Describe everything you actually see. Use factual, objective language. *Objective* means you describe only those features you can point out and other people can see. Avoid judging the work. Do not use words such as pretty, ugly, weird, sloppy and so on.

Here are some topics for your description:

ART FORM, MEDIUM, AND CONDITION. Name the kind of art and the medium used to create it. For example, is it a painting in oil or in watercolor? Is it architecture? Is it made mostly of wood? Stone? Or glass and steel? Does the artwork appear to be old, damaged or repaired? Are you looking at an original artwork or a photograph of it?

DIMENSIONS. What are the actual dimensions of the work? If you are looking at a photograph, try to visualize the size of the original art work. If the dimensions are given, the first number is the height. The second is the width. A third number will be the depth.

SUBJECT MATTER. Name things you recognize, such as a house, grass, animals, a man or a woman. Be specific, but also be cautious. For example, you may see a boy and a girl. Do not say they are a brother and sister unless there are other clues to that relationship!

SENSORY QUALITIES. Describe the visual elements you see – colors, lines, shapes, textures, spaces and the like. Combine words into sentences and phrases such as "I see a small, dull blue circle." "I see a rough border of pink near the right side," or "I see large patches of blue and yellow in the green grass," Refer to Chapter 3 for more art vocabulary.

TECHNICAL QUALITIES. Describe how the artist used materials, tools and techniques. Use what you know about art materials and processes. Here are some sample statements: "The pencil was applied lightly on a smooth paper." "I see smooth brushstrokes." "I see rough chisel marks in the wood." "The large wooden beams support the low flat roof."

Thomas Hart Benton, *Cradling Wheat,* 1938 (details). *Analysis* means that you look for relationships in the artwork. A few examples of analysis are illustrated here.

You can see two-point perspective here. You are looking into the center of the scene, then left and right.

This diagram shows the cool colors. The painting is dominated by warm colors.

There are large rhythmic curves throughout the painting. There are many smaller curves in the people and stacks of wheat.

Without the action-filled background, the painting seems stiff and incomplete.

Step 2 – Analysis: How Is the Work Planned?

Analysis means finding relationships in what you see. To find relationships in an artwork, you may refer to the principles of design. They can help you describe many of the *formal qualities* of an artwork – the planned similarities and differences in parts of the work.

Analyze the work for relationships such as these:

BALANCE. Are the main forms arranged in a symmetrical, asymmetrical or radial plan? Why? Are the main forms near the top, center, bottom or all over? How are the large negative areas balanced?

RHYTHM, MOVEMENT. Are there special rhythms in the colors, shapes or other elements? Can you see definite paths of movement? Are they vertical, horizontal or diagonal? Where do they begin and end? Why?

PROPORTIONS. Are they about normal? Are they exaggerated? Are they ideal?

EMPHASIS. What are the most dominant visual elements? Are there smaller visual elements repeated throughout the work? Is there a focal point or center of interest? Where? Why? Features like these may be the most important parts of the work.

PATTERN. Is there a pattern of light, shadow, color or other visual elements? Do you find any small designs – motifs – repeated within the work? Do the motifs create an all-over pattern, or are they repeated only in parts of the work?

UNITY AND VARIETY. What principles help to unify the work? Are some more important than others? Why? For example, is the work unified by repeated patterns, rhythms or other features? Are there other dominant elements? What parts add variety?

RELATIONSHIPS IN SUBJECT MATTER. Is there a definite subject – features you can recognize in the work? How are the features related? For example, are there implied interactions between people? Does the artist seem to invite you to walk through or around the work? How? Why? Do you seem to be an observer of a scene or part of the action?

Step 3 – Interpretation:
What are the expressive qualities?

When you interpret a work of art, you are telling about the main *expressive qualities* in the artwork and what they mean to you. Your goal is to understand how all the visual evidence fits together. Like a good detective, you should trust what you've seen – the clues or evidence – and your hunches.

Interpretations of an artwork are not like giving a right or wrong answer. Remember to think of your interpretation as a hypothesis. This is what experts do. A hypothesis is an educated guess about the meaning of the work. An educated guess includes what you have discovered by careful observation. It also includes other things you may know about art and life.

Here are some guides for interpreting art:
• A good interpretation includes *expressive language*. Expressive language is not objective. It includes lively adjectives and adverbs. For example, you might say a work has energetic lines, bold colors, velvety shadows, swirling brushstrokes, rugged forms, jagged shapes or prickly textures.
• A good interpretation includes *analogies*. An analogy tells how things you see in the work are related to other things you know or feel. Here are some examples: The delicate shading is misty, like fog. The diagonal lines seem to be marching.

Artworks can always be interpreted in more than one way. Here is one interpretation of *The Starry Night*.

"The great dark cypress tree with flame-like branches soars upward to the heavens. The heavens are filled with swirling, sparkling energy. This energy spirals and radiates throughout the sky making it seem near to us, alive, and throbbing with motion.

"A village below and mountains beyond glow with the light from the sky. The brushstrokes give life, energy, and motion to every part of the work. It is as if the artist wants us to see the world as alive and animated by a divine energy force in the heavens."

Vincent Van Gogh, *The Starry Night*, 1889. Oil on canvas, 29" x 36 ¼" (74 x 92 cm). Collection, The Museum of Modern Art, New York. Acquired through the Lillie P. Bliss Bequest.

- A good interpretation tells about causes and effects. For example, you might say: "The face looks tired (effect) because the lines and shadows are dark and droopy (cause)." You could also say "The dark, droopy lines (cause) make the face look tired (effect)."
- A good interpretation explains how the work of art is related to other ideas or events. The artist is always sending one or more wordless messages to the viewer. Make an educated guess about the message.

The message might be about the beauty of color or the power of the artist's imagination. It is often about the artist's world and culture. Some artworks send messages about human feelings, such as joy or great sorrow.

If you have difficulty in interpreting a work, think about your own experience in life. Recall other artwork you have seen – artwork from the past, artwork in a similar style or from other cultures. Your experiences in creating art may help you interpret a work.
- A good written interpretation can be as short as one paragraph or as long as several pages. It is a summary of the expressive qualities you find in a work. It tells about the most important sensations, feelings and ideas the work communicates to you.

The Starry Night

The artist wants us to see the magnificent stars swirling over the mountains and village below. The stars and moon look bright and fiery. The swirls in the sky and the curves in the tree look like they come from the wind. The cool colors and mountains covered with snow make you feel like a cold wind is blowing through the dark night.

The tall dark tree is like a shadow of a person looking out at the sky and the sleepy village below. The wintery air is filled with the fiery warmth of the moon and stars. The night is filled with swirling, falling stars from the heavens.

I think Van Gogh was awestruck by a scene like this. I think he used his imagination to express his deep emotions about the scene. His painting shows a beautiful and mysterious night. The stars swirl and whisk through the sky like angels from Heaven. The way he painted it makes me think it could be titled "Night of the Angels."

This student has used expressive language to interpret the artwork.

The Starry Night

The bright moon and stars stand out from the dark night sky. They swirl and glow with light. The brushstrokes make circles and spirals around them. They look like shooting or exploding stars. The moon is so bright it is like a sun.

The scene has a strange effect on me. The dark and light swirling colors make me feel like it is a windy and cold winter night. I feel like I'm standing on top of a hill looking at the village below. I see the snow on far-away mountains. The large dark tree near me looks scary or spooky. It's like an old tree you might see on Halloween. The tree has a shape like a devil's pitch fork.

I feel like I'm dreaming the bright circular light in the swirling sky. It scares me a little. It's like the twinkling stars and glow of the moon have been changed into giant fireballs of light. The fireballs are hanging and swirling over the earth below. There is wind and energy everywhere. It's almost like a scary scene from another planet.

This student has used expressive language and related the qualities to his own life.

Balans chair. This chair was designed for use in an office. What standards would be appropriate for judging office furniture?

Stephen Daniell, *Icarus Chair*. Criteria for judging art should be appropriate to the work. This fantasy furniture was not meant to be judged by the same standards you might use to judge office furniture. Walnut and birch. Photograph courtesy the Moira James Gallery, Green Valley, Nevada.

Step 4 – Judging Artworks

You have learned that art criticism is a process of describing, analyzing and interpreting art. Judging art is also a process. In a critical judgment of art, you state what you are judging and why, identify *criteria* (standards) for judging, and give reasons why the work does or does not meet the standards.

IDENTIFY THE KIND OF ART YOU ARE JUDGING. First, identify the kind of art you are judging, such as architecture or sculpture. Then, describe its general style, such as fantasy, realism or nonobjectivism.

This step will help you remember that you should judge things in relation to their type. You can't judge one art form or style as better or worse than another. They are different.

STATE YOUR PURPOSE IN MAKING A JUDGMENT. The purpose of making a judgment can influence the criteria you use. For example, your teacher may ask you to judge your own artwork. Your teacher may have set up the standards or criteria for you to meet. In this case, the purpose in judging art is to find out what you have learned.

In the art world, standards also vary. They depend on the purpose of making a judgment. For example, criteria might be very different if your purpose were to choose artwork for a restaurant rather than for an art museum collection.

What qualities of a tree's growth are related to saving money? Is this an effective graphic design? Why? Why not?

Blue jeans come in many styles. What are some of the criteria people use when they choose blue jeans for work clothes? For play clothes? For school clothes? Photograph by Barbara Caldwell.

IDENTIFY CRITERIA OR STANDARDS. When you know the purpose of making a judgment and kind of art to be judged, you can state criteria. There are two main sources of criteria.

First, some artworks can be judged by criteria that you learn about at home, in school and everyday life. For example, signs for stores should be easy to read. Office furniture should be comfortable and easy to adjust. Clothing for outdoor work should be durable, washable and comfortable. List the criteria as questions. Is this sign easy to read? Are these work clothes made of durable fabric? Does this office chair come in different sizes, or can it be adjusted? Is it sturdy? Is it attractive?

Second, many artworks can be judged by criteria that come from art theories that have been developed by art experts. Some of these theories and criteria are outlined on the next four pages.

CITE EVIDENCE (GIVE REASONS). After you state your criteria for judging art, give reasons why the work does or does not meet the criteria or standards. Your reasons are statements supported by evidence. For example, you might state that a chair is poorly designed because it has no adjustable seat or does not come in different sizes. Do you see how stating your criteria can help you make judgments?

STATE YOUR CONCLUSIONS. You state your conclusions by giving a summary of the major strengths and weaknesses in the work. Use sentences such as these: "I think this work is (is not) excellent because. . ." "I judge this work to be of great (little) importance because. . ." "I do (do not) think this work is well designed because. . ."

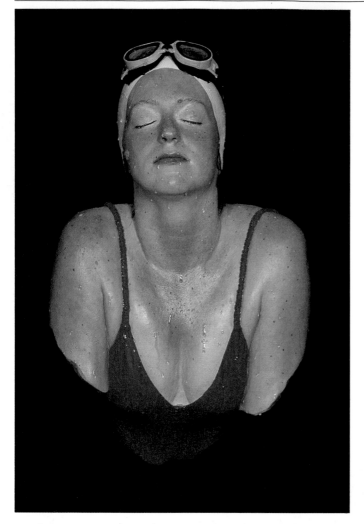

Carol Jeane Feuerman, *Catalina*, 1981. Oil painted resin, 22" x 17" x 7" (56 x 43 x 18 cm). Galerie Ninety-Nine. Photograph by Ken Spencer.

Albrecht Dürer, *Stag Beetle*, 1505. Watercolor and gouache, 5" x 4" (13 x 10 cm). The J. Paul Getty Museum, Malibu, California.

Criteria from Theories of Art

A *theory of art* states how people should think about art and judge it. Art theories are developed by philosophers called *aestheticians*. Most aestheticians agree that there are four main theories about art: art as imitation, art as formal order, art as expression and art as functional. Each theory helps people think about the value of art in a logical way.

Art as Imitation

Some experts say that art is a way to represent or imitate what you see. Accuracy and honesty in art are highly valued. Here are questions you can ask when you are judging art.

First Impression:
- Does the work look real?

Design:
- Do the proportions of parts, colors and other elements seem to be natural or lifelike?
- Is the work planned around patterns, rhythms and forms we see in nature or the human-made environment?

Subject/Theme:
- Does the subject or theme seem to be based on a real event or something the artist observed?
- Is the subject or theme more realistic than abstract? Is it honestly shown (not idealized)?

Materials:
- Can you see some of the natural qualities of the materials?
- Do the materials and techniques go with the mood? (The materials and techniques are not the first thing that you notice.)

Functional or Decorative Art:
- Can you identify the use or function of the art by looking just at the design?
- Are the decorations few or based on nature?

Apply these criteria to Dürer's *Stag Beetle* and Mondrian's *Composition* . Which artwork meets more of the criteria for art as imitation?

Art as Formal Order

Some theories are based on a respect for logical order and idealized forms in art. A work of art might be judged "good" if it met all or many of the criteria listed below.

First Impression:
• Is the work beautiful or harmonious?

Design:
• Is the work unified by a kind of invented or mathematical order?
• Are the proportions of parts, colors, and other elements more perfect or idealized then you might see in life? (The work is not filled with realistic details.)

Subject/Theme:
• Does the subject or theme seem to be idealized or have a spiritual quality?
• Is the work more abstract than realistic?

Materials:
• Does it look like the artist used extreme care using materials and finishing the work?
• Do you sense the artist knew exactly what to do with materials and techniques?

Functional or Decorative Art:
• Is this artwork elegant, refined or dignified?
• Does the design of the work seem to be just as important – or more important – than the practical use of the object?

Apply these criteria to Feuerman's *Catalina* and de Rivera's *Construction in Blue and Black*. Which artwork meets more of the criteria for art as formal order?

The Charioteer from the Sanctuary of Apollo at Delphi, ca. 470 BC The theory of art as formal order goes back to the time of the ancient Greeks. In many of their works you see idealized forms and proportions. Bronze, 71" (180 cm). Museum Delphi.

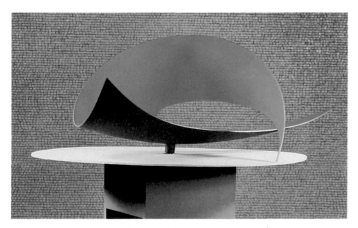

Jose de Rivera, *Construction in Blue and Black,* 1951. Why would it be inappropriate to judge these artworks by criteria for realism? The Whitney Museum of American Art, New York.

Piet Mondrian, *Composition (Blue, Red and Yellow),* 1930. Oil on canvas, 28 5/8" x 21 1/4" (73 x 54 cm). Private Collection, New York. Courtesy The Sidney Janis Gallery.

Lu Duble, *Cain*, 1953. What is the main feeling expressed in this work? What are the "clues" the artist gives you? Hydrocal, 38" x 28" x 18" (97 x 71 x 46 cm). Collection of Whitney Museum of American Art, New York. Purchase.

David Siqueiros, *Echo of a Scream*, 1937. What are the unexpected elements in this painting? What feelings does the artist express? Enamel on wood, 48" x 36" (122 x 91 cm). Collection, The Museum of Modern Art, New York. Gift of Edward M. M. Warburg.

Art as Expression

Some theories of art are based on a respect for strong human feelings and originality. Standards for judging art include:

First Impression:
• Does the work express a definite feeling?

Design:
• Are the proportions of parts, color and other elements unexpected or exaggerated?
• Is the total design dramatic or original? Does it give you a definite feeling?

Subject/Theme:
• Is the subject or theme unique, dreamlike or fantastic?

• Does the subject or theme seem to come from the artist's desire to communicate a strong feeling (the great joys, sorrows or problems of people)?

Materials:
• Is the use of materials original or unexpected?
• Are the materials and techniques an important part of the mood or feeling of the work?

Functional or Decorative Art:
• Does the work have an unusual function or combine several functions?
• Is the design of the work unexpected? Does it cause you to react in new ways?

Apply these criteria to Duble's *Cain* and the *Great Buddha of Kamakura*. Which artwork meets more of the criteria for art as expression?

Great Buddha of Kamakura, 1252. Kamakura period, Japan. Like most religious artwork, this one is meant to inspire religious faith. Many religious artworks also teach people important lessons. Cast bronze, 12.8 meters high.

Diego Rivera, *Agrarian Leader Zapata*, 1931. This painting honors Emiliano Zapata, a political leader in Mexico. Can you think of other examples of political art? What are some purposes of political art? Fresco, 7' 9 ³/₄" x 6' 2" (238 x 188 cm). Collection, The Museum of Modern Art, New York. Abby Aldrich Rockefeller Fund.

Art as Functional

Some theories of art emphasize the use of art in everyday life and for communication. Some criteria for judging art are:

First Impression:
- Does the work have an important message or function?

Design:
- Are the proportions, colors and other elements planned to help you understand the message of the work?
- Is the total design useful? Is the design an important part of the message the artist wants you to understand?

Subject/Theme
- Is the subject or theme related to the life of a particular cultural group?

- Is the subject or theme important to almost all people at sometime in their lives?

Materials:
- Do the materials and techniques help you understand the message in the artwork?
- Are the materials and techniques practical or related to the functions of the artwork?

Functional or Decorative Art:
- Does the work have an important purpose or communicate important ideas?
- Is the design or decoration well-suited for the purposes of the work? (It is not too fancy or too plain.)

Apply these criteria to Siqueiros' *Echo of a Scream* and Rivera's *Agrarian Leader Zapata*. Which artworks should be judged as functional art? Why?

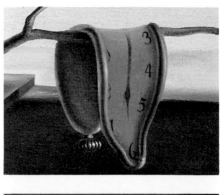

Salvador Dali, *The Persistence of Memory*, 1931 (and two details). Oil, 9 ¹/₂" x 13" (24 x 33 cm). Collection, The Museum of Modern Art, New York. Given anonymously.

How to Use Theories of Art

Most experts say that each art theory has important ideas and standards. They believe people should learn about art theories but use the ideas flexibly.

Flexibility means that you combine ideas from the theories. Flexibility is important because many works of art also combine ideas. Only a few artworks match up with the standards of a strict theory of art.

Experts often use criteria from different theories to explain and judge new kinds of art. For example, Surrealism is now a well-known style of art. It combines Realism and fantasy, or imagination. Dali's *Persistence of Memory*, shown above, is an example of Surrealism. To judge a painting in this style, you might combine criteria from two theories: art as imitation and art as expression. Can you think of other ways to use ideas from art theories?

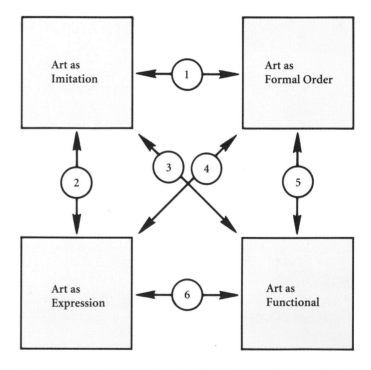

Combining ideas from art theories. This diagram and the numbered statements below show just a few ways of combining ideas to judge art. Why are combinations often helpful?

1. The work looks real, and it has a harmonious design.
2. The work looks real, and it expresses a definite feeling.
3. The work looks real, and it has an important message or function.
4. The work has a harmonious design, and it expresses a definite feeling.
5. The work has a harmonious design, and it has an important message or function.
6. The work expresses a definite feeling, and it has an important message or function.

"You're putting in too many people!"

Gahan Wilson, *"You're putting in too many people!"* The reindeer with the lamp is acting like an art critic. What criterion, or standard, does the art critic want the artist to meet? Copyright 1989 The New Yorker Magazine, Inc.

"Mrs. Hammond! I'd know you anywhere from little Billy's portrait of you."

Frascino, *"Mrs. Hammond! I'd know you anywhere from little Billy's portrait of you."* If the lady in the door *really* looks like Mrs. Hammond, what theory of art is the teacher using? Copyright 1989 The New Yorker Magazine, Inc.

Similarities and Differences in Judgments

Judgments about art, including well-known works, are not always the same. They are most likely to be the same when people use the same process of judgment and have the same theory of art. Also, when people live in the same culture and have similar personal experiences, they are more likely to judge art in the same way.

Disagreements about art are common. Even experts may disagree. There are many reasons for these differences.

DIFFERENCES IN THE PROCESS OF JUDGING. Sometimes people disagree because they do not use the same art theories and standards for judgment. In other words, people do not see and interpret the work in the same way.

DIFFERENCES IN CULTURE AND TIME. Most art experts agree that criteria or standards for judging art are not the same in every culture or time.

For example, many traditional Asian sculptures now in art museums were created for temples and religious ceremonies. The original audiences saw the works in temples and understood the religious meanings of the sculptures. Their criteria for art were different from most present-day viewers who see the works in museums.

DIFFERENCES IN PERSONAL BACKGROUND. Criteria or standards for judging art often differ within the same culture because people have different backgrounds. For example, if you are an expert in creating bronze sculpture, your standards may be different from a person who has little or no experience in making a bronze sculpture.

What Is a Masterpiece?

Some artworks are called *masterpieces.* The word masterpiece is used by art experts as a judgment about the quality of an artwork. It is the highest form of praise for an artwork.

Most experts say a masterpiece meets several criteria: (1) The artwork presents an important feeling or idea about life. (2) The artwork has a perfect design. (3) The artwork shows a highly developed technique. (4) The artwork inspires people to want to look at it again and again. (5) Many art experts agree that the work is an important achievement in art history.

The two artworks you see here are often called masterpieces. Michelangelo's *Pietà* is often praised for its superb design, crafting and expression of important religious ideas. Miyamoto's *Bird and Branch* captures in a few brush-strokes the lively form of a bird perched on a craggy branch. The work is considered a perfect example of the Zen religious idea of combining control and freedom.

Michelangelo, *The Pietà*, 1499. Marble, 5' 9" (175 cm). The Vatican, St. Peter's, Rome.

Musashi Miyamoto, *Bird and Branch*, 16th-17th century. Ink on paper, Philadelphia Museum of Art. Purchased: Fiske Kimball Fund.

Summary

Looking at your world as artists do is called aesthetic perception. Aesthetic perception is a blend of seeing, thinking, feeling and imagining. You look for very subtle qualities in art or your environment.

Art criticism is a process of using your aesthetic perception to understand and judge artwork. Art criticism is one kind of logical reasoning. The main steps in art criticism are: describing what you see, analyzing what you see, interpreting the visual evidence and judging the work.

Judging art is a logical process. You first identify the purpose and the criteria for making the judgment. Then you go back to your visual evidence and give reasons for your judgment. Some criteria for judging art come from your own experience. You can also combine criteria from four main theories about art: art as imitation, art as formal order, art as expression and art as functional.

Most experts in art today say that judgments about art are relative. This means that they are influenced by our time, our culture and our personal background.

The word masterpiece is used as the highest form of praise for an artwork. A masterpiece presents an important idea, in a perfect design, using appropriate techniques. It inspires people to look at it again and again. It is an important achievement in the history of art.

Using What You Learned

Art History

1 What are the four main theories of art?
2 What is meant when art historians call an artwork a "masterpiece"?
3 List three reasons why art historians and other experts may not agree in their judgments of the same artwork.

Aesthetics and Criticism

1 Give one example of each kind of aesthetic perception: (A) visual memory, (B) imaginative seeing, (C) shifting your point of view, (D) discovering expressive qualities.
2 What is the main difference between art criticism and expressing a personal preference?
3 What are the four steps in art criticism?
4 What are the main points to remember in judging art?
5 How can theories of art help you learn to judge art?

Creating Art

1 Choose one of your best completed artworks. Describe, analyze and interpret it. Then judge it using criteria that you think are appropriate to it.
2 Select one of the theories of art presented in this chapter. Create an artwork that meets at least three of the criteria emphasized in that theory.

Egypt, Mask of Tutankhamen, 1352 BC. Gold with precious stones and glass, life-sized. Egyptian Museum, Cairo.

Chapter 5
Art History Before 1900

Chapter Vocabulary

Terms for styles and periods in art history are listed in the time-line on page 102.

Thebes, Egypt. One of four cases for Tutankhamen's viscera, ca. 1361-1352 BC.

One of the most thrilling discoveries in the history of art was made in 1922, when the tomb of an ancient king was discovered in Egypt. Inside were thousands of dazzling objects made of silver, precious stones, inlaid wood and gold. All the treasures had been placed in the tomb over 3,000 years ago to accompany the dead ruler into his afterlife.

Scholars are still studying those treasures. They are a fascinating record of the social, political and religious history of the ancient Egyptian people. They are also important works of art in Western culture. Western culture is a heritage of beliefs and achievements beginning long ago in the lands around the Mediterranean Sea and later in Europe. When people from Europe set up colonies in North America over two hundred years ago, they brought many ideas from this heritage with them, including ideas about art.

In this chapter and the next one, you will learn about the history of art in Western culture. You will find the names of many artists. You may want to develop reports on some of them. In most cases, the names of the artists are so well known that you can easily find information. After you study this chapter, you will be better able to:

Art History
- discuss art in Western culture, noting changes in its purposes, subject matter, design and styles before the twentieth century.

Art Criticism
- use your skills in art criticism to perceive, analyze, and interpret artworks from the past.

Aesthetics
- understand the value of artworks in terms of why they were created in particular cultures and times.
- use what you know about art theories and criteria as you study art history.

Creating Art
- understand why and how artists of the past have created art.

83

Art in the Ancient World

People all over the world create art. Experts believe that making art is a basic human need. Perhaps this need inspired the first artists thousands of years ago.

Prehistoric Art 30,000–2000 BC

As far as we know, the story of art began about 30,000 years ago. Some of the earliest artworks are paintings discovered in caves of Spain, France and Africa. The cave paintings show hunting scenes with cattle, deer and bison. The animals are usually painted in profile views with lifelike proportions, details and action. People are shown as stick figures with spears.

Stonehenge, Salisbury Plain, England, ca. 2000 BC. Ancient people arranged these huge stones, called megoliths, to create a place for worship. Photograph by Claire Mowbray Golding.

Art of the Near East 3500–331 BC

One of the first known centers of civilization is Mesopotamia, a region between the Tigris and Euphrates Rivers near present-day Iraq and Iran. At different times, the region was ruled by the Sumerians, Babylonians, Hittites and Assyrians. Later, the Persians became powerful. In 331 BC Alexander the Great conquered the region and united it with Greek culture.

These ruling groups created art about their beliefs and the conquests of their leaders. Magnificent palaces and royal tombs were filled with furniture and other things crafted with gold, silver and gemstones. Some of the rulers are portrayed as animal gods. Relief and mosaic *friezes*, long horizontal compositions, tell stories of hunts, battles and ceremonies.

Palace of Darius I, Persepolis, ca. 500 BC. Many skilled workers built this palace at Persepolis, the capital of the Persian Empire under the rule of Darius I.

Ancient Egyptian Art 3000–500 BC

Ancient Egyptian civilization developed along the Nile River in Africa. This civilization grew from the earliest farming and hunting groups in Africa, before 3000 BC, and influences from the Near East.

The Egyptians believed their *pharaohs* (rulers) were gods who would live after death. Many of the pharaohs built tombs shaped like temples or pyramids. The tombs were filled with furniture, jewelry and other things the rulers might need in the afterlife. Wall paintings, relief sculptures and small models show servants bringing gifts, harvesting crops and fishing.

Egyptian art is often said to be timeless. For nearly 2,500 years, artists used many of the same artistic rules. Their portraits of pharaohs and other important people are similar in style. The subjects are usually shown with calm expressions and poses that seem to be frozen for eternity.

The Pyramid of Cheops and the Great Sphinx, ca. 2530 BC (4th dynasty). Giza. The great pyramids were once covered with smooth stone. The tomb of a pharaoh was hidden in a room deep inside the pyramid.

Hall of Bulls, left wall, Lascaux, ca. 15,000-13,000 BC. Experts believe that the cave paintings were created before a hunt to bring good luck or after a hunt to celebrate it. Could there be other explanations? Dordogne, France.

La Madeleine, *Bison*, ca. 11,000 BC. Carvings in bones and small rocks often show animals. What parts of this carving reflect a careful observation of the animal? Museé des Antiquites Nationales, St. Germaine-en-Laye, France.

Bull from the Ishtar Gate, 580 BC. The bull is a strong, powerful animal often used as a symbol for rulers. This relief is part of a ceremonial gate built for the king of Babylonia, Nebuchadnezzar. Glazed brick, 39 ³/₈" (100 cm). Staatlich Museum, Germany.

Persia, Nineveh, ca. 2340 BC. This bronze sculpture probably shows the Akkadian ruler, Sargon. What parts of the sculpture are *abstract* – not totally realistic? Bronze, 12" (30 cm). Iraq Museum.

Wall painting, 1400 BC. This Egyptian painting reflects that culture's artistic rules for showing people: Show the head, arms and lower body in profile; show the eye and upper torso in a front view. 32" (81 cm). Thebes, The British Museum, London.

Egypt, *Queen Nefertiti*, ca. 1360 BC, 18th dynasty. This ancient portrait is often said to have "timeless beauty." What does this phrase mean? Painted limestone, El Amarna, Staates Museum, Berlin.

Ancient Greece 600–150 BC

The civilization of the ancient Greeks developed from life in city-states and trade routes in the Mediterranean region, including Egypt and the Near East. Early Greek art has a stiff, geometric style. This gradually evolved to a classic style with elegant proportions and a perfection of form called ideal beauty.

The Greeks developed new ways to build temples and outdoor theaters. Many buildings included mosaic murals and sculptures decorated with paint, gold and colorful stones. Temple roofs were supported by carved columns of stone. The styles of columns are named for the system of proportions used within major regions of Greece: Doric, Ionic, and Corinthian.

Iktinos and Kallikrates, The Parthenon, 447-432 BC. The Acropolis, Athens. The Parthenon is one of the most widely admired and copied buildings in history. We know it was designed by the architects Iktinos and Kallikrates and the sculptor, Phidias. In earlier cultures artists were unknown slaves. The best Greek artists were free and are known by their names – as individuals. Photograph by David Wade.

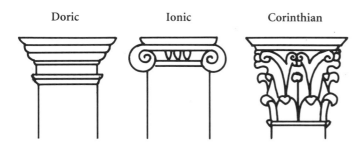

| Doric | Ionic | Corinthian |

Have you seen buildings with Greek columns?

Ancient Roman Art 753 BC–476 AD

The Romans, who conquered the Greeks and other nations, admired Greek civilization. They even copied Greek works of art. Through their conquests, the Romans helped to spread Greek culture to Europe and parts of England.

The Romans excelled in architecture and city planning. They invented concrete and combined it with stone to build large domed meeting halls, called *basilicas*, and colosseums. Similar buildings as well as forums, theaters and *aqueducts,* or water channels, were built in many parts of the vast empire. Large carved monuments were created to celebrate their triumphs.

The Romans emphasized the practical and realistic features of art. The Greeks were concerned with ideal beauty and elegant proportions. Art historians often use the term *classical* to refer to both of these traditions of art – Greek and Roman. Even today, the phrase "It's a classic" means that something has lasting merit or is nearly perfect. It is well-made and ideal in beauty, proportion or function.

The Pantheon, Rome, ca. 118-128 AD. Compare the Roman Pantheon and Greek Parthenon. What features are similar in both buildings? What are the major differences? The Romans treated their artists as skilled workers in various crafts. Many Roman artworks were actually created by Greek artists who were captured and became slaves of the Romans.

Dioskourides, *Street Musicians*, ca. 100 BC. This mosaic shows an interest in movement and detail not seen in Egyptian art. Villa of Cicero, Pompeii, Italy.

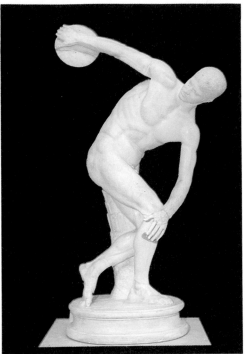

Myron, *Discobolus*. Greek gods such as Zeus, Apollo and Athena were honored in many artworks. Athletes, heroes, myths and political events were also important subjects. Myron, Polyclitus and Lysippus were well-known sculptors. Marble, 60" (152 cm) high. Museo della Terme, Rome.

Peaches and Glass Jar, ca. 50 AD. Wealthy Romans hired artists to decorate their homes with paintings, mosaics, fountains and portraits in sculpture. This kind of patronage, or employment for artists, became even more important after the Renaissance. Wall painting from Herculaneum. National Museum, Naples.

Aulus Metellus (L'Arringatore). Early 4th century BC. Bronze, 71" (180 cm). Archaeological Museum, Florence.

Early Christian Art 31–400

The Romans were still in power at the time Christ was born. Most of what we know about early Christian art comes from paintings in catacombs – secret tunnel-like burial grounds near Rome. Early Christians met in the catacombs because the Romans had laws against worshiping Christ. Although few of the paintings were created by artists, they are the first record of Christian symbols and themes in European art. Not until the rule of Emperor Constantine, about 300 years after the birth of Christ, were Christians permitted to worship in public.

Cappella di S. Giacinto, S. Sabina, Rome. The first Christian churches were Roman *basilicas* – meeting halls. They were decorated to make them places of worship.

Byzantine Art 300–1500

In 330 AD, Emperor Constantine transferred the capital of the Roman empire to an old Greek city, Byzantium, which he renamed Constantinople. This new city, near present-day Istanbul, Turkey, became the hub of Byzantine art and civilization. Byzantine architecture combines ideas from Greece, Eastern Asia and Rome.

Constantine supported art that portrayed the Byzantine rulers and people as Christians. The most impressive basilica, the Hagia Sophia, has a dome 107 feet (32 m) across. Paintings and mosaic murals were created to teach Christian doctrines. For this purpose, artists developed a simple, abstract style with clear outlines, flat shapes and decorative patterns. The Byzantine style dominated art in eastern Europe and Russia for over 1,000 years.

Byzantine, Hagia Sophia, ca. 532-537. Istanbul, Turkey.

Growth of Islamic Art 600–900

Between 400 and 900 AD many people in Europe began to fight for power. Monasteries and castles provided safety for some people, but many had no permanent homes. Migrating people created animal and flower-like designs on jewelry, belts, horse bridles and other small portable art. During this same period, the Islamic empire expanded to parts of Spain, Portugal, France and North Africa.

Islamic people follow the religious teaching recorded in the Koran by Muhammad. Islamic *mosques* are places of worship. They resemble basilicas but have *minarets* – slender towers – like those added to the Hagia Sophia. Minarets are used to call people for prayer. Islam forbids religious art that portrays people. Artistry is achieved through the use of intricate geometric and curving designs called *arabesques*.

The intricate geometric and curving patterns on this mosque are created with mosaics. Mosque of Sheikh Lutfullah, Ispahan.

Early Mediterranean, *Jonah Cast Up*, ca. 260-275. Marble, 16" x 8 $\frac{1}{2}$" x 14 $\frac{13}{16}$" (41 x 22 x 38 cm). The Cleveland Museum of Art. John L. Severance Fund.

The Good Shepherd, ca. 250-300. This painting has some of the first visual symbols for the Christian faith. The shepherd and lambs are themes in Bible stories. Catacomb of Priscilla, Rome.

Byzantine School (13th century): *Madonna and Child on a Carved Throne*. Wood, 32 $\frac{1}{8}$" x 19 $\frac{3}{8}$" (82 x 49 cm). Courtesy of National Gallery of Art, Washington, DC. Andrew W. Mellon Collection.

The Barberini Diptych: *The Emperor as Defender of the Faith*, 6th century. Experts think this carving shows the Byzantine Emperor Justinian. The small figure supporting his foot is a symbol for the earth. The figure above is a symbol for Christ. 7" x 5" (18 x 13 cm). The Louvre. Courtesy Reunion des Museés Nationaux.

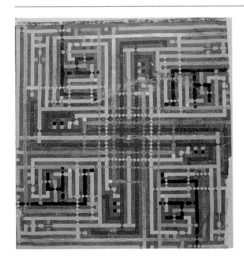

Calligraphic page from "The Album of the Conqueror" (Sultan Mohammed II). *Calligraphy* – the art of beautiful handwriting – is highly developed in Islamic art. In this example, the colorful design is geometric. Topkapi Palace Museum, Istanbul.

Mosque at Cordoba, Spain, 785. The interiors of many mosques have an open, airy feeling. The carved stones create rich patterns of solid forms and openings. Photograph courtesy of George Barford.

Romanesque Art 1000–1200

Romanesque refers to the continued use of Roman art ideas in Europe as towns began to grow and Christianity spread. In monasteries, the arts of metalworking and *illuminated,* or decorated, manuscripts were refined. Items created for use in worship were often decorated with gold, silver, pearls and gemstones.

St. Ambrogio (Interior), 11th and 12th centuries. Romanesque. Milan, Italy.

Speyer Cathedral. Begun 1030. Many new cathedrals followed the general plan of Roman basilicas. They had rounded arches, barrel vaults and thick walls with narrow windows. In Italy, builders used colored marble to brighten this heavy style. Romanesque. Germany.

Gothic Art 1100–1400

Gothic refers to a style of French art and architecture that was adopted later in other parts of Europe and England. It began as towns became cities and even larger cathedrals were built. Gothic art and architecture are often described as vertical, open, delicate and light.

Many cathedrals were built with tall columns, tapered spires and pointed arches. The walls and roofs were supported by *flying buttresses,* a system of arches and pillars outside the buildings. This new system created tall interior spaces and large openings for stained glass windows that brought glowing light inside. Paintings were usually part of illuminated manuscripts and altarpieces. Some Italian buildings have large *fresco* paintings – paintings done on plaster.

Some artists of this period are well-known. You might do research to learn more about them.

PAINTERS: *(Italy)* Giotto di Bondone, Cenni di Pepi Cimabue, Ambrogio Lorenzetti, Simone Martini, Gentile da Fabriano; *(Flanders)* The Limbourg Brothers (Paul, Jean and Herman); SCULPTORS: *(Italy)* Nicola Pisano; *(Germany)* Sabina von Steinbach, Claus Sluter.

Chartres, Cathedral of Notre-Dame, 1145. Nave looking west, Chartres, France.

Chartres Cathedral, 1145-1220. Notice the rose or wheel window on the exterior and interior. The lacy radial design is supported by metal and carved stone. Gothic. France.

Master Hugo, *The Bury Bible: Moses Expounding the Law*, ca. 1130-1140. The most common subjects for many artworks were scenes from the Bible. Color on vellum, 20" (51 cm) high. Corpus Christi College, Cambridge, England.

The Mission to the Apostles, ca. 1130. Gradually, artists added sculpture to the exterior of the church and created work for interior altars and niches. The round shapes in this *tympanum* – the top of the doorway – are typical in Romanesque art. Tympanum of the Central Portal, Vezelay, Ste. Madeleine. Romanesque.

Pietro Lorenzetti, *The Presentation in the Temple,* 1342. Tempera on panel, 102" x 67" (260 x 170 cm). Uffizi, Florence, Italy.

West Portal Tympanum, Chartres Cathedral, 1145-1220. In what ways is this different from the Romanesque tympanum of Vezelay (above)? Gothic. France.

The Renaissance 1400–1600

Renaissance means rebirth or reawakening. The Renaissance began in Italy and gradually spread to the rest of Europe. It was a time of worldwide exploration and rapid growth in knowledge about the natural world and people. Artists and other leaders also studied the history and philosophy of ancient Greek and Roman culture. Even today, anyone who has studied many subjects is called a "Renaissance" person.

Artists began to be valued as individuals. Many were creative in several fields – painting, architecture, sculpture, crafts. The church and royalty, wealthy merchants and bankers employed artists and began to collect art. New machines and engineering skills were used to create complicated forms of sculpture and architecture.

Art criticism, art history and new theories about architecture and perspective were written. Artists began to travel to other regions to create art and study it. Some artists, including women, became internationally known.

Renaissance paintings are the first to have textural details that suggest metal, wood or skin. They reflect a new interest in perspective and lighting. Artists capture action and feeling in graceful, complex works. Northern European paintings are small, highly detailed and have a strong linear quality. Smooth, glowing surfaces and clear colors were made possible by the invention of oil paint.

Many artworks are *allegories*, blending Christian ideas and classical myths. In an allegory, one subject (a myth) is a symbol for another (a religious story).

A few of the many well-known Renaissance artists are identified here. You might do more research on these artists or others.

PAINTERS: *(Italy)* Tommaso Masaccio, Fra Filippo Lippi, Fra Angelico, Piero della Francesca, Paolo Uccello, Andrea del Castagno, Andrea Mantegna, Giovanni Bellini, Sandro Botticelli, Domenico Ghirlandaio, Lavinia Fontana, Sofonisba Anguisciola, Giorgione da Castelfranco, Titian; *(Flanders)* Jan Van Eyck; *(Germany)* Mathis Grünewald, Lucas Cranach the Elder, Albrecht Altorfer, Hans Holbein; *(Netherlands)* Jerome Bosch; SCULPTORS: *(Italy)* Donatello, Andrea del Verrocchio, Luca della Robbia; *(France)* Germain Pilon; ARCHITECTS: *(Italy)* Filippo Brunelleschi, Leon Battista Alberti.

Michelangelo, *The Pietà*, 1499. Michelangelo's paintings, sculpture and architecture combine Christian emotion, classical forms and a mastery of materials. 5' 6" (175 cm). The Vatican, St. Peter's, Rome.

Donato Bramante, Michelangelo Buonarroti, Carlo Maderno, Gianlorenzo Bernini, St. Peter's and Piazza, 1506-1668. St. Peter's, the Sistine Chapel, the Piazza and other buildings within Vatican City are major achievements of the Renaissance.

Albrecht Dürer, *Knight, Death and Devil*, 1513. Dürer, a painter, also pioneered *printmaking* – making multiple copies of an original artwork. For the first time, many people could see or buy original artwork. Engraving, 9 ³/₄" x 7 ³/₈" (24.8 x 18.7 cm). Los Angeles County Museum of Art, Graphic Arts Council Fund.

Pieter Bruegel the Elder, *The Return of the Hunters*, 1565. Bruegel was among many northern European painters who explored new nonreligious subjects such as everyday life and landscape. Panel, 46" x 63 ³/₄" (117 x 162 cm). Kunsthistorisches Museum, Vienna.

Leonardo da Vinci, *Mona Lisa*, ca. 1503-1506. Leonardo da Vinci's best-known works are the *Mona Lisa, The Last Supper* and his many sketchbooks filled with drawings of inventions, nature and anatomy. Oil on panel, 30" x 20" (77 x 53 cm). The Louvre, Paris.

Donatello, *Gattamelata*, 1443-1448. Donatello's equestrian statue is an idealized portrait. It reflects the interest of Renaissance artists in ancient Greek and Roman art. Bronze, 134" (340 cm). Piazza del Santo, Padua.

Mannerism 1525–1600

Toward the end of the Renaissance, some painters began to use exaggerated lighting, unusual perspective and sweeping flame-like motions to suggest intense emotion. In architecture, massive forms were often combined with fancy carvings and detail. Art historians call this style, centered in Italy, *Mannerism.*

PAINTERS: Girolamo Parmigianino, Jacopo Tintoretto, Agnolo Bronzino, Correggio, Paulo Veronese; SCULPTOR: Benvenuto Cellini; ARCHITECT AND ART HISTORIAN: Giorgio Vasari.

Andrea Palladio, Villa Rotonda, Vicenza, Italy, ca. 1567-1570. Palladio's buildings were inspired by classical buildings like the Parthenon and Pantheon. His *Palladian style* of architecture inspired many later architects. Photograph copyright 1990 Rollie McKenna.

Baroque 1600–1700

Baroque refers to the use of exaggeration to express emotion. Lively motion, dramatic contrasts and asymmetrical design are typical of this style. Artists shaped stone and metal into fluid forms. The idea of classical beauty was refined by many French artists. In Holland, merchants bought art for their public buildings and homes. Portraits, scenes of everyday life, landscapes, still lifes and religious paintings were created in quantity, then sold by dealers.

PAINTERS: *(Italy)* Michelangelo da Carravaggio, Artemisia Gentileschi; *(Spain)* Francisco de Zurbarán, Bartolomé Murillo, Diego Velásquez; *(Flanders)* Peter Paul Rubens, Anthony van Dyck; *(France)* Nicholas Poussin, Claude Lorraine; *(Netherlands)* Frans Hals, Judith Leyster, Jan Vermeer, Jacob van Ruisdael, Clara Peeters, Rachel Ruysch, Sibylla Maria Merian; ARCHITECTS: *(Italy)* Francesco Borromini, Guarino Guarini; *(Austria)* Jakob Prandtauer; *(England)* Christopher Wren.

Louis Le Vau and Jules Hardouin-Mansart, Palace of Versailles, 1669-1685. Versailles, the palace of "Sun King" Louis XIV, is a blend of the Palladian style with the sculptural qualities of Bernini's work. It is also a major achievement in landscape architecture.

Rococo 1700–1800

Rococo art is a frilly, decorative variation of Baroque art created for aristocrats in France, Spain, England and Italy. The main subject matter is the life of leisure enjoyed by royalty. Many artists thrived by creating etchings or paintings of Rome and Venice, popular cities for tourists. Some Rococo artists were critics of the aristocracy. Their art shows the hardships of the working class. During this era, America's first artists studied art in Europe.

PAINTERS: *(Italy)* Rosalba Carriera, Canaletto, Francesco Guardi, Giovanni Battista Piranesi; *(England)* William Hogarth, Joshua Reynolds, Thomas Gainsborough; *(France)* Jean-Honoré Fragonard, François Boucher, Jean-Baptiste Chardin; *(United States)* Benjamin West, John Singleton Copley.

Balthasar Neumann, and Giovanni Tiepolo, 1719-1744. The Kaisersaal, Episcopal Palace, Wurzburg, Germany. The extreme ornateness of much Rococo art is evident here. The murals blend realism with fantastic illusions of space and distance.

El Greco, *The Burial of Count Orgaz*, 1586. El Greco, a Greek-born Spanish artist, provided drama in this religious painting. How is the drama achieved? Oil on canvas, 4.86 x 3.61 m. San Tomé, Toledo, Spain.

Michelangelo, *Moses*, ca. 1513-1515. Marble, 8'4" (254 cm) high. San Pietro in Vincoli, Rome.

Rembrandt van Rijn, *Aristotle with a Bust of Homer*. Rembrandt was a master of drawing, printmaking and painting. He skillfully controls light, detail and texture. Oil on canvas, 56 1/2" x 53 3/4" (144 x 137 cm). Metropolitan Museum of Art, New York. Purchased with special funds and gifts.

Gian Lorenzo Bernini, *Louis XIV, "The Sun King,"* ca. 1700. Italian sculptor Bernini became the most dominant sculptor of the Baroque era. His free-flowing forms also influenced architecture. Bronze, 33 1/8" x 39 3/8" x 17" (84 x 100 x 43 cm). The National Gallery of Art, Washington, DC. Samuel H. Kress Collection.

Jean Antoine Watteau, *Mezzetin*, ca. 1716. Watteau was one of many artists patronized by the French court. His art captures the closed world of the aristocracy just before it was ended by the French Revolution. Oil on canvas, 21 3/4" x 17" (55 x 43 cm). Courtesy of Metropolitan Museum of Art, New York. Munsey Fund. 1934.

Meissen Factory, The Concerto, ca. 1760. Royal patronage lead to the growth of trade in *objects d'art* – elaborate decorative items. Many were made by hand in factory-like environments. Painted porcelain, 7" (17 cm). Meissen, France.

The Modern Era

Neoclassicism 1750–1875

In 1738 and 1748, archaeologists unearthed classical art at Pompeii and Herculaneum, Italy. Both cities had been covered by volcanic ash for over 1700 years. This discovery helped inspire Neoclassical art. This style originated at the French Academy, one of many new schools that had strict rules for art. Academies held major exhibitions and favored art that was grand, yet simple and calm. Many North American artists accepted this style.

PAINTERS: *(France)* Jacques-Louis David, Jean-Auguste-Dominique Ingres, Elizabeth Vigée-Lebrun, Constance Charpentier, Adélaide Labille-Girard; *(North America)* John Trumbull, Gilbert Stuart. ARCHITECTS: *(United States)* Thomas Walter, Thomas Jefferson. SCULPTORS: *(France)* Antonio Canova.

Thomas Jefferson, Monticello, 1768-1809. Charlottesville, Virginia. Many buildings in North America were built in a Neoclassical style, often called Greek revival. Have you seen other examples?

Romanticism 1815–1875

Romantic refers to a new kind of freedom for artists to use many different ideas and to work in their own individual styles. These artists rejected Neoclassical and academic art. They explored many themes such as Bible stories, Gothic legends, foreign travel and adventure. Originality was important to Romantic artists. Architects practiced eclecticism. *Eclectic* means that ideas come from different sources. Architects designed buildings that look like Chinese temples, Swiss chalets and other styles.

PAINTERS: *(France)* Eugène Delacroix, Théodore Géricault; *(England)* William Blake, J.M.W. Turner, John Constable; *(Germany)* Caspar David Friedrich; *(Spain)* Francisco de Goya y Lucientas; *(United States)* Thomas Cole. SCULPTORS: *(France)* Antoine-Louis Barye, François Rude. ARCHITECTS: *(United States)* H.H. Richardson, Richard Morris Hunt, Sophia Hayden.

Richard Morris Hunt, Biltmore, 1895. Asheville, North Carolina. This estate in North America takes the eclectic form of a French Renaissance chateau.

Realism 1850–1900

Realist artists were rebels. They rejected the Romantic and Neoclassical styles. They portrayed city and rural life, the poor and political strife. Some artists explored reality through photography, which was invented in 1826. Painters learned to create the illusion of reality without showing tiny details. Functionalism began in architecture. *Functionalism* means that the design of a building comes from its purpose and the method of constructing it. There is little or no decoration.

PAINTERS: *(France)* Gustave Courbet, Jean-François Millet, Camille Corot, Edouard Manet, Rosa Bonheur; *(England)* Lady Elizabeth Butler; *(United States)* John Singer Sargent, Winslow Homer, Thomas Eakins, William Harnett, Henry O. Tanner. SCULPTORS: *(France)* Honoré Daumier, Rosa Bonheur. ARCHITECTS: *(England)* Joseph Paxton; *(France)* Gustave Eiffel; *(United States)* John Roebling.

Gustave Eiffel, The Eiffel Tower. The Eiffel Tower, made from cast iron, is an early example of functionalism in architecture.

Jacques-Louis David, *The Death of Socrates*. Neoclassical artists often created pageant-like historical paintings. Leaders were portrayed as heroic and idealized. Oil on canvas, 51" x 77 ¼" (130 x 196 cm). Courtesy of Metropolitan Museum of Art, New York. Wolfe Fund, 1931.

Antoine-Louis Barye, *Tiger Devouring an Antelope*, ca. 1830. Some Romantic artists found drama in untamed nature – storms, floods and wild animals. Bronze, 13 ½" x 20 ⅝" x 11" (34 x 52 x 28 cm). Hirshhorn Museum and Sculpture Garden. Gift of Joseph H. Hirshhorn, 1966.

George Stubbs, *Lion Attacking a Horse*. Mysterious, grand and haunting landscapes are popular themes in Romantic art. Oil on canvas, 40 ⅛" x 50 ¼" (102 x 128 cm). Yale University Art Gallery, New Haven, Connecticut.

Honore Daumier, The Third-Class Carriage. Oil on canvas, 25 ¾" x 35 ½" (65 x 90 cm). The Metropolitan Museum of Art. Bequest of Mrs. H.O. Havemeyer, 1929. The H.O. Havemeyer Collection.

Rosa Bonheur, *Sheep*. Bronze, 6" x 4" x 8 ½" (15 x 10 x 22 cm). Collis P. Huntington Memorial Collection. The Fine Arts Museums of San Francisco.

Impressionism 1875–1900

Impressionism began in France. An *impression* is an image or idea that comes when you look at something quickly. Impressionist compositions were inspired by the asymmetrical design in newly imported Japanese prints as well as snapshots – photographs taken quickly, often without centering the main subject.

Impressionist painters also shared an interest in capturing outdoor light and color at a particular moment in time. For the first time in history, painters could easily work outdoors. Portable, light-weight easels and oil paints in tubes were available. Many painters explored the technique of quickly applying colors to capture the shimmering light of water, trees and sky. Some developed the *pointillist* technique of mixing a color – for example, green – by placing tiny dabs of yellow and blue next to each other.

The subjects in Impressionist paintings are pleasant and attractive to many people. They include poses of dancers and young people enjoying picnics or trips to the beach. Other popular subjects are activities at racetracks or theaters, street scenes, charming interiors and colorful gardens.

Impressionism is a style name for painting, but three-dimensional art of this time was also changing. Some sculptors worked quickly in wax or clay, making models that seem to "freeze" a movement or expression. Sometimes they left the shimmering surfaces and rough grooves of fingerprints in the wax or clay models. When the model is cast in bronze, it often looks energetic without being smooth.

In architecture, there was a new understanding of engineering. This knowledge was used in the design and construction of skyscrapers. It was also used to design buildings with unusual organic forms and irregular openings.

PAINTERS: *(France)* Claude Monet, Camille Pissarro, Pierre Auguste Renoir, Berthe Morisot, Georges Seurat; *(United States)* Mary Cassatt, Julian Alden Weir, John H. Twachman, Theodore Robinson. SCULPTORS: *(France)* Edgar Degas, Auguste Rodin. ARCHITECTS: *(United States)* Daniel Burnham; *(Spain)* Antonio Gaudi.

Antoni Gaudi, Church of the Sagrada Familia, Barcelona, Spain, 1892-1930. This remarkable building has complex curves, towers and open forms that were highly innovative in the 19th century.

Auguste Rodin, *The Thinker*, 1879-1889. Rodin was one of the most innovative sculptors of the 19th century. His work is often said to be Impressionistic in technique and Romantic in theme. Bronze, 27 ½" (70 cm) high. The Metropolitan Museum of Art, New York.

Edgar Degas, *The Jockey*, 1889. Which photograph of a horse is closely related to Degas' drawing of a running horse? How does the drawing differ from the photograph? Pastel on paper, 12 ¹/₂" x 19 ¹/₄" (32 x 49 cm). Philadelphia Museum of Art. Purchase: W.P. Wilstach Collection.

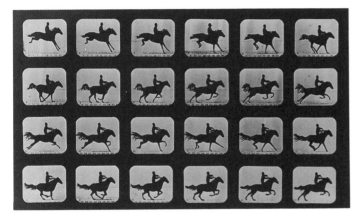

Eadweard Muybridge, *Attitudes of Animals in Motion*, 1878. Courtesy of Sotheby's Inc., 1987.

Claude Monet, *Water Lilies I.* How does the perspective in this painting differ from the perspective in the painting by Cassatt? Oil on canvas, 35 ¹/₄" x 39 ¹/₄" (90 x 100 cm). Courtesy Museum of Fine Arts, Boston. Gift of Edward Jackson Holmes.

Mary Cassatt, *The Boating Party*, ca. 1893. Many Impressionist compositions make you feel part of a scene. How is that feeling captured in Cassatt's painting? Oil on canvas, 35 ¹/₂" x 35 ¹/₄" (90 x 117 cm). Courtesy of the National Gallery of Art, Washington, DC. Chester Dale Collection.

Post-Impressionism 1880–1905

Post-Impressionism is not an art style but a period of exploring new styles, especially in painting. Artists worked in many different ways that became even more important during the twentieth century. Most of these artists worked in or near Paris, the international center for new kinds of art. People could visit museums and galleries to see art from Asia, Africa and other regions of the world. They could see the latest artwork by artists in Europe. Many collectors got advice about buying artworks from art dealers and art critics.

In addition to the influential painters whose work is shown here, you might want to find out more about some of the other artists of this era. Many of them are known for their inventive use of one or several art elements.

In France, Odilon Redon and Gustave Moreau explored visual symbols for thoughts and feelings such as solitude, fear, longing and love. Aubrey Beardsley, in England, was a master of line. Edvard Munch of Norway and James Ensor of Belgium made dramatic use of color. Gustav Klimt of Austria filled his paintings with intricate patterns. Pablo Picasso of Spain explored mood possibilities through paintings dominated by single colors – blue, then rose.

Photography continued to be explored. Eadweard Muybridge created photographs of people and animals in motion. Jacob Riis, Alfred Stieglitz, Edward Steichen, Julia Margaret Cameron and Gertrude Käsebier explored the expressive, documentary and atmospheric qualities of camera work.

Auguste Rodin is still one of the most important sculptors of this era. Others who are becoming well-known include Aristide Maillol of France, whose work was inspired by classical art. Ernst Barlach and Wilhelm Lehmbruck of Germany used exaggeration to create expressive works.

Louis Sullivan, Carson-Pirie-Scott Store; Chicago, Illinois, 1899. Sullivan's use of large windows, steel and very little ornamental work later evolved into the International Style of architecture.

Hector Guimard, *Entrance Door*, Castel Beranger, 1895. In Europe, architects, designers and craftsworkers develop a curved, linear style called *Art Nouveau* (new art). Wrought- iron and copper. Paris.

Paul Cézanne, *Mont Ste-Victoire*, 1885-1887. Cézanne used patches of color to suggest geometric forms (cone, cube, cylinder, sphere) in nature. Oil on canvas, 26" x 35" (66 x 90 cm). Courtauld Institute Galleries, London.

Georges Seurat, *Le Bec du Hoc at Grandchamp*, 1885. Seurat is known for his *pointillist* technique – blending dots of paint so the eye mixes colors. Oil on canvas, 25" x 32" (64 x 81 cm). The Tate Gallery, London.

Vincent Van Gogh, *Crows Over a Cornfield*, 1890. Van Gogh's dynamic swirling brushstrokes and use of color to express intense feelings have been inspirational to many other artists. Vincent Van Gogh Foundation/National Museum Vincent Van Gogh, Amsterdam.

Henri de Toulouse-Lautrec, *At the Moulin Rouge*, 1892. Toulouse-Lautrec observed and portrayed city life with great honesty. Oil on canvas, 48" x 56" (123 x 141 cm). The Art Institute of Chicago. Helen Birch Bartlett Memorial Collection, 1928.

Henri Rousseau, *The Sleeping Gypsy*, 1897. Rousseau was a self-taught painter. His flat style, vivid imagination and unusual subjects have fascinated many 20th century artists. Oil on canvas, 51" x 6' 7" (129 x 201 cm). Collection, The Museum of Modern Art, New York. Gift of Mrs. Simon Guggenheim.

Paul Gauguin, *Fatata te Miti*, 1892. Gauguin's color is bold, flat and often filled with symbolic meaning. His interest in a natural, spiritual way of life influenced later artists. Oil on canvas, 26 3/4" x 36" (68 x 91 cm). Courtesy of National Gallery of Art, Washington, DC. Chester Dale Collection.

Major Periods and Art Styles in Western Culture: 30,000 BC to 1900 AD

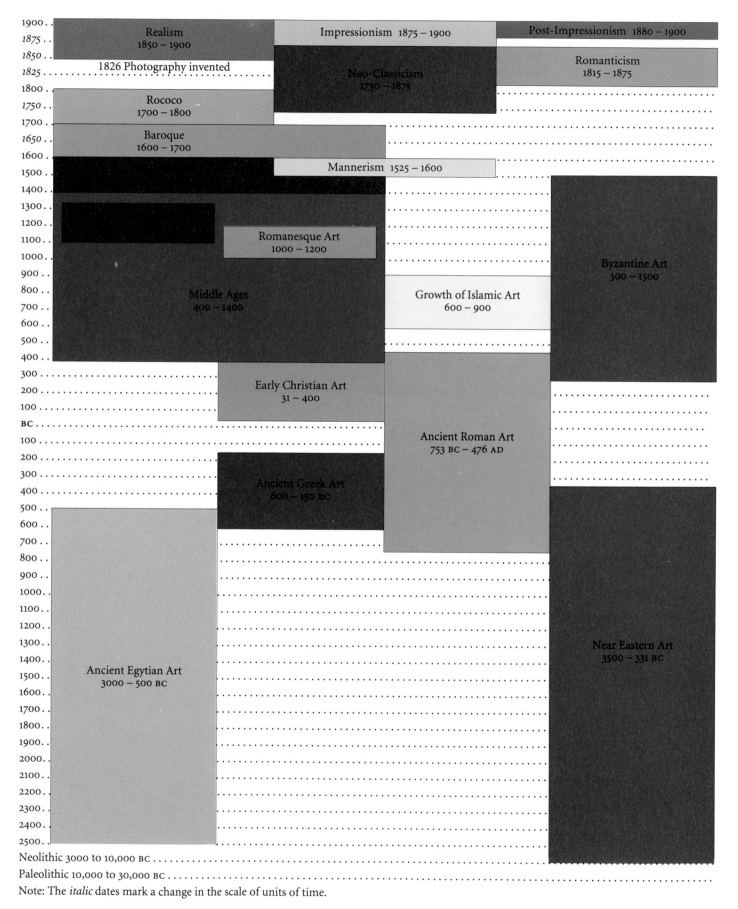

Note: The *italic* dates mark a change in the scale of units of time.

Summary

The history of art in Western culture before 1900 is the foundation for understanding art of the twentieth century. It is also a foundation for understanding art in North America and in many other cultures. Art historians have only recently begun to study the work of women artists and minority artists in Western culture.

Most of the terms for styles and periods of art history have been made up by artists, art critics, art historians or other scholars. The terms help people understand visual and cultural changes in art. Style and period names refer to common qualities and trends in art. For most styles and periods, art historians have identified major works of art or artists.

You have been introduced to many important artworks and artists in this chapter. But remember: You have only seen small photographs of the artworks. Only through visits to art museums can you fully experience the thrill of seeing original artworks.

Using What You Learned

Art History

1 Choose one style, period, artwork or artist in this chapter for a research report. Share your report in an imaginative way. You might dramatize the main points, make a poster or produce a video report.

2 Visit an art museum to see original works of art. Request a tour that will help you see the museum's collections of Western art before 1900.

3 Report on some of the oldest important examples of architecture in your community. Discuss the buildings in relation to trends in architecture before 1900.

Aesthetics and Art Criticism

1 With other students, choose one artwork introduced in this chapter that you find especially fascinating. Discuss the work using the steps in art criticism to describe, analyze and interpret the artwork. Present your interpretation to the class.

2 Art historians often use the word *masterpiece* to describe art that has many admirable qualities. Choose one artwork in this chapter that you admire. List your criteria for a masterpiece. Explain how the work does or does not meet the criteria.

3 The terms for styles and periods of art history are often used in the art world and in discussions of Western culture. Write down the names of the style periods introduced in this chapter. Next to each one, write several phrases that will help you remember important ideas about the period or style.

Creating Art

1 Imagine that you are living in the prehistoric era. Create an artwork using only natural materials. Choose a theme that you think prehistoric artists would care deeply about.

2 Draw the *facade* or front, of your school or home. Show how it might be redesigned by an architect who favors a style of the past such as the Classical or Rococo style.

3 Choose one artist introduced in this chapter. Prepare a report on the artist's background, training in art and most important artwork.

Careers and Art History

A knowledge of art history is valuable in almost every art-related career. It can also increase your appreciation and enjoyment of art, regardless of your choice of a career.

Art historians enjoy doing research and writing about art in an accurate way. Many art historians are also art teachers, or work as curators in art museums. Curators are experts on the origin, artistic importance and condition of artworks. Most architectural historians write, teach and do research on buildings. Some work for groups that preserve historic buildings.

Henri Matisse, *The Green Stripe (Madame Matisse)*, 1905. Many of the artworks you will study in this chapter are not realistic. The brilliant, illogical colors in this portrait tell you that Matisse's painting is not a photograph. Along with many other artists, Matisse explored the idea that works of art can be adventures in looking and thinking about art. Oil on canvas. Statens Museum for Kunst, Copenhagen. J. Rump Collection.

Chapter 6
Art History: The Twentieth Century

Chapter Vocabulary

The most important terms and style names are presented in bold italic type within the chapter and appear in the time line on page 124.

You are living in the twentieth century – the period between 1900 and 2000. It is one of the most remarkable and rapidly changing times in history. It was first called "The Age of Electricity." After the first explorations of outer space, people spoke of "The Space Age." It is now sometimes called "The Information Age" because knowledge is expanding so fast. It is also a period of many changes in European and North American art. In this chapter, you will learn about a few of these changes, discussed in two time divisions: 1900 to 1950, and 1950 to the present.

Some of the new directions in art build on the past, especially the Post-Impressionist era. In some artwork, you can find ideas from the Romantic, Realist and Neoclassical periods. The Renaissance idea of individual creativity is the foundation for all the new directions.

As this century has unfolded, some artists have been influenced by scientific discoveries, the growth of technology and mass-produced items. Artists began to use plastics, welded steel and other new materials. Studies of human behavior – how people look at their world and how they think about art – have influenced many artists. Some artists care deeply about social problems. Others explore dreams and random events in their art. In fact, many of the new directions in twentieth-century art are aimed at redefining what art is.

In this chapter, you will find the names of many artists. This will help you do research on some of them. After you study this chapter, you will be better able to:

Art History
- discuss developments in twentieth-century European and North American art, noting major changes in styles.

Art Criticism
- use your skills in art criticism to perceive, analyze, and interpret twentieth-century art.

Aesthetics
- understand that style names are invented to discuss groups of related artworks.
- appreciate the many different styles and new ideas in twentieth-century art.
- use what you know about art theories and criteria as you study art history.

Creating Art
- understand why and how twentieth-century artists have created art.

1900–1950

Post-Impressionist Influences

The beginning of twentieth-century art is linked to several of the styles you learned about in Chapter 5. Post-Impressionist influences are one important bridge between styles of painting. Art critic Roger Fry used this term in 1910 to describe an exhibit of work by Paul Cézanne, Paul Gauguin, Vincent Van Gogh and other artists who used Impressionist ideas but developed their own styles.

A second bridge is *Art Nouveau,* or "New Art." In architecture, graphic and interior design, many artists use flowing lines and organic forms. Architects Frank Lloyd Wright and Peter Behrens moved away from this style. Both had a major influence on architecture later in the century. Art Nouveau artists: Henri de Toulouse-Lautrec, Aubrey Beardsley (drawings, posters); Louis C. Tiffany (silver and glassware); Victor Horta, Antonio Gaudi (architecture).

A third bridge is *Expressionism.* This term refers to a bold, often colorful style of twentieth-century art about feelings such as grief, joy and fear. You might do research on: PAINTERS: Paula Modersohn-Becker, Oskar Kokoschka, Egon Schiele. ARCHITECT: Eric Mendelsohn. SCULPTORS: Wilhelm Lehmbruck and Käthe Kollwitz.

Some Expressionists formed groups to share ideas and exhibit their work. *The Fauves* (1905-1907) were named by art critic Louis Vauxcelles. Fauve is French for "wild beasts." The term sums up the "wild" use of brilliant colors and vigorous brushstrokes by Henri Matisse and other artists who explored *arbitrary* color – the way colors look in paintings, not the colors you see in nature. Other Fauves: André Derain, Maurice de Vlaminck, Georges Rouault, Raoul Dufy.

Die Brücke, or "The Bridge," (1905-1913) was a community of artists who used clashing colors and unusual textures to express the stressful feeling of city life. ARTISTS: Emil Nolde, Otto Mueller, Ernst Ludwig Kirchner, Erich Heckel, Karl Schmidt-Rottluff, Max Pechstein.

The name *Der Blaue Reiter,* or "The Blue Rider," (1911-1914) came from a painting by Wassily Kandinsky, a leader of this group. He believed that the "creative spirit is concealed within matter" and is best expressed with abstract colors and forms. ARTISTS: Alexej von Jawlensky, August Macke, Franz Marc, Paul Klee, Gabriele Münter.

Antonio Gaudi, Façade, Casa Mila, Barcelona, 1905-1910. Gaudi's apartments show the typical curved forms of Art Nouveau.

Edvard Munch, *The Scream,* 1893. Munch's painting is related to the work of Van Gogh, James Ensor, Emil Nolde and other leaders of Expressionism. Oil on canvas, 36" x 29" (92 x 74 cm). Munch-museet, Oslo.

Frank Lloyd Wright, Robie House, Chicago, Illinois, 1909. Wright, one of America's famous architects, believed a building should fit into its natural environment. His Prairie-style houses were influenced by the flat plains of the Midwest and traditional Japanese houses.

Karl Schmidt-Rottluff, *Two Heads,* 1918. Some members of *Die Brücke* revived the art of woodcut printing, creating powerful images. Woodcut. Brücke-Museum, Berlin.

Ernst Barlach, *Avenger,* 1914. Barlach was a well-known Expressionist sculptor. Others were Wilhelm Lehmbruck and Käthe Kollwitz. Bronze, 17 1/8" x 23 1/2" x 9" (43 x 60 x 23 cm). Hirshhorn Museum and Sculpture Garden, Smithsonian Institution. Gift of Joseph H. Hirshhorn, 1966.

Wassily Kandinsky, *Improvisation 31 (Sea Battle),* 1918. Kandinsky, a leader of the *Der Blaue Reiter* or *"The Blue Rider,"* said that abstract visual designs are similar to the abstract qualities in instrumental music. Oil on canvas, 55 3/8" x 47 1/8" (145 x 120 cm). Courtesy of National Gallery of Art, Washington, DC. Ailsa Mellon Bruce Fund.

Cubism and Early Abstract Art

Cubism (1907-1914) is a style first developed by Pablo Picasso and Georges Braque. The style was named by Matisse to point out the cubes and other geometric shapes in their paintings. Cubism builds on Cézanne's work and other abstract art, especially African masks. Shapes are often fractured, then locked together and rearranged so that one picture seems to include many points of view. Picasso and Braque worked together so closely that both are given credit for this new direction. It soon influenced many other artists.

Picasso and Braque also invented collage, the use of pasted paper and other materials in two-dimensional art. These collage elements help us see the paintings as objects to investigate, not just as window-like views of reality. PAINTERS: Fernand Léger, Juan Gris, Robert Delaunay, Sonia Delaunay-Terk, Jacques Villon. SCULPTORS: Pablo Picasso, Alexander Archipenko, Jacques Lipchitz, Henri Laurens, Ossip Zadkine, Raymond Duchamp-Villon, Constantin Brancusi.

Until 1913, few North American artists knew about Cubism or other new directions in European art. The most well-known group of American artists was the *Ashcan School* (1908-1914). The group was named by critics to sum up the subjects they painted – alleys, tenements and slum dwellers. ARTISTS: Robert Henri, John Sloan, William Glackens, George Luks, Maurice Prendergast, Arthur B. Davis, Ernest Lawson.

Artists in the Ashcan School were Realists, but they were interested in other kinds of art. They helped organize the famous *1913 Armory Show,* the first large exhibition of modern European art in America, held at the Armory building in New York City. After the Armory Show, many North American artists created work with simplified or rearranged elements. This direction is called varieties of abstract art (1913-1950). PAINTERS: John Marin, Marsden Hartley, Max Weber, Arthur Dove, Georgia O'Keeffe, Joseph Stella, Rufino Tamayo.

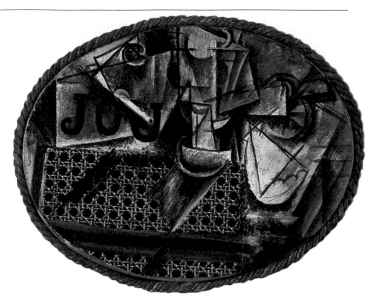

Pablo Picasso, *Still Life with Chair Caning*, 1912. A collage includes bits of paper, cloth and other real objects. The artwork becomes an invented object instead of a window-like view. Oil and pasted oilcloth, 10 ⁵/₈" x 13 ³/₄" (27 x 35 cm). NY/SPADEM.

Marcel Duchamp, *Nude Descending a Staircase, No. 2*, 1912. This well-known painting was part of the 1913 Armory Show. It is based on Cubism but portrays movement in a way that became more widespread with Futurism (page 110). Oil on canvas, 58" x 35" (147 x 89 cm). Philadelphia Museum of Art. Louise and Walter Arensberg Collection.

Pablo Picasso, *Woman's Head (Fernande)*, 1909. Picasso developed Cubist ideas in painting and sculpture. Bronze, 16 ³/₄" x 9 ³/₄" x 10 ¹/₂" (41 x 25 x 280 cm). Collection, The Museum of Modern Art, New York. Purchase.

Georges Braque, *Violin and Palette*, 1909-1910. Braque's painting has the fractured, angular forms typical of early Cubist works. Oil on canvas, 36 ¹/₈" x 16 ⁷/₈" (92 x 43 cm). Solomon R. Guggenheim Museum, New York. Photograph by David Heald.

Georgia O'Keeffe, *Corn Dark I*, 1924. Oil on composition board, 31 ³/₄" x 11 ⁷/₈" (81 x 30 cm). The Metropolitan Museum of Art. The Alfred Stieglitz Collection, 1950. Photograph by Malcolm Varon.

Max Weber, *Spiral Rhythm*, 1915. Bronze, 24 ¹/₈" x 14 ¹/₄" x 14 ⁷/₈" (61 x 36 x 38 cm). Hirshhorn Museum and Sculpture Garden, Smithsonian Institution. Gift of Joseph H. Hirshhorn, 1966.

The Future, Fantasy and Change

Just before and after World War I (1914-1918), several groups of artists explored the future, fantasy and change as subjects for art. Some also explored new methods of creating art.

Futurism (1909-1914) was an Italian movement. These artists used Cubist ideas to express the beauty of speed, the dynamic energy of modern life and rapid change in the modern industrial age. ARTISTS: Giacomo Balla, Umberto Boccioni, Carlo Carrà, Gino Severini. ARCHITECT: Antonio Sant'Elia.

Dada (1915-1923) is a nonsense word chosen by artists who questioned traditional definitions of art. Some created work based on chance and accidental effects in materials. Others altered or combined ready-made objects. Montage – a collage made from photographs – was another invention of this group. Many Dada artists

later explored Surrealism. The experimental attitude of the Dada artists set the stage for later artists to question whether art must always be made in traditional ways. ARTISTS: Marcel Duchamp, Max Ernst, Kurt Schwitters, Jean (Hans) Arp, Man Ray, Francis Picabia. SCULPTORS: Julio Gonzáles, Sophie Taeuber-Arp.

Surrealism (1924-1940) refers to realistic or abstract images of dream-like events. Some artists developed their ideas from unusual Dada-like techniques such as dripping or blotting paint. Interest in dreams and other invented images fascinated many later artists. ARTISTS: Henri Rousseau, Marc Chagall, Joan Miró, André Masson, Yves Tanguy, Roberto Matta, Salvador Dali, Kay Sage Tanguy, René Magritte, Giorgio de Chirico, Meret Oppenheim, Oscar Dominguez.

Salvador Dali, *The Persistence of Memory*, 1931. Dali's painting has been called a masterpiece of Surrealist art. He has used realist techniques to create a strange dream-like environment. Oil on canvas, 9 ¹/₂" x 13" (24 x 33 cm). Collection, The Museum of Modern Art, New York. Given anonymously.

Antonio Sant'Elia, *Project for "The Inner City,"* 1914. What features of this Futurist plan for a city might be seen in large cities today? How long ago was this plan made? Watercolor. Marcherita G. Sarfatti Collection, Rome.

Meret Oppenheim, *Object*, 1936. Surrealist artist Oppenheim placed her unexpected materials around ordinary objects. This kind of experimentation inspired many later artists. Fur-covered cup, saucer and spoon, overall height: 2 7/8" (7.5 cm). Collection, The Museum of Modern Art, New York. Purchase.

Oscar Dominquez, *Untitled*, 1936. Dada artists were interested in the kind of order that can be created by chance or random placements of shapes. Gouache transfer on paper, 14 1/8" x 11 1/2" (36 x 30 cm). Collection, The Museum of Modern Art, New York. Purchase.

Umberto Boccioni, *States of Mind I: The Farewells*, 1911. Futurists adapted Cubist ideas to express the "force lines" of energy. The subject in this work is a steam locomotive. Oil on canvas, 27 3/4" x 37 3/8" (70 x 95 cm). Collection, The Museum of Modern Art, New York. Gift of Nelson A. Rockefeller.

Marcel Duchamp, *Bicycle Wheel*, 1951. In this Dada work, Duchamp created an *assemblage* and used *ready-made objects* for a *kinetic* sculpture. Artists later in the century have become very interested in all three of these inventions. Metal and wood, 50 1/2" x 25 1/2" x 16 5/8" (128 x 43 x 65 cm). Collection, The Museum of Modern Art, New York. The Sidney and Harriet Janis Collection.

Nonobjective and Geometric Art

Many early twentieth-century artists developed new concepts and goals for art. Some art has no subject you can recognize – it is nonobjective. The ideas behind a nonobjective artwork can be an important part of its purpose. Several groups of artists developed geometric art – forms based on precise, measured relationships and the qualities of machine-made products.

The concept for Dutch artists in *De Stijl,* which means "The Style," (1917-1932) was that simple forms and primary colors could be used to express the harmony and order in the universe. ARTISTS: Piet Mondrian, Theo Van Doesburg, Georges Vantongerloo, J.J.P. Oud, Gerrit Rietveld.

The goal of Russian *Constructivism* (1917-1920) was to use machine-made materials to create art that looked industrial. ARTISTS: Vladimir Tatlin, Alexander Rodchenko, Olga Rozanova, Antoine Pevsner. Other Russians combined several styles to explore spiritual or scientific concepts. ARTISTS: Mikhail Larionov, Natalia Goncharova, Lyubov Popova, Kasimir Malevich.

Purism (1918-1930) is a related French style based on simple forms painted with sharp edges and a smooth finish. In a similar American style, *Precisionism* (1920-1930), artists focused on urban and industrial scenes. ARTISTS: Charles Demuth, Charles Sheeler, Niles Spencer, Amédeé Ozenfant.

All of these new "geometric" directions in art had a great influence on an important new German art school, the *Bauhaus* (1919-1933), set up by architect Walter Gropius. The program combined ideas from art, crafts and architecture with manufacturing. It emphasized experiments with materials and ideas for an industrial era. When the Nazis closed the Bauhaus before World War II, similar schools were set up in North America. ARTIST-TEACHERS: Walter Gropius, Marcel Breuer, Herbert Bayer, Johannes Itten, László Moholy-Nagy, Lyonel Feininger.

The Bauhaus also taught that "form follows function." This means that the style of functional art comes from its practical use – not from decorations. This idea started a new *International Style* of architecture (1930-1970). ARCHITECTS: Walter Gropius, Eliel Saarinen, Le Corbusier, Miës van der Rohe, Richard Neutra, Philip Johnson.

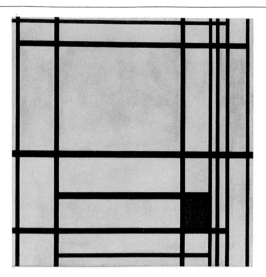

Piet Mondrian, *Composition with Blue,* 1937. Courtesy Sidney Janis Galleries.

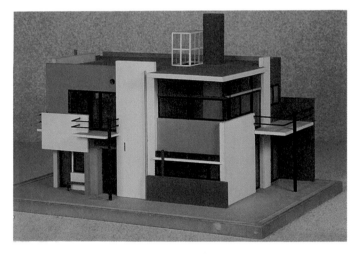

Gerrit Rietveld, Model of the Schröder House, 1923-1924. Glass and wood, 17 ³/₈" x 28 ³/₈" x 19 ¹/₄" (44 x 72 x 49 cm). Stedelijk Museum, Amsterdam.

Charles Demuth, *I Saw the Figure 5 in Gold*, 1928. Oil on canvas, 36" x 29 ³/₄" (91 x 76 cm). Courtesy of the Metropolitan Museum of Art. The Alfred Stieglitz Collection, 1949.

Joost Schmidt, Poster for the Bauhaus Art and Technology Exhibition, 1923. The Bauhaus approach to graphic and product design was influenced by DeStijl, Constructivism, and related styles based on geometric and industrial forms. Courtesy Bauhaus Archive, Berlin.

Amédeé Ozenfant, *The Jug*, 1926. Notice the sharp edges in this Purist painting. Oil on canvas, 199 ³/₄" x 58 ¹/₂" (507 x 149 cm). Museum of Art, Rhode Island School of Design. Mary B. Jackson Fund.

Skidmore, Owings and Merrill, Lever Brothers Building, 1952. New York.

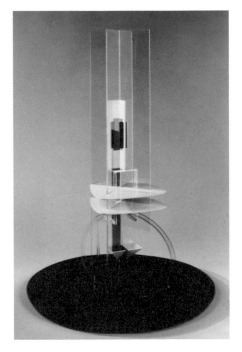

Naum Gabo, *Column*, ca. 1923. Constructivist sculptors pioneered the use of industrial materials such as plate glass, plastic and sheet metal for fine art. Perspex, wood, metal and glass, 41 ¹/₂" x 29" x 29" (105 x 74 x 74 cm). Solomon R. Guggenheim Museum, New York. Photograph by David Heald.

Varieties of Realism and Abstraction

After World War I, artists continued to create realistic and abstract art. Varieties of realism were especially evident in the United States during the Great Depression (1930's).

American Scene Painters captured the way of life in rural areas and cities. Their work often centers on one main theme within a realistic or semiabstract style. ARTISTS: Thomas Hart Benton, John Steuart Curry, Grant Wood, Charles Burchfield, Isabel Bishop, Walt Kuhn, Edward Hopper, Raphael Soyer, Horace Pippin.

Some artists created paintings with recognizable themes but added a Surrealistic quality. Their work is called *Magic* or *Poetic Realism.* ARTISTS: Loren MacIver, Pavel Tchelitchew, Morris Graves, Ivan Albright, Andrew Wyeth, Robert Vickery.

In *social commentary art,* North American and European artists expressed their feelings about poverty and other social problems. ARTISTS: Otto Dix, George Grosz, Peter Blume, Ben Shahn, George Tooker, Robert Gwathmey.

Powerful *documentary photographs* that showed life in the United States were made by artists who worked under the Federal Art Project. They helped make documentary photography a fine art. PHOTOGRAPHERS: Gordon Parks, Walker Evans, Berenice Abbott, Dorothea Lange, James Van Der Zee, Margaret Bourke-White.

The *Mexican muralists* revived the art of mural painting, expressing their political beliefs with dramatic forms and colors. ARTISTS: José Clemente Orozco, Diego Rivera, David Alfaro Siqueíros.

Dorothea Lange, *Migrant Mother, Nipomo, California,* 1936. One critic called this documentary photograph "The Madonna of the Depression." What do you think the critic meant? Photograph. Dorothea Lange Collection. The Oakland Museum.

Stuart Davis, *Rapt at Rappaport's,* 1952. Many Americans created abstract art. Can you see the influence of Cubism in this painting? Oil on canvas, 52" x 40" (132 x 101 cm). Hirshhorn Museum and Sculpture Garden, Smithsonian Institution, Gift of Joseph H. Hirshhorn, 1966.

In Europe, Paris had become an international art center. Artists who worked there until the end of World War II are known as the *School of Paris*. Many had helped develop earlier styles of art. Now they explored personal variations on those styles. Fantasy, memories and people were common themes. ARTISTS: Jules Pascin, Marie Laurencin, Amedeo Modigliani, Chaim Soutine, Julio Gonzáles, Maurice Utrillo, Raoul Dufy.

In England and North America, some artists worked with abstract organic forms. Others created geometric work. PAINTER: *(England)* Ben Nicholson; SCULPTORS: Barbara Hepworth, Henry Moore. PAINTER: *(North America)* Stuart Davis; SCULPTORS: Isamu Noguchi, Elie Nadelman, John Flannagan, Alexander Calder.

Henry Moore, *Carving*, 1935. English sculptor Moore developed smooth organic forms with voids that lead through and around the whole work. Cumberland alabaster, 11 ½" x 11 ⅝" x 6 ¾" (29 x 30 x 17 cm). Hirshhorn Museum and Sculpture Garden, Smithsonian Institution. Gift of Joseph Hirshhorn, 1966.

David Siqueiros, *Echo of a Scream*, 1937. Mexican artist Siqueiros created this powerful image about the disasters of war. Enamel on wood, 48" x 36" (122 x 91 cm). Collection, The Museum of Modern Art, New York. Gift of Edward M. M. Warburg.

Grant Wood, *American Gothic*, 1930. This well-known American Scene painting has many details that refer to the values and daily life of the people who are shown. What are some of these details and values? Oil on beaver board, 30" x 25" (76 x 63 cm). Friends of American Art Collection, The Art Institute of Chicago.

Marie Laurencin, *Nymph and Hind*, 1925. What earlier styles seem to have influenced this School of Paris artist? Oil on canvas, 28" x 20 ½" (71 x 52 cm). Philadelphia Museum of Art. Given by Mr. and Mrs. Herbert Cameron Morris.

1950 – Present

Abstract Expressionism, Pop Art and New Directions in Sculpture

Since World War II (1939-1945), the center of new, exciting art has shifted from Paris to New York. Style names for new trends often refer to painting, but some apply to sculpture or design. The International Style of architecture has been refined. Some architects design buildings with complex, curved forms.

In *Abstract Expressionism,* artists explore unusual ways of applying paint to express feelings and moods. Most of these *action* or *gestural paintings* have no familiar subject or theme. ARTISTS: Hans Hofmann, Arshile Gorky, Willem de Kooning, Franz Kline, Hale Woodruff, Lee Krasner, Mark Tobey.

Many sculptors combine expressive and abstract forms in traditional media. ARTISTS: Eduardo Chillida, Germaine Richier, César Baldaccini, Marino Marini, Giacomo Manzù.

Constructed sculptures are created from industrial materials such as plastic and metal sheets or rods. Some sculptors join ready-made or salvaged items to create assemblages. *Combines* are paintings that include ready-made objects. SCULPTORS: David Smith, Reuben Nakian, Theodore Roszak, Joseph Cornell, Louise Nevelson, Louise Bourgeois, John Chamberlain, Lee Bontecou, Jackie Winsor, Nancy Graves.

Pop art refers to art based on the impersonal products and images of popular culture. Favorite subjects are brand-name products, comics, famous people and other things you often see or use without much thought. You might think of Pop art as a new form of social commentary art. ARTISTS: Richard Hamilton, Larry Rivers, Jasper Johns, Robert Rauschenberg, Jim Dine, James Rosenquist, Tom Wesselmann, Andy Warhol, Robert Indiana, Claes Oldenburg, David Hockney.

Around 1965, even more adventurous forms of sculpture appeared. Some artists created theater-like environments with sculptural elements. *Happenings* are theater-like events with planned and unplanned activities and audience participation. Around 1970, *performance* artists expanded on the Dada idea that sculpture can be an event in time, not just an object. ARTISTS: Allan Kaprow, Claes Oldenburg, Jim Dine, Red Grooms, Marisol, Edward and Nancy Kienholz, Lucas Samaras, George Segal, Joseph Beuys, Gilbert and George, Hans Haacke.

Andy Warhol, *Marilyn,* 1967. Warhol became the most well-known Pop artist. Why might his work be called a form of social commentary art? Silkscreen print, 36" x 36" (91 x 91 cm). Courtesy of Ronald Feldman Fine Arts, New York.

Louise Nevelson, *Sky Cathedral,* 1958. The elements in this assemblage are pieces of wood salvaged from old furniture and buildings. Why do you think the artist painted the whole sculpture one color? Wood construction painted black, 11' 3 ¹/₂" x 10 ¹/₄" x 18" (344 x 26 x 46 cm). Collection, The Museum of Modern Art, New York. Gift of Mr. and Mrs. Ben Mildwoff.

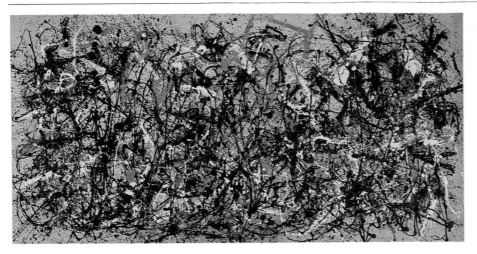

Jackson Pollock, *Autumn Rhythm,* 1950. Oil on canvas, 105″ x 207″ (267 x 526 cm). The Metropolitan Museum of Art. George A. Hearn Fund, 1957.

George Segal, *Cinema,* 1963. Segal's sculpture seems to "freeze" a moment in time and space. Why wouldn't you find a sculpture of this kind before the 20th century? Plaster, illuminated plexiglass and metal, 118" x 96" x 30" (300 x 244 x 76 cm). Albright-Knox Art Gallery, Buffalo, New York. Gift of Seymour H. Knox, 1964.

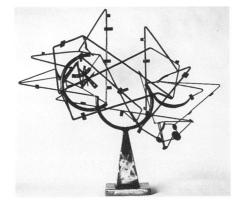

David Smith, *Star Cage,* 1950. A drawing by artist Dorothy Dehner, Smith's wife, was the inspiration for this sculpture. Various metals, welded, painted blue, 44 ⁷/₈" x 51 ¹/₄" x 25 ³/₄" (114 x 130 x 65 cm). University Art Museum, University of Minnesota, John Rood Sculpture Collection.

Le Corbusier, Ronchamp Church. Unlike most buildings in the International style, this chapel is designed around curved forms and spaces. Stone. Courtesy French Embassy Press & Information Division.

Varieties of Geometric and Conceptual Art

Around 1960, some artists became well known for moving away from action painting and Pop art. Some created art with geometric qualities. Others worked with the idea that art is an idea more than an object.

Color field paintings are a variation on abstract expressionism. Large *fields* (areas) of color are applied to canvas by staining it or using subtle brushstrokes. Many paintings have a few dominant colors or color interactions. ARTISTS: Mark Rothko, Barnett Newman, Ad Reinhardt, Adolph Gottlieb, Clyfford Still, Sam Francis, Joan Mitchell, Helen Frankenthaler, Morris Lewis, Jules Olitski, Cy Twombly, Alfred Jensen, Sam Gilliam, Alma Thomas.

Hard-edged paintings have geometric shapes, "hard," or very clear, edges and subtle color interactions. The vigorous brushstrokes and textured surfaces of abstract expressionism are rejected. ARTISTS: Ellsworth Kelly, Helen Lundeberg, Frank Stella, Al Held, Ad Reinhardt, Kenneth Noland, Jack Youngerman.

Op, kinetic and light art are directions that were first explored in the Bauhaus program. *Op* is a short form of *optical illusion*. These artists create illusions of change, motion or illogical space in paintings. ARTISTS: Victor Vasarely, Josef Albers, Larry Poons, Bridget Riley, M.C. Escher, Richard Anuszkiewicz, Yaacov Agam.

Kinetic refers to sculpture with parts set in motion by natural or mechanical energy. Alexander Calder, who invented mobiles, was the first well-known kinetic sculptor. ARTISTS: George Rickey, Jean Tinguely, Pol Bury, Jesús-Raphael Soto, Lin Emery. Some artists use forms of light (neon, fluorescent, lasers) to create sculpture and environments. ARTISTS: Otto Piene, Richard Lippold, Chryssa, Dan Flavin, Robert Irwin.

Minimal art is based on a very few art elements or materials, such as a brick, so that you become aware of other art elements, such as the colors, textures and spaces between the bricks. ARTISTS: Agnes Martin, Robert Mangold, Dorothea Rockburne, Anthony Caro, Mathias Goeritz, Tony Smith, Donald Judd, Robert Morris, Sol LeWitt, Carl Andre, Richard Serra.

In *conceptual* work, only the record of having an idea for art is important. ARTISTS: Joseph Kosuth, Daniel Buren, Robert Barry, John Baldessari.

Mark Rothko, *Blue, Orange, Red*, 1961. Rothko's color field paintings are meant to inspire quiet meditation of the simple shapes and subtle variations in colors and textures. Oil on canvas, 90 ¼" x 81 ¼" (229 x 206 cm). Hirshhorn Museum and Sculpture Garden, Smithsonian Institution. Gift of Joseph H. Hirshhorn Foundation, 1966.

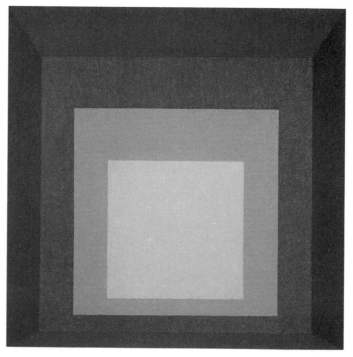

Josef Albers, *Homage to the Square: Apparition*, 1959. Albers used hard-edged squares in many paintings. He explored the idea of color interaction in greater depth than any previous artist. Oil on board, 47 ½" x 47 ½" (121 x 121 cm). Solomon R. Guggenheim Museum, New York. Photograph by David Heald.

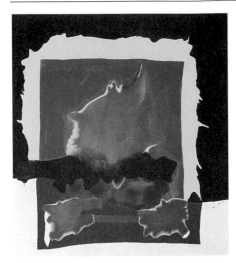

Helen Frankenthaler, *Interior Landscape*, 1964. Frankenthaler's color field paintings have fluid edges created by staining the canvas. Acrylic on canvas, 92 ⁵/₈" x 104 ⁷/₈" (235 x 267 cm). San Francisco Museum of Modern Art. Gift of the Women's Board.

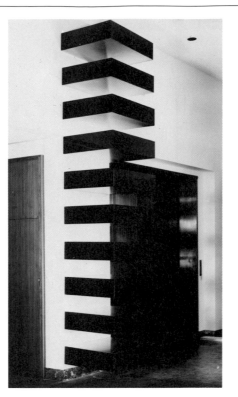

Donald Judd, *Stack*, 1969. The simple forms in Judd's minimalist sculpture make viewers look at related visual elements such as the shadows and space between the forms. Stainless steel and laminated plastic. Courtesy of the Detroit Institute of Art.

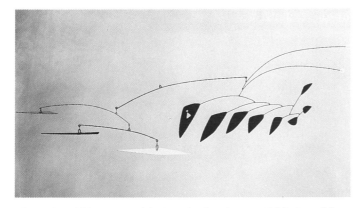

Alexander Calder, *Two White Dots in the Air*, 1958. Calder's mobiles are a form of suspended kinetic sculpture. Parts move gently in air currents. Sheet metal and wire, 100" (250 cm) long. Copyright 1990. Indianapolis Museum of Art. Gift of Joseph Cantor.

Bridget Riley, *Drift No. 2*, 1966. Op art creates optical sensations in the viewer. What sensations do you get when you look at this work? How large is Riley's painting? Acrylic on canvas, 91 ¹/₂" x 89 ¹/₂" (232 x 227 cm). Albright-Knox Art Gallery, Buffalo, New York. Gift of Seymour H. Knox, 1967.

Realism, Environmental and Heritage-Based Art

Since about 1970, artists and the larger art world have shown a growing interest in art about people, the environment and the past.

Artists who work in the tradition of realism have become well known. Critics refer to newer directions as *Super-Realism,* or *New Realism.* In *photorealism,* painters render the exact details and distortions often seen in photographs. Sculptors also explore new ways to create realistic or "fool-the-eye" sculpture. PAINTERS: Richard Estes, Alice Neel, Chuck Close, Ralph Goings, Audrey Flack, Robert Cottingham, Don Eddy, Alex Katz, Janet Fish, Alfred Leslie. SCULPTORS: Duane Hanson, John De Andrea.

Land or *earth* art refers to several directions in sculpture. Some artists record changes caused by natural forces such as decay or erosion. Others use the earth, wind and water as sculptural media. Many create permanent changes in urban spaces that include fountains, gardens and the like. ARTISTS: Walter De Maria, Robert Smithson, Richard Long, Jan Dibbets, Dennis Oppenheim, Charles Simonds, Mary Miss, Alice Aycock, Christo, Arman, Athena Tacha, Helen Escobedo, Nancy Holt.

Heritage-based art describes artists who are inspired by themes linked to their personal heritage or quest for recognition in today's culture. Only a few of many are noted here. *(Feminist Artists):* Judy Chicago, Lynda Benglis, Lucy Lippard, Miriam Schapiro. *(African-American)* Charles White, Elizabeth Catlett, Jacob Lawrence, Betye Saar, Romare Bearden. *(Mexico)* Frida Kahlo, Judy Baca, Carmen Lomas Garza, José Luis Cuevas, Luis Jiménez. *(Puerto Rico)* Rafael Tufiño, Myrna Báes, Rafael Ferrer. *(Cuba)* Amelia Paláez. *(Haitian-Hispanic)* Jean-Michel Basquiat. *(Native North American)* Kimberly Ponca Stock, George Hunt, Joyce Growing Thunder Fogarty, Fritz Scholder, Kevin Red Star, Bill Reid.

Post-modern architecture is a reaction against the uniformity of the International Style. Architects plan buildings that have unexpected combinations of materials, design elements, and ideas from older styles. In the *historic preservation* movement, architects are working to preserve historic buildings and other landmarks. ARCHITECTS: Robert Venturi, Denise Scott Brown, Charles Moore, Hans Hollein, Robert A.M. Stern, Michael Graves, Philip Johnson, John Burgee, Ricardo Bofill, James Stirling.

Public Services Building, Portland, Oregon. Architect: Michael Graves. Photograph courtesy of Tom Clark Architectural Associates.

A. Hamilton and E. Wooley, Independence Hall, Philadelphia, Pennsylvania, 1732-1754. Urban planning and the preservation of historic buildings are new fields of architecture. Why are they important?

Robert Smithson, *Spiral Jetty*, 1970. This earthwork was created with the aid of bulldozers. Algae that thrive in the water are a natural source of color. How do you think the work might change over a long period of time? Black rock, salt crystals, earth and red water (algae) composing a coil, 1,500' x 15' (457 x 5 m). Great Salt Lake, Utah. Photograph by Gianfranco Gorgoni. Courtesy Contact Press Images New York.

Duane Hanson, *Football Player*, 1981. This "fool the eye" sculpture looks realistic. Why do you think it might startle people who see it in an art gallery? Oil on polyvinyl, 43 1/4" x 30" x 31 1/2" (110 x 76 x 80 cm). The Lowe Art Museum, Coral Gables, Florida. Museum purchase through funds from the Friends of Art and Public Subscription.

Elizabeth Catlett, *Homage to My Young Black Sisters*, 1969. *Homage* means respect. What forms in the work go with its theme? Cedar, 71" x 14" (180 x 36 cm). Courtesy of the artist.

Chuck Close, *Self-Portrait*, 1976-1977. Many photorealists portray the distortions in photographs in large paintings. What parts of the face are distorted in this painting? Watercolor on paper mounted on canvas, 81" x 58 3/4" (206 x 149 cm). The Pace Gallery, New York.

Art of the Present and Future

Since 1980, much of the art being shown in galleries has been called eclectic or pluralistic. *Eclecticism* means that ideas from different sources, including earlier styles, are used in a planned way. *Pluralism* means that art galleries and art critics are more willing to promote several new styles of art instead of just one dominant style.

Eclecticism began in the 1970's with post-modern architecture. Today, architects are interested in how buildings work together in a larger environment. They consider the meaning of the building in relation to the people who will use it. Some architects are designing communities of the future, often with the aid of computers.

There is a similar trend in painting and sculpture. Many artists are reinterpreting ideas from past styles. The styles of this new direction are still being named.

New abstraction is a term for paintings based on new combinations of brushstrokes and other visual elements, usually without any subject matter you can clearly recognize. PAINTERS: Elizabeth Murray, Howard Hodgkin, Nancy Graves, Gerhard Richter, David Reed, Susan Laufer, Gary Stephan, Will Mentor, Sherry Levine.

SCULPTORS: Donald Lipski, Scott Burton, Siah Armajani, Tong Cragg, Bill Woodrow, Judy Pfaff.

New expressionism is influenced by the earlier styles of expressionism, Dada and Surrealism. The subject matter is often about historical events, myths and heroic symbols of culture. ARTISTS: Markus Lüpertz, Sigmar Polke, Anselm Kiefer, Francesco Clemente, Sandro Chia, Julian Schnabel, David Salle, Robert Longo, Sue Coe, Tom Otterness, John Ahern.

New Image refers to artists who have picked a single topic of personal interest and explored it through a series of related works. Many artists use subjects you can recognize, such as the human figure, ordinary objects or an animal. ARTISTS: Susan Rothenberg, Nicholas Africano, Joe Zucker, Robert Moskowitz, Donald Sultan, Jonothan Borofsky, Jennifer Bartlett, Pat Steir, Barry Flanagan, William Wegman, Kenny Scharf, Keith Haring, Rodney Alan Greenblat.

High tech art is a general term for the artists who create images with computers, lasers, television and other technologies. Many video artists, filmmakers, and performing artists *collaborate*, or work together, on projects. ARTISTS: Charles Csuri, Nam June Paik, Twyla Tharp, Laurie Anderson.

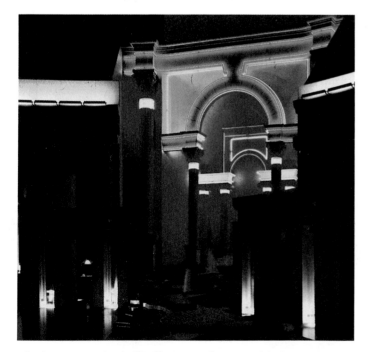

Charles Moore, Piazza D'Italia, New Orleans, Louisiana, 1975-1980. Post-modern architects inventively use ideas from many different styles. What architectural ideas from the past are included in this plaza? Courtesy of Perez Architects.

Lawrence Goodridge, Kinetic Light Sculpture, 1988. Helium, Neon laser source, 38" x 38" x 10" (97 x 97 x 25 cm).

David Salle, *Miner*, 1985. Salle combines ideas from different styles. Can you identify some styles he has borrowed ideas from? Acrylic, oil, table, fabric and canvas, 96" x 162 ¼" (244 x 412 cm). Courtesy Mary Boone Gallery, New York.

Judy Pfaff, *Deepwater*, 1980. Pfaff's environmental works have been compared to Jackson Pollock's Abstract Expressionist paintings. What similarities do you see? How is this work unlike Pollock's *Autumn Rhythm*? Mixed media. Courtesy Holly Solomon Gallery, New York. Photograph by Julius Kozlowski.

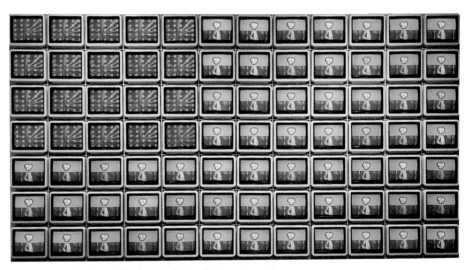

Nam June Paik, *Video Flag 2*, 1985. Korean-born Nam June Paik pioneered the use of television images and television sets for art. What makes this work a unique example of 20th century art? Moving painting. The Los Angeles County Museum. Gift of the Art Museum Council.

Maya Ying Lin, Vietnam Veterans' Memorial, 1980-1982. Maya Ying Lin was still a student in architecture when her proposal for this memorial was selected. How is the design different from many other war memorials? Black granite. Constitution Gardens, Washington, DC. Photograph courtesy National Park Service.

Major Trends: 20th Century European and North American Art

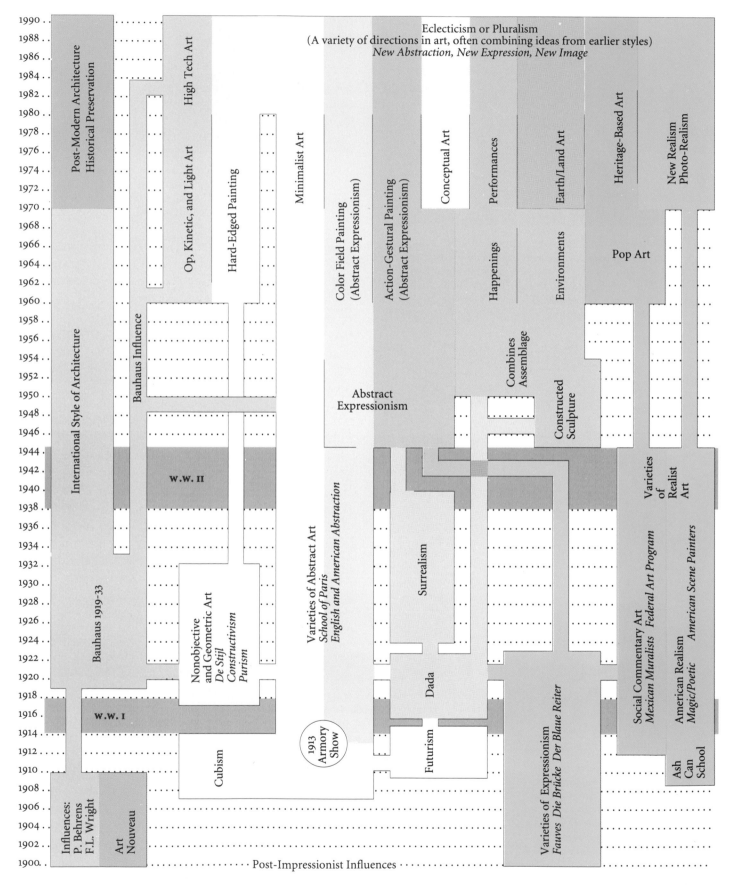

Note: The beginning dates and ending dates for each development in art becomes less precise after World War II. The pathways and color coding illustrate some general relationships among the styles or directions.

Summary

The twentieth-century has been a time of rapid changes. The art styles introduced in this chapter are just a few of many that have become well-known. Many of these styles came from directions in art prior to 1900. In the same way, some styles of art from the last half of the twentieth-century have roots in the first half of the century.

Most of the styles recorded in this century have come from the idea that art must look new or different to be important. Today, some scholars and artists are questioning this way of thinking about art. They realize that artists often change their styles of working over their lifetimes. They recognize that some artists' work does not fit into well-known styles.

There is no doubt that there are many different styles of art today. Style names are a useful way to think about them.

Using What You Learned

Art History

1 Choose a style, period, artwork or artist presented in this chapter for a research report. You may dramatize the main points, create a slide show, make a poster or produce a video.

2 Visit an art museum to see original works of art. Ask for a tour or guidance that will help you see the collections of European or North American art after 1900.

3 Choose one style in this chapter and invent a different name for it. Write down several features of artworks in this style. Can your classmates identify some artworks that go with the name you have invented?

Creating Art

1 Art of the present is said to be eclectic – based on an inventive use of ideas from the past. Choose a medium and create an original eclectic artwork. Before you begin, write down the sources of ideas you will use.

2 Futurist artists were interested in change and the future. Create an artwork based on a related theme. Develop your own style.

Aesthetics and Art Criticism

1 Choose one artwork in this chapter that you find especially fascinating. Use the steps in art criticism to describe, analyze and interpret the artwork. Present your interpretation to the class.

2 Does your local paper print critiques of current art exhibits? Clip some of these, and note the art critics' names. Perhaps your teacher can arrange for an art critic to visit the class and discuss how and why critics make judgments about contemporary art. Find out how their judgments are influenced by the history of twentieth-century art.

Careers and Art Criticism

In the twentieth-century written art criticism has become an important way for artists to become well-known to art collectors, museums and the public. Today, many artists depend on critical reviews of their work to gain recognition.

Art critics enjoy looking at art and writing about it. Many people who write about art for newspapers and popular magazines study journalism. They often report facts about art events prepared by artists, art dealers or museums. Art critics who write books, essays for exhibition catalogs and other publications almost always have a background in art history and aesthetics.

Skills in art criticism, whether shown in writing or not, are important for everyone who creates or enjoys art. They allow you to make judgments on your own. Good criticism helps us see and appreciate art that might be hard to understand.

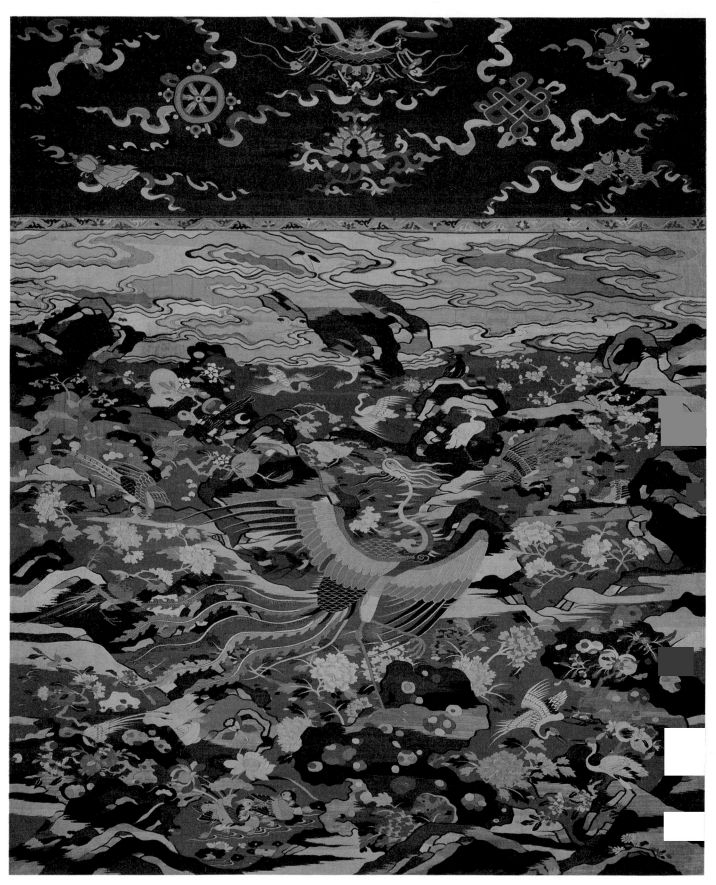

K'o ssu panel, with main figure feng huang; rest of ground covered with birds, rocks and flowers, Ming dynasty. Textile, 7'4 ¹/₂"" x 5'11" (225 x 180 cm). The Metropolitan Museum of Art. Seymour Fund, 1960.

Chapter 7
Art: A Global View

Chapter Vocabulary

Pre-Columbian art
Latin American art
Native North American art
African art
Oceanic art
Indian art
Southeast Asian art
Chinese art
Japanese art
Korean art
Islamic art

Much of what you learn in art classes is based on the Western tradition of art and culture. This tradition began in ancient Egypt, Greece and Rome. It was renewed during the Renaissance and has continued for the last 400 years. In this Western tradition, you learn to see art mainly as objects created to display and enjoy aesthetically.

But much of the art you see in museums was not created just to be displayed as art. It was first created for use in everyday life and special ceremonies. The process of creating the artwork was filled with ritual or spiritual meanings. The people who made the objects might have thought the objects had powers to help or harm people. The way people used objects was just as important as the objects' appearance. If you had grown up in these cultures, you would have learned the traditional meanings of the art forms. You would have known when and how to use them.

In this chapter, you will learn about some of the arts of non-Western cultures. Most of these cultures have beliefs and values very different from those in the West. Learning about each culture can help you understand and appreciate its art. It is equally important to imagine living in cultures where people have beliefs and ways of life very different from your own.

Studying this chapter will help you:

Art History   • become familiar with art of non-Western cultures.

Aesthetics   • learn more about art terms, concepts and values related to non-Western art.

Creating Art   • understand that art is created around the world.

Pre-Columbian and Latin American Art

The ancient arts of Mexico, Central and South America, and the Caribbean Islands are called *Pre-Columbian* (before the voyages of Christopher Columbus and John Cabot to North America). The art of this region was influenced by the artists' religious and political beliefs and the natural resources available to them. Around 1500, most of this area was conquered by France, Spain, Italy and Portugal. Because the languages of those countries are based on Latin, the region south of the United States is now called *Latin America.*

In Mexico and Central America, pyramids with steps were created for religious rites. Animal and human forms were often combined in fabrics, ceramics and metal-working. The Olmec people created sculptures of people and catlike creatures. The Mayans built big cities. Many buildings had sculptured facades covered with mosaic or paint. The Toltecs and Aztecs borrowed Mayan art ideas. They recorded their beliefs and conquests in carvings and illuminated manuscripts.

In the Andes region of South America, the Inca people created planned communities, including the city of Machu Picchu. They excelled in elaborate work in gold, silver and finely woven and tie-dyed fabrics.

In the Caribbean Islands, early Mayan influences have been found in large stone plazas. Spanish, Mexican and African art also influenced artists in Puerto Rico, Haiti, Cuba and the Dominican Republic.

Teotihuacan, Avenue of the Dead. In Central America, the Mayans and other groups built large cities with plazas and pyramids for use in religious rites. Many pyramids had elaborate painted carvings. Courtesy of the Mexican National Tourist Council.

When Europeans conquered these regions, much of the artwork was destroyed. In most of Latin America, European art styles were combined with the local art traditions. Spanish influences on art are called *Hispanic*.

After the Mexican Revolution (1910-1920), Diego Rivera, José Clemente Orozco and David Alfaro Siqueiros revived the art of fresco murals. Their powerful work illustrates the history, problems and hopes of the Mexican people.

Orozco and Rivera also created murals in the United States. Their work stimulated the government to employ North American artists to create murals in public buildings. Today, Mexican-American, Caribbean and Latin American artists are working in a variety of styles and art forms.

Mexico, Aztec, *Jaguar*, 15th century. Stone, 11" x 4 ¹⁵/₁₆" x 5 ¹¹/₁₆" (28 x 13 x 15 cm). The Brooklyn Museum. The DeSilver Fund.

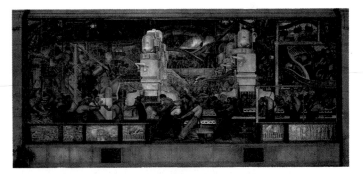

Diego Rivera, *Detroit Industry*, 1932-1933 (detail). Fresco, mural. The Detroit Institute of Arts. Founders Society Purchase: Edsel B. Ford Fund and Gift of Edsel B. Ford.

Tapestry Poncho, ca. 1438-1532. The patterns in this Incan textile are thought to be a form of writing. Notice the subtle variations in the repeated elements. Containing silver tinsel yoru. Neg. #10127. Courtesy Department of Library Services, American Museum of Natural History.

Right. Eastern Mexico, Huaster, *Quetzalcoatl*, 900-1250 AD. Quetzalcoatl is a cultural hero in Mesoamerican history. He was a Toltec prince named for an ancient Mayan feather-covered serpent-god. He fostered art and learning, was banished, but promised to return at the dawn of a new golden age. Limestone, 62 ¹/₄" (158 cm) high. The Brooklyn Museum. Henry L. Batterman, Frank S. Benson Funds.

Native North American Art

The art of Native North Americans reflects their ancient traditions and religious beliefs. Archaeologists think that the first groups in North America crossed the Bering Straits from Siberia to Alaska around 15,000 years ago. The way of life of these peoples has always been closely tied to a deep respect for nature. For this reason, most Native North American art has been inspired by the plants, animals and landscapes they found around them.

Along the Pacific coast and in the Northwest, wood was plentiful. Artists used it to create carved masks and many other forms of art. Plank houses were built, often with carved and painted doorposts. Large sculptured totem poles were erected to honor ancestors. Groups in the Arctic region created tools and jewelry of animal bone. They created clothing from hides and carved ivory to create sculpture.

In the Southwest, dwellings called pueblos were built of adobe, a mixture of clay and straw. Decorated pottery, woven blankets, sand painting, kachina dolls and silver jewelry were made for ritual use.

Bark-covered houses were built by groups living along the East coast. Work in ceramics, metal and leather was highly developed. Woven work included small beads and porcupine quills.

Nomadic groups living in the Great Plains created small portable artifacts from animal hides, including clothing and decorated tent shelters called tepees. Basketry, bead and feather work, painted tools and weapons were also made.

When Europeans settled in North America, the culture of many Native North American groups was changed and in some cases nearly destroyed. Some museums have preserved early examples of Native North American art. When you see the work in a museum, it is important to find out about its original purposes. Try to imagine its origin and use in the culture.

Among many Native North American groups, traditional art forms are being revived for ceremonial pur-

Cliff Palace, Mesa Verde National Park, Colorado, ca. 1100 AD. The Anasazi were ancient Navajo people. The *pueblo* is an apartment-like dwelling with rounded ceremonial rooms, called *kivas*, often decorated with murals. Photograph courtesy Department of Interior, Bureau of Reclamation.

Kwakiutl Mechanical Headdress, 1875-1900. This complex mask, carved from wood, has hinged sections. The wearer opened and closed sections to add dramatic meaning to ceremonies. Carved wood with painted muslin backing, 40" x 52" (102 x 132 cm). Museum of the American Indian, New York. Collected by George Heye. Photograph by Carmelo Guadagno.

poses. Some Native North Americans also use traditional designs and techniques to create work for sale.

Some Native North American artists prefer to use modern methods to express important themes from their heritage. Among these are a respect for nature, the survival of their traditions and the meaning of their heritage in today's world.

Crow Beaded Bridle Decoration. Courtesy of the Carnegie Museum of Natural History, Pittsburgh, Pennsylvania.

Native American, Pomo Feather Basket. Some baskets have 26 stitches per inch (10 stiches per cm). Fibre, buttons and quail topknots, 12" (30 cm) diameter. Courtesy of the Hurst Gallery.

Navajo, Bertha Stevens weaving outside hogan, 1963. Many hard-edge painters were inspired by the masterful designs in Navajo blankets woven by women. Museum of the American Indian, Heye Foundation. Photograph by George Hight.

Large Zia Polychrome Jar, Trinidad Medina. Pottery of the Zia, Acoma, Zuni, Hopi and other groups in New Mexico and Arizona, often include geometric motifs based on clouds, water serpents, rain, deer, birds and flowers. 19" x 13 1/2" (48 x 34 cm).

African Art

The arts of ancient Egypt are major achievements in African history. You learned about this north African civilization as an early source of Western culture.

In parts of Africa below the equator, the record of artistic work is less complete. Much of the art was destroyed by the damp environment and wood-eating insects. In addition, almost all of the art was created for use in everyday life and rituals. Forms have been re-painted, repaired or replaced as needed.

Within many groups of the past and present, art has been created to communicate with powerful spirits – natural forces and individuals, including ancestors and guardians. The materials and style of the artwork have many levels of meaning. Sculptures of figures or animals, many household objects and body adornments are "homes," or resting places, for spirits. Ritual masks and costumes have been created to communicate with a spirit world.

Representational art in ceramic clay was created by people of the early Nok culture (about 500 BC). Artists of the kingdoms of Benin (southern Nigeria) and Ife (west of Benin) mastered bronze casting during the 1400's and 1500's. Discovered in the 1890's, the bronze works are striking in detail, crafting and the information they reveal about the Ife and Benin kingdoms.

Masks and other art forms from Africa were first displayed in Europe during the late 1800's. The abstract forms influenced Pablo Picasso, Henri Matisse and other artists early in the twentieth century. Today, many museums have collections of African art in wood, ivory and bronze. Decorated gourds, baskets, beadwork, textiles, musical instruments, hairstyles and other art forms are now being studied by historians.

Warrior, Zaire; Lulua, 19th century. Wood, pigment, 29 ¹/₈" (74 cm) high. Collected by Hermann von Wissmann, 1865.

Benin, *Warrior and Attendants*, 17th century. This bronze relief once decorated the king's palace in Benin. The king is shown in the center, wearing a tall, beaded collar. On each side are soldiers and children making music. Bronze plaque, 14 ³/₄" x 15 ¹/₂" (37 x 39 cm). The Nelson-Atkins Museum of Art, Kansas City, Missouri. Nelson Fund.

African-American artists have often used their cultural heritage as a source of ideas for art. Some express their historical and personal experiences in America. Their work often deals with the themes of racial injustice, social concerns and hopes for the future. Some have used design concepts from Africa. Others explore artistic problems of personal interest. There is not just one kind of art or set of interests among African-American artists.

Make Mask (Mulwalwa). Zaire, Southern Kuba, 19th century. When you see masks in an art museum, it is important to remember they were part of a costume and used in ceremonies along with chants, music and dancing. Wood, raffia, fiber, paint, metal, 21 1/4" (54 cm). Collected by H. Salomon, 1910.

Zaire, Songye peoples, Power Figure, 19th-20th century. Wood, raffia, metal, leather, horn and beads, 30" x 9" (76 x 23 cm). The Brooklyn Museum, New York. Museum Purchase Fund.

Bamana, Mali, Chi Wara Headdress, late 19th-early 20th century. According to African legend, the antelope-spirit is the source of human knowledge about agriculture. Antelope masks vary in style but are usually worn at fertility rites. Wood, 42" (107 cm). The Brooklyn Museum. Gift of Mr. and Mrs. Ernst Anspach.

Oceanic Art

Easter Island, Male Figure, Moai Kavakava, ca. 1880. These Polynesian sculptures are thought to be memorials to important clan-members. Wood, 26" (66 cm). The Brooklyn Museum. Ella C. Woodward Fund.

Kangaroo. Australian aborigines create paintings on bark in a unique "x-ray" style that often shows animals with their inner organs and skeletons.

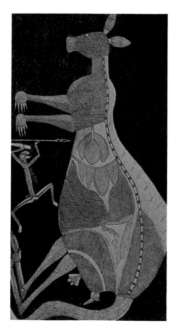

Oceanic art refers to the traditional arts of people who live almost isolated in Australia and the groups of Pacific islands known as Micronesia, Polynesia and Melanesia.

All art within this region was originally made from natural materials, without using metal technologies. It was made mainly for ceremonies or as decoration. Images in art usually refer to local religious beliefs, myths, ancestors, heroes or leaders. These traditional ways of creating art are still practiced by many groups, especially those living far from cities and towns.

Melanesia is an area about 3,000 miles (4839 km) long in the southwest Pacific Ocean. It includes many islands from New Guinea to Fiji. Religious beliefs include faith in supernatural spirits, myths, magic and the power of ancestors.

Crocodiles, birds, snakes, fish and pigs are common images in artworks. Raffia (fiber of a palm tree), bark cloth, tusks, shells, feathers and paint are often combined in dramatic ways. Architecture and household items are decorated with paint and modeled or carved forms.

Micronesia is an area including many small Pacific islands north of Melanesia and east of the Philippines. Strong traditions of crafts are evident in sculptured figures, tattooing and ornamental utensils. Woven textiles, canoe and house-building are also highly developed.

Polynesia stretches east and southeast from Micronesia in a triangle about 5,000 miles (8064 km) on each side. It is within the area from Hawaii to New Zealand and Easter Island. Many cultures believe in worshiping ancestors and a social ranking based on ancestors.

Human figures, man-bird images and lizards are symbols in sculpture, carving and *tapa cloth* – bark fibers pounded into a firm, matted cloth. Tapa designs are applied with stamps, stencils or by freehand painting.

Missionaries arrived in Hawaii in 1820. Before this time, one of the most unusual native arts was the creation of large, basket-woven head masks, covered with feathers. These images, usually of the war-god Kukailimoku, were taken into battle.

Today, Maori artists of New Zealand continue their artistic traditions. They are skilled woodcarvers, tattooists and makers of textiles. Intricate curved designs often include stylized human figures of ancestors.

Australian *aboriginal* (native) art is created by people who live as nomads. Much of the art is based on a belief in *Dreamtime*, the time of creation, when giant animals with human and supernatural powers arose from the earth. They had the power to change the world and take different forms. When they died, they went to the sky and became stars. These spirits are the source of aboriginal customs and art.

New Ireland, Mask, 19th century. Wood, paint, fiber, sea snail opercula, 18 ⁷/₈" x 9 ³/₄" (48 x 25 cm). The Brooklyn Museum. Gift of Frieda and Milton F. Rosenthal.

Wooden face mask from Mortlock, central Carolines. Painted with lime and soot, 17 ³/₄" x 19 ³/₄" (45 x 50 cm). Hamburgisches Museum fur Volkerkunde und Vorgeschichte.

Hawaiian War God, Kukailimoku, 7 feet tall. The simple, powerful forms in this traditional Hawaiian sculpture emphasize the aggressive pose and snarling mouth of the war-god Kukailimoku. Feather-covered versions were carried into battle. Peabody Museum of Salem. Photograph by Mark Sexton.

Indian Art

About 5,000 years ago, Indian civilization developed around great cities in the Indus valley. Early forms of art included clay, stone and bronze sculptures as well as murals in caves. Cattle, scenes of bull-wrestling and images of single male dancers in the company of animals are common.

Many early artworks are based on the Hindu religious concept of reincarnation and elaborate myths about *Brahma* (the creator), *Vishnu* (the preserver) and *Siva* (the destroyer). Siva is often shown entwined with snakes or dancing in a circle of fire.

The next great influence on art came from Buddha, a teacher who founded the religion of Buddhism. Many Buddhist artworks show Buddha sitting crosslegged under a tree, with royal attendants. One hand is often raised in a gesture that symbolizes pushing away fear. He is also shown with a third "all-seeing" eye on the forehead and large "all-hearing" ears. The lotus, or water lily, symbolizes purity.

Some images of Buddha reflect the spread of Greek artistic ideas by Alexander the Great, who invaded India in 326 BC. Islamic influences (see page 145) can be seen in Indian art from the twelfth to sixteenth centuries. Indian artistic traditions also influenced China, Tibet, parts of Russia and other neighboring countries.

Ranganathaswanny Temple, Tamilnadi, South India.

Seated Buddha Preaching the First Sermon, Sarnath, 5th century AD. Buddha compared the laws of right conduct to the spokes of a wheel. His hand gestures symbolize the turning of the Wheel of the Law. The sculpture visually explains some of the laws. Stele, sandstone, 63" (160 cm) high. Archaelogical Museum, Sarnath.

The Descent of the River Ganges from Heaven. 10th century. During the rainy season, water from the Ganges River flows from a cleft in this massive rock carving. The whole work tells about the rewards given to a *sage,* or honored wise person, for living a simple, austere life. Live rock carving at Mamallapuram, India.

Tamilnada, *Siva, King of the Dancers, Performing the Nataraja,* Chola dynasty, India, 10th century. Siva, one of many subjects in Hindu art, is a destructive force who can take many forms. This Siva is dancing in a circle of fire. Bronze, 30" x 22 ¹/₂" x 76 ¹/₂" (76 x 57 x 18 cm). The Los Angeles County Museum of Art.

Punjab Hills, Guler. Kaliya Damana: *Krishna Overcoming the Naga Demon, Kaliya.* Elaborate myths and legends are combined with religious teachings in this and many other paintings from India. Gouache on paper, 7 ³/₈" x 10 ³/₈" (19 x 26 cm). The Metropolitan Museum of Art. Rogers Fund, 1927.

Angkor Thom. Sculpted Faces of Jayavarmin VII, ca. 1190. This Buddhist monument has great towers with human faces thought to represent the ruler who built it and a *Bodhisattva* – a guardian to whom the temple is dedicated. Cambodia.

Vietnam, Mi Son Cham School, *Celestial Dancer*, ca. 900 AD. The Mon, Khmer and Champa people lived in the region around present-day Vietnam, Thailand and Cambodia. To see the Indian influence in this region, compare this work and the *Siva*, King of the Dancers on page 137. Sandstone, 24" (62 cm) high. Museum of Cham Sculpture, Da Nang, Vietnam.

Southeast Asian Art

Southeast Asia includes the mainland region around the countries of Vietnam, Cambodia, Thailand, Burma and the islands of Indonesia. This region has a long history of artistic influences from China, India, the ancient Vietnam civilization known as Dong-son and other early groups (Mon, Pyu, Cham, Khmer).

The major influences on the art of mainland Southeast Asia came from Buddhism and Hinduism. Temples and sculptures combine features from Indian and Chinese art. In smaller sculpture and decorative arts, local myths and legends are featured.

Indonesia is a large crescent-shaped region to the east and northeast of the southeastern tip of Asia. It includes Sumatra, Java, Bali, Borneo, the Philippines and many smaller islands. The art forms, subjects and design traditions of people in this region are varied. Some arts are practiced today as they were centuries ago. Artists often use curving lines and surfaces, and shapes based on plant forms.

Human and animal figures are usually symbols for protective spirits or ancestors. The dominant religious art form is sculpture. It is often decorated with sea snails, colored fibers and barks, or clay-based paints. In many isolated regions, the art shares characteristics with Oceanic art.

Later Indonesian art shows the influence of migrations of people from Asia, especially China. Hindu and Buddhist influences from India, as well as Islamic features, are also present in later art.

Kris Balinese Sword Stand, 18th century. Wood, 23 ¹/₄" (59 cm) high. The Metropolitan Museum of Art. Bequest of George C. Stone, 1936.

Chinese Art

Buddhists have a deep respect for nature and ancestor worship. These themes are prominent in the traditional arts of China. Bronze artifacts from 1100 BC have been found. Between 221 and 210 BC, the Great Wall was built to keep out invaders. Large tombs filled with realistic clay sculptures of emperors and their armies were created 2,000 years ago.

The T'ang dynasty was a period of intense scholarship comparable to the European Renaissance. The arts of calligraphy, wood block printing and ceramics flourished. Paintings of birds, flowers and landscapes were highly developed.

During the Yüan and Ming dynasties, urban life expanded and art – especially ceramics and silk – was created to be sent to other countries. In the Qing dynasty, a more flamboyant, exotic and highly decorative art emerged – comparable to Baroque art in Europe.

Through trade, conquest and settlement, Chinese art influenced art in Japan, Korea, Southeast Asia and parts of Indonesia.

Terra-cotta army guards at the grave mount of Qin Shihuangdi, the first emperor of China. Hidden for 2,000 years, it includes thousands of individually modeled and painted warriors, horses, chariots and metal weapons.

Ming period, Offering Hall at the Altar of Heaven. The Emperor used this hall for seasonal offerings. It is filled with number symbolism. Eight flights of stairs represent eight directions of the universe. The three-stage roof and terraces come from a symbol for heaven. Twelve columns stand for months in a year. Ch'in-nien-tien, Peking.

Hsu Tao-ning, *Fishermen (Yu-fu)*, Northern Sung dynasty. In general, Chinese landscape paintings are idealized. The mountains tower above, overlap and vanish into the distance. The river meanders below. People are often shown as small details in the larger scheme of nature. Scrolls like these are meant to be unrolled slowly and studied in sections. Handscroll, ink and slight color on silk, 19" x 82 ½" (49 x 210 cm). The Nelson-Atkins Museum of Art, Kansas City, Missouri. Nelson Fund.

China, *Great Spiritual Chaser of Demons* , 1873. The British Museum, London.

China, Shoulder Jar, Ming Dynasty (Chia-Ching period, 1522-1566). The powerful dragon on this jar means that it was probably made in an imperial ceramic factory. Porcelain, 8 ¼" (21 cm). Ostasiatische Kunstabteilung-Staatliche Musees, Berlin.

141

Japanese Art

Traditional Japanese art is often more decorative and detailed than Chinese art. It is often used for storytelling. Two-dimensional art is most often linear and asymmetrical. Space is thought of as a positive part of the design, not just a background.

Paintings often take the form of poems on scrolls and screens created with calligraphic brushstrokes. Atmospheric and parallel perspective are often used to suggest space. Ceramic arts are admired around the world because their design, material and function work together so well. Hiroshige, Hokusai, Utamaro and Harunobu are among the masters of multicolor woodcut printing.

Arts inspired by a Japanese religious sect called *Zen* include the tea ceremony, monochrome ink painting, flower arranging and large or miniature garden design. Many people practice these arts for private reflection or meditation. The arts reflect three Japanese aesthetic ideals: *wabi* (quiet, honest integrity), *sabi* (reserved, mellowed by time), and *shibui* (moderate but refreshing and energizing).

Sculptures in bronze, wood, clay and dry-lacquer (layers of hemp bound together with lacquer) often feature Buddhist themes and characters. In some periods, sculptures were painted, gilded or decorated with inlaid stone. Masks for traditional dramas and dances are also an important form of sculpture.

Architecture ranges from multi-tiered, fortress-like castles to complex shrines and grand palaces. It also includes the simple Zen-inspired modular home with room spaces created by sliding screens.

Around 1800, trade and artistic influences increased between Asia and Europe. The French Impressionists and Post-Impressionists explored the linear asymmetrical design and flat spaces in Japanese prints. American architect Frank Lloyd Wright was inspired by Japanese architecture. European influences on Oriental art also became stronger, especially in work created to be sold in the West.

Ando Hiroshige, *Evening Rain on the Karasaki Pine*. From the series "Eight Views of Omi Province." Multicolored woodcuts of great subtlety are a unique art form highly developed in Japan. Prints of familiar landmarks and activities were especially popular as gifts. Woodblock print, 10 ¼" x 15" (26 x 38 cm). The Metropolitan Museum of Art. Bequest of Mrs. H.O. Havemeyer, 1929. The H.O. Havemeyer Collection.

Golden Pavilion, Kyoto, 1398. This was a study for a shogun, a military ruler who brought Zen religious ideas into everyday life. He used it to read, to enjoy his art collection and view the pond-garden.

Jizo Seated on a Lotus Dais, Kamakura period. This figure is a symbol for a guardian of travelers and warriors. He is dressed as a beggar, seated on a lotus petal. Wood, 43 ³/₄" (111 cm). The Metropolitan Museum of Art. The Harry G.C. Packard Collection of Asian Art. Gift of Harry G.C. Packard and Purchase.

Tokugawa period, porcelain ewer with dragons. The dragon motif is a Chinese influence on Japanese art. The direct brushwork has a freedom admired by European artists of the 20th century. Kutani enamelled porcelain, 8" (20 cm) high. Victoria and Albert Museum, London.

Korean Art

Traditional Korean art is gentle and refined. It often reflects Buddhist influences from China.

Temple forms and sculpture for shrines are graceful. Many have a floating decorative quality that is rare in Chinese art. These qualities are also seen in Japanese art, which owes much to early Korean work.

Korean ceramic artists invented the use of inlaid designs of different colored clays. The subtle contours and colors of many of the ceramic works are distinctive.

Under the Yi dynasty (1392-1910) official studios for artists were set up. Many of the official artists were employed to create portraits and work on architectural projects.

In the late 1500s, Korea became a battlefield. Many of its early art treasures were destroyed. Many Korean artists went to Japan and influenced its art, especially ceramics. In later Korean art, there was a tendency to go back to Chinese sources for inspiration.

Wine pot, late 12th century. This winepot shows the graceful, delicate forms created by Korean potters. In the 1500's, Korea was invaded by Japan. Korean potters were sent to Japan where they helped revitalize Japanese ceramics. Porcelain. Toksu Palace Museum, Seoul.

Paekche, *Maitreya*, early 7th century. Korean images of Buddha often have delicate curves and a calm grace not seen in related images from China, Japan or India. Gilt bronze, 37" (93.5 cm) high. Toksu Palace Museum, Seoul.

Kyungbok gung Palace, Seoul, early Yi period. The interior of this double-roofed temple is elaborately decorated. It combines ideas from China and Japan. Find the stone markers in the courtyard. Officials stood at these, according to rank, for imperial events.

Islamic Art

Islam is a religion founded in 622 AD by the Arabian prophet Muhammad. Within the next one hundred years, the Moslem faith spread from Arabia (now Iran) westward to Spain and eastward to India. This religion brought about an artistic and cultural unity in the many regions where it was practiced.

In Islamic religious art, representation of people and the Moslem god, Allah, is forbidden. This explains why many Islamic artworks are richly ornamented with curved and geometric abstract designs. People are only shown in *secular art*, about everyday life or the court.

Fine, detailed designs in enameled glass, metalwork, ceramics and illuminated manuscripts are characteristic of Islamic art. Textile arts, especially Persian carpets, were also highly developed by the 900's.

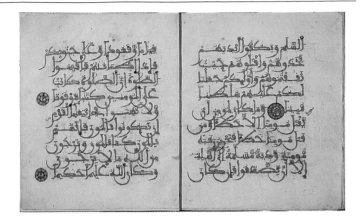

Text from the Koran, 11th century. This page is from the Koran – the holy book of Moslems. The calligraphy of the Arabic script is bold, rounded, and precisely laid out. Gilt on vellum, 11" x 9" (28 x 23 cm). Reproduced by courtesy of the Trustees of the Chester Beatty Library, Dublin.

The Taj Mahal is an Islamic tomb, built in 1632 by Shah Jahan for his wife.

Mosque Lamp from the Dome of the Rock, Jersualem, 1549. Ceramic, 15" (38 cm) high. Isnik, Turkey. The British Museum, London.

Heritage-Based Art Today

In many of the cultures in this chapter, there is no word for art. But people still create beautiful or visually powerful things for personal and cultural reasons. If you wanted to see important art in these cultures you would not go to a museum! You would go to their communities to learn why and how the art is used.

If you were to visit places around the world today, you could find artists who work in a variety of styles. Some create art that is directly related to the artistic traditions and beliefs in their culture. Some of the art might reflect only some of the artistic traditions in the culture, such as the use of traditional media, themes or qualities of design.

Other artists might be working in an *international style*. An international style is one that cannot be linked to just one culture or tradition of art. International styles have come about from exchanges of ideas among artists of many nations and cultures.

In some regions of the world, cultures are changing very rapidly and traditional art forms are in danger of being lost. In Australia, museums have been set up to preserve examples of traditional aboriginal art. In Latin America, efforts are being made to protect and preserve Pre-Columbian architecture and other outdoor works of art. Similar steps are being taken in many other regions.

Critical Thinking Suppose you could save one work of art in this chapter so that it could be seen by future generations. Which artwork would you choose? Why? What would you want other people to know or value when they saw the work?

Andrew Tsinahjinnie, *Pastoral Scene*, Navajo. Kiva Gallery, Gallup, New Mexico.

Left, Alejandro Otero, *Color-rhythm I*, 1955. This Venezuelan artist has been active in the international art world. His primary interest is the optical effect of color rhythms. Enamel on plywood, 6' 6 3/4" x 19" (200 x 48 cm). Collection, The Museum of Modern Art, New York. Inter-American Fund.

Right, Faith Ringgold, *Mrs. Jones and Family*, 1973. This African-American sculptor draws inspiration from African masks and garments, and her experience as a woman. Sewn fabric and embroidery. Courtesy Bernice Steinbaum Gallery, New York City.

Summary

There are remarkable artistic traditions around the world. You have been introduced to a few examples of this artwork. It is called non-Western art because much of it was created to express values or beliefs that have not been dominant in European and North American culture.

This chapter has pointed out some of the traditional arts of many cultural groups. In countries around the world, there are artists who work in different ways. Some create traditional art based on their unique cultural heritage. Others create art that shows some cultural influence but is not in a traditional style. There are also many contemporary artists whose work is international in character.

Using What You Learned

Art History

1 On a world map, identify the geographic regions that are included by each cultural style term:
- *Pre-Columbian art*
- *Latin American art*
- *Native North American art*
- *African art*
- *Oceanic art*
- *Indian art*
- *Southeast Asian art*
- *Chinese art*
- *Japanese art*
- *Korean art*
- *Islamic art*

2 Give three reasons why art historians think Western and non-Western traditions of art are different.

Aesthetics and Criticism

1 Identify three works of art in this chapter that have visual similarities but were created in different cultural regions. Describe the main ways they are similar and possible reasons for these.

2 Why is it important for you to learn about non-Western traditions of art?

3 Identify one of the artworks in this chapter that you find fascinating. Fascinating means you want to look at it even if you do not fully understand or like it. Give three reasons why you find it fascinating.

Creating Art

1 Every person has a cultural heritage. Your heritage may go back to one of the cultures discussed in this chapter. It may have roots in Europe and North America or be a combination of several cultures. You may only know about your cultural heritage from the people you have lived and grown up with. Create a work of art in any medium. In this work, try to express the best part of your cultural heritage.

2 Look back through this chapter. You will find many works created by unknown artists. Explain why the names of artists are often unknown to us.

Albrecht Dürer, *Dürer at Thirteen*, 1484. Dürer was thirteen when he created this self-portrait. He later became one of the best-known artists of the Renaissance (1400-1600). Albertina, Vienna.

Chapter 8

Drawing

Chapter Vocabulary

thumb-nail sketch
contour
gesture
whole-to-part
dry media
fixative
wet media
wash
collage
mixed media
silverpoint
negative shape
positive shape
silhouette
light source
highlight
cast shadow
perspective
vanishing point
horizon line
proportion

Fifteen thousand years ago, a cave dweller took a burned stick out of the fire and used it to draw animals on a cave wall. Why were these drawings made? Did they give the artist some power over the animals? Was it part of a magic ceremony? Or was the cave dweller simply moved by the animals' beauty and movement? We'll never know the answer to these questions, but one thing is certain: that ancient person was drawing.

Sketches are quick drawings – visual notes or plans for artwork. With a sketch you can record things you see and want to remember. Drawings can be used to plan other artwork. They can also be created as finished works of art. In this case, artists use drawing materials to express feelings and ideas.

Many artists draw or sketch in books every day. Sometimes they also write notes on the pages. Their sketchbooks become a visual diary. If you have not yet started a sketchbook, begin today. Draw what you see, feel and imagine. Sketch your classmates and things you see in your neighborhood. Use your sketchbook as a way to develop ideas and strengthen your visual skills.

In this chapter, you will learn about tools and materials for drawing. You will also learn new ways to think about drawings. You will make drawings to help you learn to see and understand design. Most importantly, you will create drawings to express your ideas, feelings and imagination.

After you have studied this chapter and completed some of the activities, you will be better able to:

Creating Art   • create drawings using different media and approaches.

Art Criticism   • evaluate different kinds of drawings in relation to their design and expressive qualities.

Aesthetics   • understand terms used to describe drawing media and approaches to drawing.

Art History   • understand traditional and experimental approaches to drawing.

Gallery

Artists create drawings for many reasons. Sometimes they are making a record of things they see and want to remember. Others use drawings to explore ideas. Some are plans for artwork in another medium.

Drawings can also be created as finished artworks. Some drawings are realistic. Some are abstract, and some are nonobjective, which means that they aren't pictures of any particular object or scene.

Sometimes it is difficult to say whether an artwork is a drawing or a painting. When artists draw with inks and a brush, their drawings may have a "painterly" quality. Painterly means a work looks like it was painted with a brush.

Critical Thinking Which of the drawings shown here is the most realistic? Why do you think so? Which one expresses the most powerful idea or feeling? Why do you think so? Which one do you most enjoy looking at? Why?

John Biggers, *The Cradle*, ca. 1950. Charcoal on paper, 22 ³/₈" x 21 ¹/₂" (57 x 55 cm). The Museum of Fine Art, Houston. Twenty-fifth Annual Houston Art Exhibition, Museum Purchase.

Michelangelo, *Damned Soul, A Fury*, 1475-1564. Black chalk, 11 ⁵/₈" x 8" (295 x 203 cm). Royal Library, Windsor Castle.

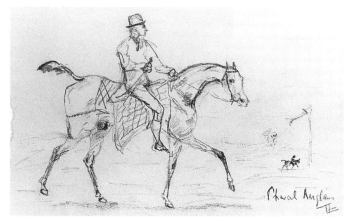

Henri de Toulouse-Lautrec, *English Horseman*, Pencil on paper. Marion Koogler McNay Art Museum, San Antonio, Texas. Bequest of Marion Koogler McNay.

Edgar Degas, *The Violinist*, 1877-1878. Pastel and charcoal on green paper, 15 ⁷/₁₆" x 11 ³/₄" (39 x 40 cm). The Metropolitan Museum of Art. Rogers Fund, 1918.

Paula Modersohn-Becker, *Peasant Woman*, 1900. Charcoal on buff wove paper, 17" x 25" (43 x 64 cm). The Art Institute of Chicago. Gift of the Donnelley Family, 1978.

Rajput, Rajasthani School, *Head of Krishna*. Cartoon for mural painting, from illustration to the "Rasa Lila." Color on paper. The Metropolitan Museum of Art. Rogers Fund, 1918. Photography by Otto Nelson.

Earle Horter, *The Chrysler Building Under Construction*, 1931. Ink and watercolor on paper, 20 $^1/_4$" x 14 $^3/_4$" (51 x 37 cm). Collection of Whitney Musem of American Art. Purchase. Photograph by Gamma One Conversions.

Diego Rivera, *Sleep*, 1933 (detail). The Metropolitan Museum of Art. Harris Brisbane Dick Fund.

Meet the Artist

Leonardo da Vinci

1452–1519

He believed that if you looked hard enough at the world, you would understand everything. He never stopped looking and never stopped drawing the things he saw. This great artist, inventor and scientist filled sketchbooks with hundreds of drawings. He drew pictures of everything around him and didn't stop there. He sketched ideas that no one else had thought about – a submarine, a helicopter, an airplane, even a parachute. And this was nearly 500 years ago!

Leonardo da Vinci was born in Italy and lived during the Renaissance, a time between 1400 and 1600 when people became very interested in the world of science and exploration. He was a student of anatomy, an inventor and engineer, a mathematician and a philosopher. He was also a gifted painter, sculptor and architect. Leonardo was interested in city planning, astronomy, botany, geology and optics. He was a skilled musician and a designer who designed both weapons and women's fashions. From his example, people today call someone who can do many things well a "Renaissance" person.

Leonardo da Vinci, *Studies of Cats and Dragons*, ca. 1513-1514. Pen and ink and wash over black chalk, 10 ³/₈" x 8 ¹/₄" (26 x 21 cm). Royal Library, Windsor Castle.

Leonardo da Vinci, *Self-portrait*, ca. 1512. Royal Library, Windsor Castle.

Leonardo da Vinci, Sketch of a parachute.

This amazing man began his career at the age of fifteen, when he became an apprentice to the artist Andrea del Verrocchio. He became well known in his lifetime and worked for many kings and leaders in Italy and France. When he died at the age of 67, he was one of the most respected people in Europe.

He wrote many notes in his sketchbooks, including his thoughts on drawing itself. Here is some of his advice: "(You should practice) watching and taking notes of the attitudes and actions of men as they talk and dispute, or laugh or come to blows...noting these down with rapid strokes, in a little pocket-book which you ought always to carry with you (because) the memory is incapable of preserving them."

Leonardo was a master at showing the natural expressions and inner character of people. His best known works are the paintings *Mona Lisa* and *The Last Supper*. His sketchbooks show us that an artist must be a creative thinker, not just a skilled craftsperson.

Critical Thinking Many artists keep sketchbooks with written notes. Leonardo's sketchbooks are a record not only of the things he saw, but of his many thoughts as well. What are some other uses for a sketchbook?

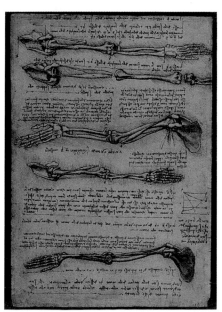

Leonardo da Vinci, *Study of a Star-of-Bethlehem.* Red chalk and pen and ink, 7 3/4" x 6 1/4" (20 x 16 cm). Royal Library, Windsor Castle.

Leonardo da Vinci, *Anatomical Bones of Arm, Hand and Shoulder,* 1510. Pen and ink, 11 1/3" x 7 3/4" (29 x 20 cm). Royal Collection, Windsor Castle.

What ideas for drawing are of interest to you? Student art.

Glenn O. Coleman, *Street Bathers*, ca. 1906. Can you see the variety of lines and shadows in this lively streetscape? What medium did the artist use? Crayon on paper, 11 ¹³/₁₆" x 15 ¹⁵/₁₆" (28 x 40 cm). Collection of Whitney Museum of American Art, New York.

Ideas for Drawing

When you sketch something you see, you are making a visual record of the important or interesting parts of your subject. Sometimes artists fill one page with ***thumbnail sketches*** – small drawings of people, landscapes or other ideas for art.

Where do you get ideas for drawings? You might remember exciting, unusual or funny events in your life. Maybe you care deeply about poor people and injustice, or have strong hopes for the future. Thinking about these memories, beliefs and feelings can give you ideas for drawing.

Sometimes you can get ideas by using your imagination. For example, look at your shoe as if it were an imaginary creature. Can you draw it so that other people will see your idea?

Try experimenting with drawing materials and tools, Use them in new ways, maybe even in ways you've never seen before. Express yourself through a variety of materials. Can you think of other techniques that might help you develop ideas for drawings?

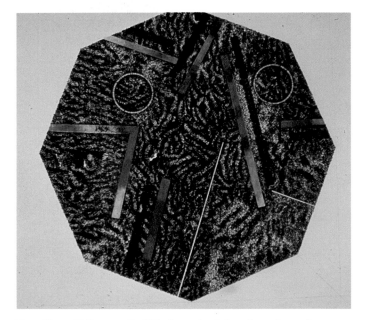

Tom Shaw, *Tribute to Cecil Taylor*, 1980. Ink and magic marker. Courtesy of the artist.

154

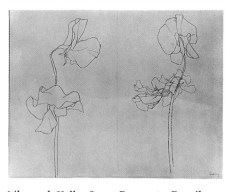

Ellsworth Kelly, *Sweet Pea*, 1960. Pencil on heavy white wove paper, 22 ⁹/₁₆" x 28 ¹/₂" (57 x 72 cm). The Baltimore Museum of Art. Thomas E. Benesch Memorial Collection.

Rembrandt van Rijn, *Study of Saskia Lying in Bed,* ca. 1638. Rembrandt used quickly placed lines to capture his subject in a few strokes. Pen and brush in bistre, wash, 5 ¾" x 7" (145 x 178 cm). National Gallery of Art, Washington. Ailsa Mellon Bruce Fund, 1966.

Methods of Drawing

There are three ways of drawing – contour, gesture and whole-to-part – that artists have used for hundreds of years. About 50 years ago, artist-teacher Kimon Nicholaides (KEE-mon nick-oh-LIE-dees) wrote about them in a book called *The Natural Way to Draw.* You can practice these methods.

Contour drawing improves your eye-hand coordination. This is important if you want to draw things you see and show them in great detail. Artists usually do contour drawings to develop and practice their skill in seeing, but sometimes they become finished artwork.

The main ideas in contour drawing are these: Look at the edges *(contours)* of the object you are drawing. Don't look at the lines you are making on your paper. Don't take your eyes off the object. Draw slowly and carefully. Imagine that your drawing tool is slowly touching and tracing around each edge of the object you are studying.

Gesture drawing is just the opposite of contour drawing. Gesture drawings are done quickly, without any attention to details.

The aim in gesture drawing is to draw the main "action lines" in an object, scene or person. Use a wide, soft pencil or the side of a crayon. Have extra paper on hand. Draw quickly. Most gesture drawings should only take about 30 seconds. A complex scene might take three minutes. Remember, most gesture drawings are sketches. Just feel and record the main action lines or movement of the subject.

Whole-to-part drawing helps you compose a drawing so that the larger and smaller parts are unified. This method has three steps:

1. Lightly draw the largest shapes. Do not worry about detail. Just show the main angles, positions and proportions of the shapes.

2. Add lines or correct them to show the edges (contours) of objects. Rearrange lines or shapes if you need to.

3. Now look at the smaller parts of your subject. Add details. Develop textures, values and colors if you want them.

Marcia Isaacson, *Bellsmith's Family Members*, 1970. A graphite (lead) pencil has been used to create textures that seem to flow from the dog to the person, uniting them as a "family." Pencil, 29 1/4" x 41" (74 x 104 cm). Collection Minnesota Museum of Art, St. Paul. Gift of her children in memory of Miriam Holman Bend.

Yin-t'o-lo, *The Monk from Tan-hsia Burning of a Wooden Image of the Buddha*, 13-14th century.

Media for Drawing

Dry Media

Dry media for drawing include pencils, charcoal, chalk or pastels, and crayons (wax or oil). You can also scratch lines into prepared cardboard and other surfaces.

Graphite pencils are often called lead pencils. The numbers on the pencil tell you what type of line it will make, from 6B (soft, dark) to 9H (hard, light). To remove lines, rub the paper lightly with a soft rubber eraser.

Charcoal is available in natural sticks (vine charcoal), compressed sticks, or pencils. Use soft charcoal for dark values and a hard charcoal for light values. Create shades of gray by smudging areas with a cloth, a tissue or your fingers. A kneaded eraser will remove charcoal. Textured papers are best for charcoal drawings.

Colored chalk, often called pastels, can be used on wet or dry paper. Dip the chalk into water or liquid starch if you want to make clean sharp lines. Charcoal and chalk are soft and smear easily. A *fixative* is a clear spray that protects charcoal or chalk drawings from smears.

With wax crayons, you can draw lightly or press hard. Make a crayon etching by scratching through a dark color placed over a light color. Make crayon rubbings by placing paper over a textured surface, then rubbing over the paper. For a crayon resist, brush water-diluted ink or paint over a drawing. The paint "rolls away" from the wax crayon.

Oil pastels are a greasy, stick-like medium. You can blend colors on paper or build them up in layers. Some crayons are made of chalky pigments mixed with wax and oil. They are called crayon-pastel or pastel-oil.

Choose one dry medium for drawing. Experiment with lines, shapes, values and textures. Try using a light pressure and a heavy pressure. Use the point, edge and side. Try smudging and erasing. Work on different kinds and colors of paper.

Safety Note Chalk and charcoal are dusty materials. If you are allergic to dust, tell your teacher. Use spray fixative only in well-ventilated areas outside the class-room. Follow all directions.

Wet Media

Pens and inks are wet media. Pens come in many sizes and with different kinds of points. Some are natural materials – such as reed, bamboo or quills. Some have flexible or rigid steel points that you push into a handle. Some pens, such as ballpoint pens, felt-tip markers and fountain pens have their own ink supply

Inks for artwork are available in many colors. A permanent ink, like India ink, will not smear after it is dry. Unwanted spots are very difficult to remove.

A *wash* is a thin, watery ink applied with a brush or swab. Wash drawings often combine lines and fluid shapes. You might experiment, using ink on tools such as twigs, cotton-tip swabs, the edges of cardboard or small pieces of sponge.

Wet media can be used on many kinds of paper. Textured papers that absorb liquids are usually best. Pens make very precise lines on a smooth paper. Try drawing with ink on wet paper. Allow it to dry as you continue drawing. How does the line change as the paper dries?

Safety Note Most permanent felt-tip markers contain extremely harmful fumes. Because these fumes can be hazardous to your health, they are not recommended for use in any art activity.

Collage and Mixed Media

Many art experts include collage as a form of drawing. A *collage* is made from pasted paper or other flat materials. When some artists cut out collage shapes, they call it "drawing" with scissors. Many artists combine collage with drawing or painting media.

You can get very interesting results when you put different types of materials together in the same drawing. This is called *mixed media* drawing. Try combining dry media such as charcoal and pencil, or chalk and crayon. Try combining wet media. For example, create a wash drawing. Let it dry. Then use felt-tip markers on top. Try drawing with water-base markers, and then brushing clear water over the lines.

There are many other drawing media that artists have used in the past and continue to use today. *Silverpoint* drawings are scratched into thick paper with a piece of silver wire. In time, the silver lines tarnish and become dark.

In some cultures, artists draw with natural materials such as chalk or colored clay. Some use sharp tools to incise lines into bark, wood, stones, slabs of clay or leather. Other artists are exploring the use of computers to create drawings.

Ida Kohlmeyer, *Synthesis No. 49*, 1982. Mixed media, 70" x 68 ¹/₂" (178 x 174 cm). Courtesy of the artist.

Romare Bearden, *Eastern Barn*, 1968. Collage of glue, lacquer, oil and paper, 55 ¹/₂" x 44" (141 x 112 cm). Collection of Whitney Museum of American Art. Purchase.

Exploring Design Concepts

Line

The way a line is drawn, or the medium it is drawn with, affects the way you feel about the subject of the drawing. Lines can show anger or sadness. They can show how delicate, solid or transparent an object is.

Artists say that each drawing medium has unique qualities and possibilities. Each medium – even one as simple as a pencil – can be used in many different ways.

Explore these ideas about drawing. Set up a still life or find an object to draw such as your shoe or purse. You could draw a natural form such as a leaf, weed, acorn or shell.

Create a series of drawings of your subject using different types of lines. For example, one drawing might show only the contours of the objects. A second might use dots or lines to suggest values and shading. A third drawing might suggest the overall lines of movement and gestural quality of the object. Could you also use lines to capture patterns? How?

Now choose a simple object. Create a series of drawings of it, each in a different medium. What qualities of line can you develop in each medium? How does each medium help you express something different about the object?

What media might you use to create a drawing with colored lines? What happens to the mood of a drawing if you use soft, fuzzy lines? Precise, thin lines? Jagged lines? What media might you choose for other special qualities of line? When might you want to create lines with qualities like these?

Student art.

Linear Shading Techniques

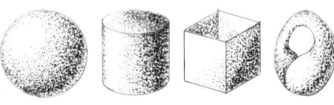

Stippling

Hatching

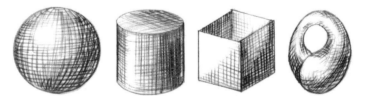

Crosshatching

Notice how the lines in hatched and crosshatched shading are parallel to the curve of the surface. To stipple, begin with wide spaces between the dots, then gradually add more dots.

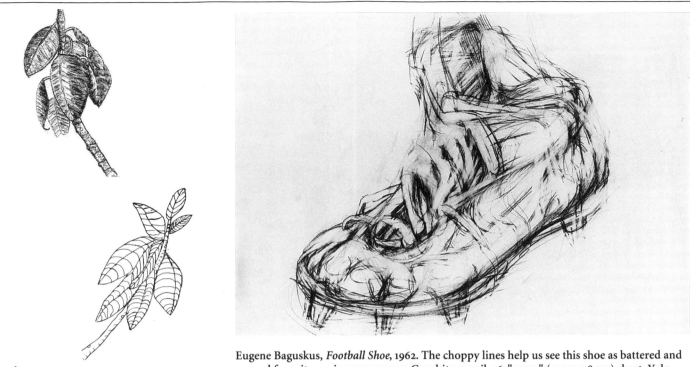

Student art.

Eugene Baguskus, *Football Shoe*, 1962. The choppy lines help us see this shoe as battered and scarred from its use in many games. Graphite pencil, 165" x 172" (419 x 438 cm) sheet. Yale University Art Gallery.

Student art. This drawing is based on a *stipple* technique. The whole work is made of tiny dots. How did the artist place the dots to create a feeling of near and distant elements? What is the center of interest?

What makes the shapes stand out clearly? Student art.

Alexander Calder, *Four Black Dots*, 1974. The broad flat lines create strong positive and negative shapes. Gouache on paper, 29 ½" x 43" (75 x 109 cm). Collection of Whitney Museum of American Art. Purchase.

Repeated shapes focus our attention on the central object. Student art.

Shape

Most of the drawings you create will contain shapes. A shape is made when a line encloses a space. Shapes can be organic or geometric. They can have soft, fuzzy edges or hard, precise edges.

Shapes can be drawn so they seem active or passive. They can be drawn so the *negative* shapes are as important as the *positive* shapes. Shapes can overlap and change in size or contour (edge). You can create gradual changes in value within a shape to make it look three-dimensional.

If you outline a shape and then fill it in with a solid value, you have a *silhouette.* The silhouettes of most objects look very different from the front, sides, top and other angles.

Shapes can be an important part of an overall compo-

sition. A landscape might be drawn in a horizontal or a vertical rectangle. Drawings can be made to fit inside circles, squares and other shapes.

Small shapes grouped together can be used to create patterns and suggest textures. You can base an entire drawing on repeated shapes. All of these qualities of shapes can be used to suggest moods, space or ideas in your drawing. Can you explain how and why?

Draw some positive and negative shapes without using outlines. Use a short piece of crayon, chalk or charcoal. Hold it flat against the paper and draw the main or positive shapes. Then draw the same subject again, but show only the negative shapes or "air" around the forms.

To introduce a strong feeling of shape, fill in areas of a drawing with solid, flat color. You might try some drawings based on a stencil. Fill in and overlap the open (cut out) shapes of your stencil.

Amédeé Ozenfant, *Untitled*, 1924. What values stand out and seem to come toward you? Which ones seem to recede? Why? Pastel on paper, 11" x 8 ³/₄" (30 x 22 cm). Collection of the Modern Art Museum of Fort Worth Memorial Fund. Purchased in Memory of Jewell Nail Boman. Photograph by David Wharton.

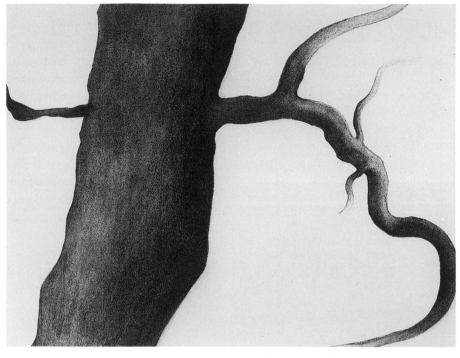

Georgia O'Keeffe, *Drawing IV*, 1959. Where is the implied source of light in this drawing? How can you tell? Charcoal, 18 ¹/₂" x 24 ¹/₂" (47 x 62 cm). Collection of Whitney Museum of American Art, New York. Gift of Chauncy L. Wadell in honor of John I. H. Baur.

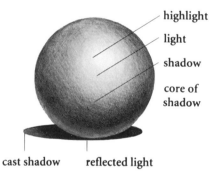

highlight
light
shadow
core of shadow

cast shadow   reflected light

Changes in value within a curved form.

A value scale.

Blending.

Value and Form

Value is the word artists use to describe light and dark areas in artwork. Black is the darkest value; white is the lightest value. There are many shades of gray in between (see the value scale above).

Shading is a gradual change in value. Shading is often used to create the illusion of three-dimensional form. The arrangement of values is planned so you can identify the actual or implied *light source.* Shading, *highlights,* shadows, and *cast shadows* are clues to the light source (see the curved forms and O'Keeffe's *Drawing IV,* above).

Drawings dominated by light values tend to look delicate, misty or filled with light. Dark values tend to make a drawing look somber, mysterious, stormy or heavy. Some drawings have abstract patterns of values.

The values may be flat, contrasting areas or have gradual changes.

Try some drawings based on geometric forms (boxes, cans, balls, paper bags). Place them in a strong light. Shade your drawing of the forms as accurately as you can. Angular geometric forms often have sharp, well-defined changes in value. How might you suggest the values you see on smooth or rough organic forms?

Try other ways to work with value. For example, create a drawing on gray paper. Use white and black chalk to create a drawing with only three main values (the gray paper, black and white areas).

Texture and Pattern

Have you ever placed paper over a surface and rubbed over it with the flat side of a pencil or crayon? Try this with several surfaces. The result is called a *texture rubbing*. The effect you see is a record of an actual texture.

In drawings you will often create *simulated* texture. This means that you make the drawing look as if it has texture. A simulated texture of fur or hair might be created by drawing fine lines. How might you simulate the rough surface of burlap? The smooth surface of glass or shiny metal?

In drawings, you can also create *invented* textural effects. Try putting small marks of various kinds side by side. Repeat them to suggest irregular surfaces such as a pebbled beach or leaves on trees.

In some drawing media you can create *actual* textures: textures that you can feel if you touch the drawing surface. For example, if you combine wax or oily crayons with chalk or watercolor, each medium has a subtle texture of its own.

You can make larger patterns by repeating elements such as stripes, plaids, swirls or diamonds. Smaller patterns can suggest a texture or decorative surface. Artists often use large and small patterns to unify their work.

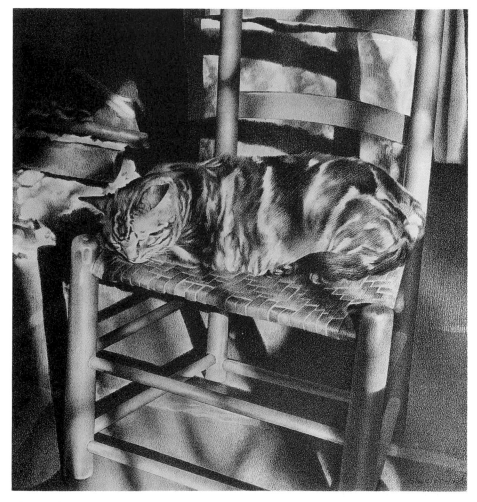

Charles Sheeler, *Feline Felicity*, 1934. The texture of the cat's fur is shown, in part, by the pattern of the cat's stripes. You can also see a pattern in the woven reed seat. How is the texture of the reed suggested? Conte crayon on white paper, 559 x 457 mm. Courtesy of the Fogg Art Museum, Harvard University, Cambridge, Massachusetts. Gift of Mr. and Mrs. Joseph Pulitzer, Jr., Louise E. Bettens.

Student art.

Action Figures

How can you draw figures that seem to be moving? It is a skill many artists use in sketches. Sometimes the sketches become finished works of art. Often they are made as visual studies – to plan another artwork.

Try drawing people in action poses. Have classmates pose in costumes or with props such as sports equipment. Begin with a gesture drawing to set up the main action lines. Then add details.

You can also create a feeling of action in an abstract drawing. Diagonal lines usually suggest action. Vertical lines seem to stretch upward. Horizontal lines often create a restful mood. They can also suggest a plunging action, left and right. What action lines might create a graceful, flowing movement? A flittering movement?

Francis de Erdely, *Football Players.* Lines have been scratched in thick layers of crayon in this action-packed drawing. Crayon etching, 21" x 27" (53 x 69 cm). Courtesy, The Snow Gallery, San Marino, California.

Edgar Degas, *Ballet Dancer Standing*, ca. 1886-1890. Where do you see evidence of the artist's interest in capturing action? Black crayon heightened with white and pink chalk on gray-brown wove paper, 11 15/16" x 9 1/2" (30 x 24 cm). The Baltimore Museum of Art. The Cone Collection.

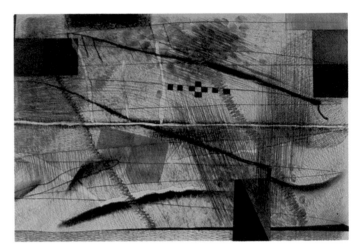

Robert Straight, *Crossfire*, 1975. Do you think the title of this drawing fits the way the artist has composed the work and used his media? Pastel and collage on paper, 27" x 40" (69 x 102 cm). Collection of the artist.

Space

Drawings are two-dimensional, which means they are flat. There are many ways to create the illusion of three-dimensional space in drawings and other two-dimensional artworks. Almost all of the techniques shown in the diagrams at the right were known to Renaissance artists.

You have probably used some of these techniques in your drawings. They are called techniques of *perspective* drawing.

Here are some ways to explore the possibilities of perspective drawing:

Try drawing a row of houses, trucks or people so they overlap and seem to go back in space and get smaller.

Try drawing a person, still life or landscape from an unusual point of view (above, below, extremely close).

Find an old magazine photograph of a city or street. Paste it down on a much larger piece of paper, leaving wide borders on all sides. Use a ruler to draw lines beyond the edges of the photograph. This will help you find the *vanishing points* and the *horizon line*.

Practice drawing objects and scenes in perspective. Begin with simple forms. Follow the guides in the diagrams on these two pages.

Ways to Create the Illusion of Depth

Overlap. Which shapes seem nearest to you? Why?

Size. Make distant objects of the same size smaller.

Placement. Place distant objects higher in the picture.

Detail. Show less detail in distant objects.

Color. Light, dull greyed colors usually suggest distance.

Converging Lines. Use linear perspective to suggest space.

Henry Lee McFee, *House Tops*, 1931. *Perspective* means that you have a point of view when you see something. Pencil on paper, 19 ⁷/₈" x 16 ⁷/₈" (50 x 43 cm). Collection of Whitney Museum of American Art, New York. Purchase.

Ibram Lassaw, *Untitled*, 1967. This artist has used perspective techniques inventively. Ink on paper, 13 ³/₈" x 16" (34 x 41 cm). Collection of Whitney Museum of American Art, New York. Purchase.

Meindert Hobbema, *The Avenue, Middleharnis*, 1689. This painting has one-point perspective. It also has other perspective techniques. Can you name six of them? Oil on canvas, 41" x 56" (104 x 141 cm). National Gallery, London.

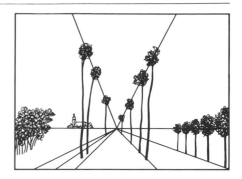

One-point Perspective
The symbol VP means vanishing point. It is a point anywhere on the horizon line where the edges of lines converge.

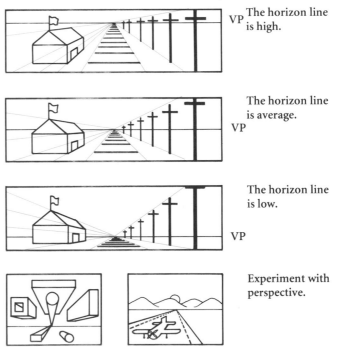

VP   The horizon line is high.

The horizon line is average.
VP

The horizon line is low.

VP

Experiment with perspective.

Robert Hubert, *Landscape with Large Tree*, ca. 1763. This drawing uses atmospheric perspective. The distant elements are less detailed and lighter than the foreground elements. Red chalk on laid paper, 20" x 15 ¼" (508 x 388 cm). Gift of Elizabeth Paine Card and Richard C. Paine. Courtesy Museum of Fine Arts, Boston.

Charles White, Sketchbook study. Courtesy of the artist.

William Artis, *Michael*. What proportions can you identify in this sculpture? Do you see similar proportions in many faces? Why?

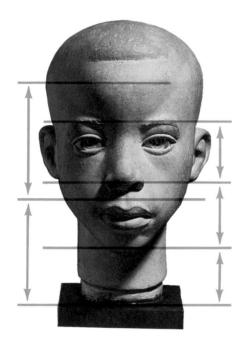

Proportions: Drawing People

People differ in many ways. There are big-boned people and delicate people, tall and short people. But all people are surprisingly alike in their *proportions,* which is the relation between one part of the body and another. A good self-portrait or portrait of a person captures their general proportions and individuality. For example, although most faces are oval-shaped, the oval may be broad or thin.

Faces If you want to draw the front view or profile of a head, you can begin with the general proportions. Sketch them lightly as guidelines. Then draw the unique features of the person. Try a drawing of yourself – a self-portrait – or a portrait of another person.

You might begin a front view of a face within a 5" x 8" (13 x 20 cm) grid. This will help you see the relative proportions and placement of major features. Notice that:

• The eyes are about halfway between the top of the head and chin.
• The forehead is partly covered with hair.
• The bottom of the nose is about halfway between the eyes and chin.
• The ears are about parallel to the eyebrows and bottom of the nose.
• The neck flows down from the jaw below the ears.
• The mouth is slightly higher than halfway between the chin and nose.
• The space between the eyes is about the same as the width of an eye.
• The mouth extends to a line directly under each eye.
• The iris of the eye is partly covered by the eyelid.

You might draw a profile of a face within a 8" or 9" (20 or 23 cm) square. Although the proportions are similar to the front view, notice these differences:

• The lower part of the ear is about halfway between the top of the nose and back of the head.
• The bridge of the nose and front of the chin are nearly parallel (in a vertical line).

Can you find the foreshortened parts in this drawing? Student art.

Figures The height of most adults is about seven or eight times the length of the head. Find some of these proportions in Ingres' drawing and in your own body as well.

- The knees are about halfway between the heel and the hip.
- The hip is about halfway between the heel and the top of the head.
- The elbows are about level with the waist.
- The hands are about as large as the face.

For a challenge, try drawing an action figure with arms or other parts of the body *foreshortened.* Foreshortened means that the nearest part of a form looks large, or exaggerated. The intermediate and distant parts look shorter (compressed) in size. In addition, the near parts often overlap the distant parts. Where do you see foreshortening in Demuth's artwork?

Jean-August-Dominique Ingres, *Portrait of Lord Grantham*, 1816. Pencil, 16" x 10" (40 x 25 cm). The J. Paul Getty Museum, Malibu, California.

Charles Demuth, *Bicycle Act, Vaudeville*, 1916. Brush and watercolor over chalk and pencil on off-white paper, 10 ¹⁵/₁₆" x 8" (28 x 20 cm). The Baltimore Museum of Art. Edward Joseph Gallagher II Memorial Collection.

Other Ideas to Explore

Imaginative Drawing

Leonardo da Vinci thought that accidental or unplanned effects could be a source of inspiration for art. For example, the irregular cracks in the sidewalk may remind you of a face or a giant river seen from outer space. Clouds might remind you of strange creatures.

Unusual ways of getting ideas have fascinated many twentieth-century artists. Some artists make "doodles" or scribbles – lines and shapes without any obvious plan. They study the lines and shapes for ideas, then color them, outline them or fill them with patterns. Dada and Surrealist artists used dreams and other illogical experiences as sources of ideas for art.

Start an unplanned drawing. You might begin with a crayon rubbing of cracks in a sidewalk or the grain of weathered wood. You could start with a random pattern of dots and connect them with lines.

Now study your "unplanned" drawing. Rotate it to see if the first marks suggest other ideas. Look at the marks until you see something you hadn't expected. Add lines, shapes, shadows or other details to develop an abstract work or one with a recognizable theme.

If you prefer, create another kind of imaginative drawing. It might be based on a dream, a fantastic idea about the future, or an imaginary time in the past. Try combining two or more objects to create another.

Close-Ups

There are wonderful possibilities for close-up drawings. The idea is to make a small part of something look as if it is only a few inches away.

You can capture this close-up feeling by choosing something small and drawing it large. If you include many small details and textures the drawing will look even more convincing.

Try a close-up drawing. If you have a mirror, try drawing your eye so that it fills the paper. Show every detail you can. You can also capture a definite mood or feeling, even if you don't include details. When you watch television, look for close-ups. Try some sketches of the close-ups you see.

Jonathan Borofsky, *2,342,041*, 1976. Ball point pen on 4 sheets graph paper, 8" x 12 ¼" (20 x 31 cm). Collection Kunst Museum, Basel, Switzerland. Photograph courtesy Paula Cooper Gallery, New York.

What is shown in this close-up drawing? Student art.

Expressing Feelings and Moods

People feel many emotions: great joy, deep despair, loneliness, respect, love, anger, peace. Drawing is a wonderful way to express these feelings and moods.

Drawings about feelings and moods can be realistic or abstract. They can also be imaginative. Faces are one of the best subjects, but your work can have other subjects, too. For example, a tree or a cityscape might be a way for you to express a feeling.

If you experiment with media, you may discover a mood or feeling to express. Cover several papers with watercolor washes. Select color schemes to set up a different mood on each paper. Let the paper dry. Create drawings on top of the paper. Use lines and other visual qualities that bring out a definite mood or feeling.

Geometric and Optical Effects

Some artists are fascinated by the use of line and other visual elements to create optical effects. Geometric lines and shapes are often used for this purpose, because we expect geometric elements to be precise, clear and easy to appreciate. The surprise comes when we find unexpected rhythms, tensions or movements.

You can see some of these unexpected effects in Pearson's work, below. The straight line is a place where wavy, circular lines meet. The circular lines on the left and right seem to radiate toward the line. What other features create a sensation of movement?

Try an optical illusion drawing. It might be based on precise geometric lines that you draw with a ruler, compass or other tools. You might combine irregular or soft-edged lines with even lines. You might include some perspective ideas too.

Many optical illusion drawings are done on a computer. If you get to use a computer, try different optical effects.

Leonard Baskin, *Tormented Man*, 1956. Ink on paper, 39 ¹/₂" x 26 ¹/₂" (100 x 67 cm). Collection of Whitney Museum of American Art, New York. Purchase.

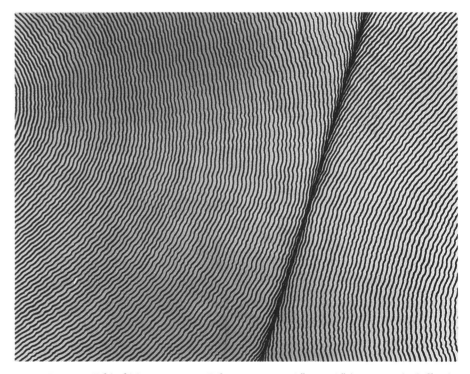

Henry Pearson, *Ethical Movement*, 1914. Ink on paper, 15 ⁵/₈" x 20 ¹/₄" (40 x 51 cm). Collection of Whitney Museum of American Art, New York. Purchase.

Caricature

A caricature is an exaggeration of something. People draw caricatures for humor and satire. Satire is a way of poking fun at ideas by showing them in exaggerated form.

You see this in comic strips where animals behave like people. You also see this in drawings of people who have very, very long chins or extra wide grins. In editorial cartoons in newspapers, exaggeration is often used to persuade you to think about political or social issues.

Draw a caricature of yourself or another person. First, exaggerate the proportions of the whole shape of the head and hair. Then exaggerate the proportions of the most dominant features. If the eyes look small, make them very small. If the chin is wide, make it very wide.

Find an old black-and-white photograph of a face that you can cut up. Cut the photograph into strips and spread them slightly apart. Paste the strips down. Then use a pencil to fill in the spaces between the strips so the whole face looks like one photograph. Do you see the exaggerated proportions?

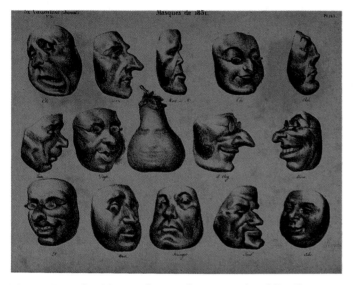

Honore Daumier, *Masques de 1813*. The New York Public Library, Print Collection. Miriam and Ira D. Wallach Division of Art, Prints and Photographs. Astor, Lenox and Tilden Foundations.

What features of the face look exaggerated? Why? Student art.

Student art.

Student art.

Student art.

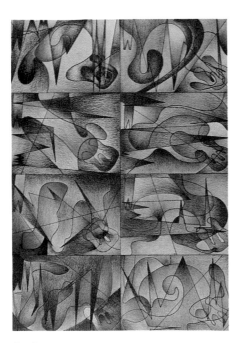

Student art.

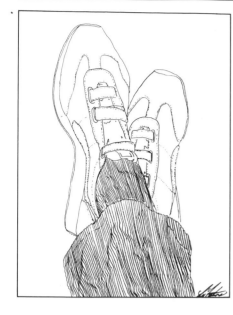

Student art.

Student art.

Student art.

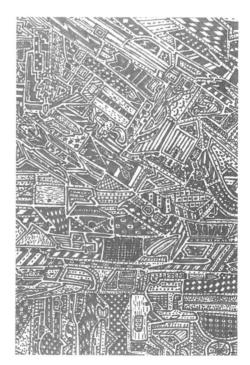

Student art.

Summary

Drawing is one of the most direct ways of recording what you see and exploring other ideas for artwork. A sketch is usually made just for the artist's own reference, but some sketches are so important they are displayed as final artwork.

Some drawings are created as final artworks. Drawings may be done in a dry medium, a wet medium or with mixed media. They may have characteristics that we traditionally associate with drawing. Sometimes drawings resemble paintings or other art forms.

Kimon Nicolaides became one of the most well-known teachers of drawing in this century. His methods are still used in most art schools. They are known as contour drawing, gesture drawing and whole-to-part drawing.

Drawing is one of the most important ways of quickly exploring the visual elements of art. These include line, shape, the illusion of form, color, texture, and the illusion of space. Systems for creating the illusion of space are called perspective systems.

Using What You Learned

Creating Art

1 Create a drawing that shows at least three drawing skills you have learned. Use a subject or theme of your choice.

2 Select one of your best sketches. Redevelop the ideas in a final drawing. Use a medium of your choice.

3 Choose one of the following activities. (A) Select, compose and draw items in your pocket, desk or purse. Strive for accuracy in proportions, details and textures. (B) Choose a view in your room, in the hall, or a view you see from the window. Draw it using at least four techniques of perspective.

Aesthetics and Criticism

1 Look through the artwork presented in this chapter. Choose one that you judge to be excellent. Write down your criteria for judging it. Then give reasons for your judgment. Be sure to state reasons that are based on a careful use of your skills in describing, analyzing and interpreting art.

2 Select one of your best drawings. Explain why you think it is one of the best you created.

Art History

1 What do we mean when we call someone a "Renaissance" person?

2 What are three approaches to drawing that artists have used for centuries?

3 Why has Leonardo da Vinci been called a genius? List at least three reasons.

Career Awareness

Drawing is one skill that applies to almost every field of art. In fact, most art schools teach two or more years of drawing to all students. The type of drawing students learn may be slightly different after the first year. For example, architects and designers must learn skills in drafting. Painters and printmakers usually explore creative drawing.

Drawing skills are also valuable in many other occupations. Carpenters, welders, and mechanics who can sketch ideas have an advantage in solving problems. The ability to diagram accident scenes or sketch people is an asset for police officers. Medical illustrators can show clearly in drawings some of the body structures that photographs do not reveal. In what other occupations is drawing an asset?

Hans Hofmann, *Flowering Swamp*, 1957. Oil on wood, 48 ⅛" x 36 ⅛" (122 x 91 cm). Hirshhorn Museum and Sculpture Garden, Washington, DC. Gift of the Joseph H. Hirshhorn Foundation, 1966.

Chapter 9
Painting

Chapter Vocabulary

fresco
hard-edge
soft-edge
linear style
painterly style
Pointillism
chiaroscuro
trompe l'oeil
monochromatic
analogous
complementary
atmospheric perspective
transparent
opaque

Subject matter for painting is often said to be "as varied as life itself." This statement means that artists have created paintings of almost anything you can imagine. But how can you choose a subject?

The answer is, of course, you can choose anything you want. This is what artists do. You can create paintings of things you see – people, animals, birds, tools, plants. You can paint landscapes, seascapes, cityscapes, still life. In a painting, you can show things you dream about, things that exist only in your imagination. Or you can create paintings about things you recall or know about, such as myths and historical events. Whatever your subject you can interpret it in your own way in a painting.

How will you plan and develop your paintings? You might plan them carefully by making sketches. You might pick up your brush and start painting without having a plan for each color and shape. You might experiment with some brushstrokes and ideas for color to get started.

Sometimes the kind of paint or style you want to use suggests how to begin. For example, before the 1800's most artists built up their paintings slowly, using many coats of oil paint. Some artists still do this to create glowing highlights and shadows.

Fresco paintings also need to be planned. They are done on a fresh layer of plaster before the plaster sets. Fresco means "fresh." Can you think of other reasons why artists might have a detailed plan before they begin to paint?

Less planning became common when the Impressionists started to paint outdoors. Many of these artists liked to work directly on their canvas. They planned their work as they painted it. Twentieth-century painters have also experimented with materials. For example, Georges Braque and Pablo Picasso combined collage and painting.

Painting is an art form in which brushstrokes, color and light are especially important. After you study this chapter and try some of the activities, you will be better able to:

Creating Art
- create original paintings using a variety of ideas and approaches.
- use painting media, tools, and techniques expressively.
- effectively design your paintings.

Aesthetics
- use art terms to describe, analyze and interpret your own and others' paintings.
- apply your knowledge of art theories and criteria when you create and judge paintings.

Art History
- discuss some of the major subjects, purposes and styles in the history of painting.

Art Criticism
- apply your skills in art criticism to evaluate your own and others' paintings.

Gallery

Artists today create paintings in their own ways. We say they have different methods of painting. Some prefer to plan their paintings carefully by making drawings first. Others work more spontaneously – they have a general idea but are not exactly sure how the final painting will look.

Study the examples of painting methods here. Notice how methods of painting depend in part on the artist's general style (realistic, abstract, expressionistic, imaginative). The artist's choice and use of painting media influences how his or her paintings will look. The traditions of art in a culture can also influence how paintings are created.

Critical Thinking Which of the eight paintings create the illusion of reality? Why do you think so? Which paintings are abstract but express a definite idea and mood? Which paintings do you find most interesting? Why?

Linda Stevens, *Haiku #4*, 1984. Watercolor, 29 ½" x 60" (75 x 152 cm).

Fidelia Bridges, *Milkweeds*, 1876. Watercolor on paper, 16" x 9 ½" (41 x 24 cm). Courtesy Munson-Williams-Proctor Institute Museum of Art, Utica, New York.

Wang Yidong, *Tobacco House*, 1987. Oil on canvas, 30" x 23 ¾" (76 x 60 cm).

Cosimo Rosselli, *Portrait of a Young Man*, ca. 1480. Tempera on panel. Private Collection. Photograph courtesy The Bridgeman Art Library, London.

Morris Louis, *Point of Tranquility*, 1958. Synthetic polymer oil on canvas, 102" x 135" (259 x 343 cm). Hirshhorn Museum and Sculpture Garden, Washington, DC.

A.Y. Jackson, *Algoma, November, 1935*. Oil on canvas, 32" x 40" (81 x 102 cm). National Gallery of Canada, Ottawa. Gift of H.S. Southam, Ottawa, 1945.

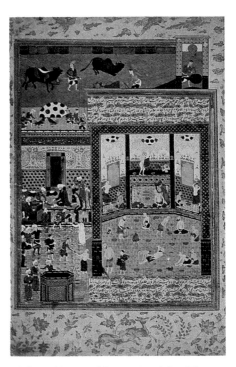

Nagasawa Rosetsu, *Tiger*, ca. 1792. Ink and color on paper, 78 ¹/₄" x 14" (199 x 36 cm). Dallas Museum of Art, General Acquisitions Fund.

Firduousi in a Bathhouse, Receiving Wages for having written the Shah Nama, 16th century. Watercolor on paper, 17" x 11" (44 x 28 cm). Los Angeles County Museum of Art. Nasli Heeramaneck Collection.

Georgia O'Keeffe

1887–1986

She had been a good student. She was taught to paint like European artists, and did it well. But something was wrong. One day she put her paintings on the wall and sat down to look at them. This one, she thought, was to please so-and-so. And that one was to please so-and-so. Each one had been painted to please somebody. There wasn't anything that seemed to say, "This is what interests Georgia O'Keeffe. This is the way she likes to work. This is her art."

So, at the age of 29, Georgia O'Keeffe put all her work away and started over. She began with charcoal and vowed not to use color until she had learned to express her ideas with charcoal. Within one year, her work burst into color and she never painted like anyone else again.

O'Keeffe grew up on a 600-acre farm in Sun Prairie, Wisconsin. By the age of ten, she knew she wanted to become a painter. She studied art in Chicago and then in New York. In New York, she met Alfred Stieglitz, a well-known photographer and gallery owner. He exhibited her work and helped her meet other artists. After seven years of friendship, they married. During the course of their life together, he photographed her over 500 times.

O'Keeffe lived in New York for thirty years, but she felt she really belonged in the country. She spent her summers in New Mexico and it was this desert land that she loved and painted. "I had never seen anything like it," she said, "but it fitted me exactly." After Stieglitz died in 1946, she moved permanently to New Mexico.

Georgia O'Keeffe is best known for her flower paintings. They are painted so large that one flower – sometimes just the center of one flower – fills the whole picture. Because they are painted in such extreme close-up, the forms and colors flow together in a striking design that is abstract and realistic at the same time.

She preferred to paint natural forms: skulls of horses and cows, mountains, clouds and the changing colors of the desert. She loved to work with soft, muted colors of paint and large, simple shapes.

In 1984, at the age of 97, Georgia O'Keeffe was honored with a major exhibition in New York. The exhibition showed viewers how hard O'Keeffe worked to paint what she saw in her mind's eye. She once said, "I decided I was a very stupid fool not to at least paint as I wanted to and say what I wanted to when I painted, as that seemed to be the only thing I could do that didn't concern anybody but myself – that was nobody's business but my own." O'Keeffe did indeed paint what she wanted to. It is her voice – no one else's – that speaks from her canvases.

Critical Thinking Experts in art invent style names to help people remember how one group of artworks is related to others like it. Each style name also helps people remember some characteristics of an artist's work. Look for similarities in the paintings of O'Keeffe shown here. Then invent a style name that you think is appropriate for them. Try to limit your style name to three words or less.

Alfred Stieglitz, *Georgia O'Keeffe*, 1933. Photograph, 9 ⁷/₁₆" x 7 ¹¹/₁₆" (24 x 19 cm). The Cleveland Museum of Art. Gift of Cary Ross.

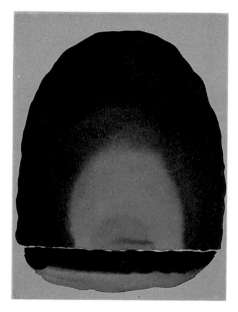

Georgia O'Keeffe, *Light Coming on the Plains II*, 1917. Watercolor on paper, 11" x 9" (28 x 22 cm). Amon Carter Museum, Fort Worth, Texas.

Georgia O'Keeffe, *Yellow Hickory Leaves with Daisy*, 1928. Oil on canvas, 30" x 40" (76 x 101 cm). The Art Institute of Chicago. Gift of Georgia O'Keeffe to the Alfred Stieglitz Collection.

Georgia O'Keeffe, *The Mountain, New Mexico*, 1931. Oil on canvas, 30" x 36" (76 x 91 cm). Collection of Whitney Museum of American Art. Purchase.

How has this student inventively combined lines, colors and shapes? Student art.

Paul Klee, *Twittering Machine,* 1922. Each medium has special qualities. In this watercolor, Klee has created the colors and shapes to appear transparent. Watercolor and ink, 16 ¼" x 12" (41 x 30 cm). Collection, The Museum of Modern Art, New York. Purchase.

The Visual Elements of Painting

The visual elements of art apply to all kinds of painting. When you create paintings of your own, or look at paintings, you'll find that the visual elements are always there, helping you and other artists express ideas.

Lines in paintings can be sharp and have clear outlines. They can be the soft, blurred edges where two colors meet. When a whole painting is done almost entirely in one type of line, it is called a *hard-edge* or a *soft-edge* painting. Some paintings are done in a *linear style,* which means they are often dominated by outlines and fine detail. Others are dominated by patches of color and free brushstrokes in a *painterly style.*

Paintings may have few or many different *hues.* When analogous colors are placed close together, a painting "glows" with color. In a technique called *Pointillism,* you put small dots of pure colors next to each other. To the eye of the viewer, the dots seem to be mixed. You can use colors to create a flat, abstract design or to capture qualities of light and space.

Colors can range from light to very dark in *value.* A painting can be planned with dramatic lighting and shadows. This effect is called *chiaroscuro* (ki-AR-roh-SKUH-roh), Italian for "light and dark." A painting with closely related values will usually have a definite mood. The dominant colors might be very bright or very dull.

Textures in paintings can be uniform or varied, smooth or rough. Acrylic and oil paints can be built up in thick layers to create actual textures. Paintings with very realistic details and textures are called *trompe l'oeil* (say tromp LOY), French for "fool the eye."

Shapes, forms, and *spaces* in paintings can be planned to create flat, abstract paintings that are unlike a scene. They can also be designed to give the illusion of a three-dimensional world. Highlights, shadows, and overlapping shapes help to suggest form and distance.

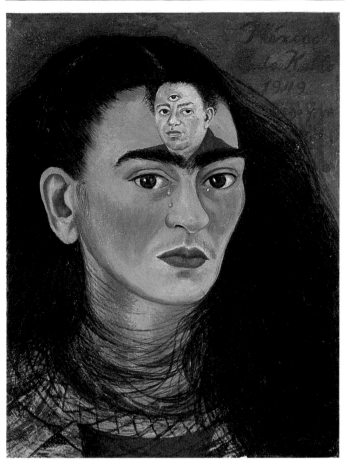

Frida Kahlo, *Diego y yo*, 1949. Oil on masonite, 11 ⁵/₈" x 8 ¹³/₁₆" (30 x 22 cm). Courtesy Mary Anne Martin/Fine Art, New York.

How has this student used the elements and principles of design? Student art.

Ways to Design Paintings

Artists develop their own methods of painting. Some plan their paintings by making drawings and slowly building up the painting. Others work more directly with paint and develop a plan while they are working.

When you create paintings, try to interpret your subject in a personal way. Think about the *principles of design* in relation to your general aim in painting.

For example, suppose you want to create a realistic painting. To create the illusion of reality, you will think about proportions and other design principles in a naturalistic way. If you want to create an expressive painting about a definite, intense feeling, your proportions and colors might be exaggerated. For an idea based on fantasy, you will think about design in another way. You can combine ideas from these approaches.

Once you have decided on a general theme or aim for your painting, you can decide how to use the principles of design. Would exaggerated, normal or ideal *proportions* work best for your painting? Should the *balance* be asymmetrical or symmetrical? Your decisions about *movement, pattern,* and *emphasis* will also be influenced by your aim.

Activities later in this chapter will help you explore different subjects and methods of painting. These will help you discover your own style of painting. Think about the principles you might use and how they can make your painting effective.

Studies in Color

Experimenting with color can be exciting. It can give you ideas for other paintings. Sometimes color experiments are so attractive they are displayed as final artwork.

Choose a simple subject for your color experiments with paint. The main idea is to learn about color by doing several variations on one idea.

Set up several objects for a still life. Create a *monochromatic* painting of it. Your painting should have many values of only one hue. The hue might be a primary, secondary or neutral color.

Try a painting with *analogous* colors (next to each other on the color wheel). Mix different values of each color you choose. Plan your painting so that major areas are dominated by warm hues or by cool hues. You might create two paintings with different sets of analogous colors and compare the expressive qualities of each.

Find out what happens when you use bright, intense, unmixed colors. Mix some dull, muted colors like browns by mixing complements (for example, a blue with a small amount of orange).

Try an Op Art experiment by using *complementary* colors side by side. For a Pointillist experiment, place small dots of primary colors side by side.

Learn to use color for *atmospheric perspective.* Atmospheric perspective shows the idea of a hazy distance. The background areas are usually painted first with light, cool hues and only a little detail. In the middleground and foreground, colors are brighter and warmer, with more detail. What other color experiments can you set up?

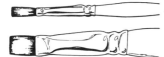

Stiff bristle brush for thick paint.

Soft hair-type brush for fluid paints, washes and details.

Stiff bristle brush for stencil work.

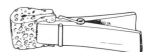

Improvised sponge brush.

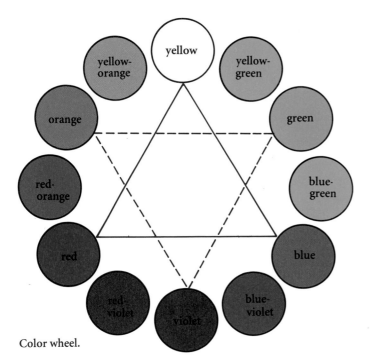

Color wheel.

Helen Lundeberg, *Tree Shadows*, 1982. A monochromatic color scheme unifies this work. Acrylic on canvas, 35" x 50" (89 x 127 cm). Courtesy Tobey C. Moss Gallery, Los Angeles. From the Collection of Colet Seiler.

Vincent Van Gogh, *Le Crau – Peach Trees in Blossom,* 1889. Oil on canvas. Courtauld Institute Galleries, London. The Courtauld Collection.

Sonia Terk Delaunay, *Electric Prisms,* 1914. Abstract arrangements of color harmonies have been used in this work. Oil on canvas, 93 ³/₄" x 98 ³/₄ (238 x 251 cm). Musée National d'Art Moderne, Centre Georges Pompidou, Paris.

Papers.

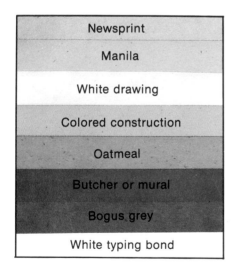

| Newsprint |
| Manila |
| White drawing |
| Colored construction |
| Oatmeal |
| Butcher or mural |
| Bogus grey |
| White typing bond |

Try a variety of papers for painting. You can also paint on other materials such as cotton cloth or canvas, gesso-covered masonite, thick cardboard and many three-dimensional surfaces.

Mixing Secondary and Intermediate Hues.

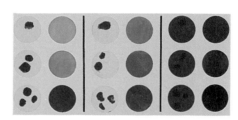

For practice, paint several circles of a primary color. Add a different number of dots of another primary color. Mix the paint in each circle. Wash, wipe and blot the brush when you change colors.

Wash   Wipe   Dry   Next Color

Mixing Values.

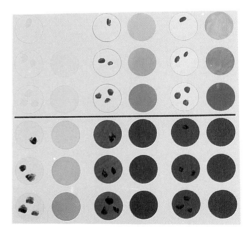

Top. To mix a *tint,* begin with white. Add dots of a hue and mix the paint. Why is it usually best to begin with white?
Bottom. To mix a *shade,* begin with a hue. Add dots of black and mix the paint. What happens if you begin with black instead of a hue?

Media and Techniques

Each painting medium has special qualities and limitations. Look at the samples of painting media. Paints may be matte or shiny. They may be *transparent* or *opaque.* Some are fluid and thin. Others are dense and thick. Paint is applied to a surface or support such as paper, canvas or wood.

Paint colors come from pigments. *Pigments* are powdered coloring materials from earth, plants or chemicals. Pigments are held together by a binder such as glue, egg, wax, oil or latex. You will probably use water-based paints such as tempera, acrylic or watercolor. Chalk, oil and wax pastels are dry painting media.

Tempera paints are thick and opaque. Wet paint will tend to soften and mix with any dry paint underneath. Related paints are poster colors, gouache and casein or designer colors.

Acrylic paints are thick, like oil paints, but can be diluted with water. Add water to create transparent glazes. Wet paint will not mix with dry paint underneath. Clean up your brushes before the acrylic paint dries on them.

Watercolors are diluted with lots of water and applied in a light-to-dark sequence. You leave the paper unpainted for white. Always begin with light washes of color and gradually add darker values. For a wash, lightly dampen the paper with a brush or sponge. Then put a lot of water in your brush and just a little paint. Brush the paper quickly. You can let the colors blend and fuse. For fine details, paint on top of dry colors. Try for a transparent quality in the whole painting.

Stiff, bristle brushes are often used for oil, acrylic and tempera. Soft, hair brushes are usually best for watercolor. You can also apply paint with a palette knife, roller, sponge, strip of cardboard and other tools.

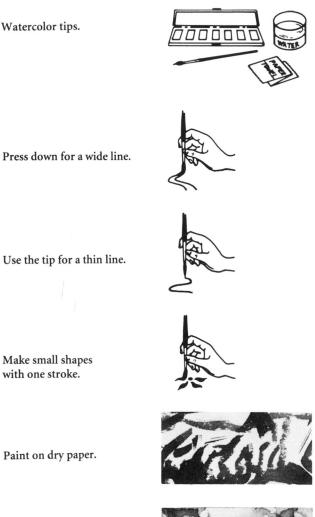

Watercolor tips.

Press down for a wide line.

Use the tip for a thin line.

Make small shapes with one stroke.

Paint on dry paper.

Paint on wet paper.

David Hockney, *Backyard, Echo Park*, 1984. Gouache on paper, 61" x 44" (155 x 112 cm). Courtesy of David Hockney.

184

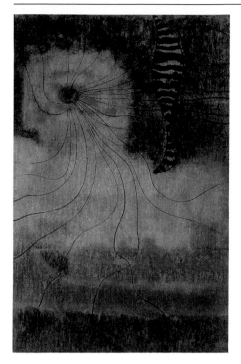

William Baziotes, *Sea Forms,* 1951. Soft blended washes can be used as a background for other shapes, lines and textures. Pastel on paper, 38 ¹/₈" x 25 ¹/₈" (97 x 64 cm). Collection of Whitney Museum of American Art. Purchase.

Winslow Homer. *Sloop, Nassau.* Letting the white paper show and keeping the colors well-diluted are important watercolor techniques in Homer's painting. Watercolor on paper, 15" x 21 ¹/₂" (38 x 55 cm). The Metropolitan Museum of Art, Amelia B. Lazarus Fund, 1910.

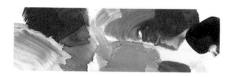

Acrylic paint. Available in jars or tubes. Usually thick like oil paint but can be diluted with water to create glazes – semi-transparent layers of colors. (Allow each coat to dry.) Wash brushes before paint dries.

Tempera paint. Dilute with water as desired. Similar to poster paint or gouache. Has a dull, chalky appearance when dry. Available as a liquid, powder (mix with water) or compressed cake.

Watercolor. Available in pans or tubes. Dilute the color with a water-filled brush. For white, let the white paper show. Apply light colors first. Try for a clear transparent quality in the whole painting.

Water-based felt markers. Apply to damp or dry paper. Use a wet brush at top of lines, shapes or textures for a watercolor effect.

Wash and ink. Dampen the paper with water. Brush well-diluted paint on the paper. Allow colors to blend. Blot the "pools" of paint. Outline some of the colors and shapes with pen and ink. Add final details when the paint is dry.

Chalk or pastels. A painting medium when colors are blended. Experiment. Blend with a tissue. Erase areas. Apply to damp paper or paper covered with diluted liquid starch. **Safety Note** *Do not use chalk if you have a dust allergy.*

Mixed Media and Processes

Today, paintings often include collage and montage. Mosaics and paintings with three-dimensional elements are often called paintings, although they are not simply paint on a flat surface. Many artists have explored techniques that combine painting with drawing and other media.

A *collage* is made by gluing down paper, fabrics or found objects. A *montage* is a collage made of photographic images. Select your collage and montage materials for a reason. They may have comical, literary or political meaning for you. You may be fascinated by their colors or textures. Many collages and montages have overlapped shapes with drawn or painted elements.

Combining wet and dry media is one way to achieve rich, textural effects. Try several resist techniques for painting. Try painting on different kinds of paper, cardboard, or cloth. Make mosaic-like paintings with small bits of colored paper. Try a tissue paper collage.

Paintings can also include three-dimensional objects. Paintings on three-dimensional objects (boxes, cylinders or found objects) are usually called *combines* or *assemblages* (an extension of collage). Paint is often used to unify the work.

Critical Thinking You can make endless experiments with painting media. What are some of the main reasons why experiments are valuable? Are there some disadvantages if you are only interested in experimenting all the time? If so, what are they?

Henry Moore, *Madonna and Child.* What advantages can be gained by combining media? Crayon resist with pencil, pen and India ink wash on white paper, 8 7/8" x 6 7/8" (23 x 17 cm). The Cleveland Museum of Art.

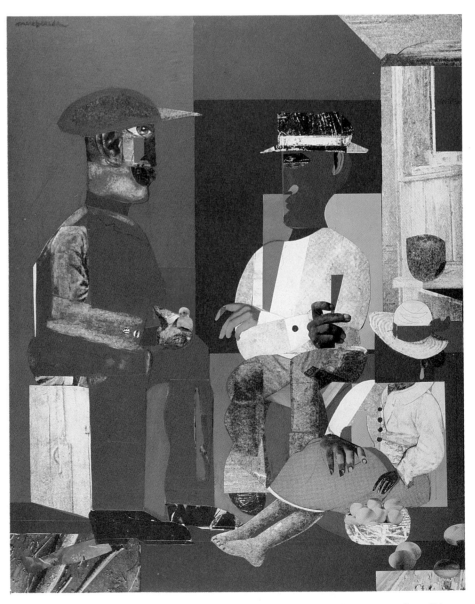

Romare Bearden, *Eastern Barn*, 1968. Collage of glue, lacquer, oil and paper, 55 1/2" x 44" (141 x 112 cm). Collection of Whitney Museum of American Art. Purchase.

Henri Matisse, *Sorrows of the King*, 1952. Matisse painted sheets of paper, then cut the sheets into shapes for his collages. This allowed him to have full control of the color in his work. Gouaches decoupes, 113" x 157" (287 x 399 cm). Musée National d'art Moderne, Centre Georges Pompidou, Paris.

Tissue collage. Cut or tear colored tissue paper for a collage. Brush diluted white glue on the entire paper and on each shape as it is glued down. Overlap shapes and allow colors to blend. Student art.

Collage. Made from a wide range of papers, often combined with paint or other media.

Mosaic. Made by placing small bits of material (stones, glass, wood) next to each other.

Tempera resist. Create a painting with thick tempera. Leave some of the paper unpainted. Allow the paint to dry. Apply waterproof ink to the entire surface. Allow the ink to dry. Wash the painting under running water, gently rubbing it with a soft brush.

Chalk or oil pastel with tempera. Create a tempera painting. Allow it to dry. Add details and other colors with chalk or oil pastels. **Safety Note** *Do not use chalk if you have a dust allergy.*

Montage. A collage created with photographic images.

Oil or wax-based pastels. Mix and blend colors without dust. Build up textures and scratch into the surface with a pointed tool.

Tempera with crayon or oil pastel. Begin with a thick layer of crayon or oil pastels. Use light colors. Apply a second layer of dark tempera paint mixed with a drop or two of liquid soap. Allow the paint to dry. Draw into the black layer with a nail or similar tool.

Crayon resist. Apply wax crayons or oil pastels with firm pressure, then brush the entire paper with diluted tempera or ink. The wax (or oil) will "resist" paint or ink.

George Agnew Reid, *Evening, Lake Temagami*, 1941. Government of Ontario Art Collection.

Charles Burchfield, *Nasturtiums and the Barn*, 1917. Watercolor, charcoal, gouache, wash, crayon, ink, pencil on paper, 22" x 18" (55.9 x 45.7 cm). McNay Art Institute.

Other Ideas to Explore

Environments

Views of environments – natural and human-made – have been a popular subject for paintings. Scenes of the land and sea are called *landscapes* or *seascapes*. Scenes of cities are called *cityscapes*.

Paintings of environments can suggest any weather, season of the year, or time of day. They can be beautifully calm or hint at danger. They can be scientifically accurate, abstract or totally imaginative.

To get ideas for an environmental painting, you might list a number of places you are familiar with (your city or town, a farm, a bus station, etc.). Next, list all the main seasons, times of day and kinds of weather you can imagine.

Here is a starter list. Add ideas to each column separately. Then select one entry in each column at random and combine them.

Place	*Season*	*Time*	*Weather*	*Details*
city	winter	night	snowy	people
park	spring	dawn	foggy	animals

Can you envision, for example, a park in autumn, at night, with foggy weather and streetlights? What other ideas can you develop from this technique for creative thinking?

A traditional method for painting environments – called *back-to-front* painting – has been used since the Renaissance. Compose a scene with a hazy, far-away background that needs atmospheric perspective.

First, paint the large, background areas such as the sky and very distant objects. Use white to make light, dull background colors. Bluish hues and few details will help you suggest a distant space.

Second, in the middleground in your painting, use brighter colors related to those in the background. Finally, mix brighter, darker and warmer colors for the foreground.

Add details to the nearest sections. These subtle gradations in color, value and detail help to create the illusion of space and distance.

Paintings can often be effective if you leave out tiny details. Student art.

David Alfaro Siqueiros, *The Challenge*, 1954. Pyroxylin on masonite, 79 ¼" x 69 ⅝" (201 x 157 cm). Galeria Arvil, Mexico City.

Paintings of People

People are fascinating subjects for artists. Many paintings show the whole figure alone or in groups, in active or quiet poses.

In *portraits*, artists try to capture the personality of real people. *Caricatures* exaggerate the features or expressions of a person. *Self-portraits* are artworks that you create of yourself. Paintings of people can focus on their features, personality, activities or environments.

You might create a self-portrait or a close-up portrait of a classmate. Close-up portraits usually focus on the head and shoulders. You might try action figures – people dancing, playing a game, lounging on the beach or working at a trade.

If correct proportions are important, sketch the main shapes first. How long are the arms compared to the legs? Compare the length of the upper arm to the lower arm, the length of the hand to the face, and so on.

The flesh is often painted first with one basic color. Then highlights and shadows are painted on top of the basic color. Some artists begin by mixing colors for all the highlights. After these lightest figures areas are painted, they paint all the shadows. They finish up by using a basic flesh tone to blend the light and darker tones together.

Your paintings of people can be effective without trying for exact realism. You might try analyzing the geometric forms of noses, faces, or whole figures. Cézanne and other artists did this. Look beyond the details for forms similar to cones, rectangles, or cylinders.

Painting imaginary people in exotic costumes and patterned environments may appeal to you. What other paintings could you create using people as a subject?

Strong contrasts and patterns help to make this work effective. Student art.

Reginald Marsh, *Twenty Cent Movie*, 1936. Egg tempera on composition board, 30" x 40" (76 x 102 cm). Collection of Whitney Museum of American Art. Purchase.

Jan Vermeer, *The Little Street in Delft*, ca. 1700. Oil on canvas. Rijksmuseum, Amsterdam.

Everyday Life

For many years in Europe, only wealthy people could afford to own paintings. They usually wanted paintings of "noble" subjects such as history, religious stories, myths, or idealized portraits.

As the aristocracy declined and democracy grew, paintings about the everyday life of merchants, workers and poor people became popular. In countries like Holland, the merchants and business people could afford paintings. Many wanted paintings about ordinary people at home, work and play. Experts call this kind of subject matter *genre* (say ZHANN-rah).

Genre paintings often show people in their homes. The interior space might be a kitchen, living room or parlor where people gather. Exterior genre paintings often show life in the city, suburbs or farm. They may focus on people at work or play.

You might create a genre painting. Choose a subject from your own life. It could be your favorite weekend activity. Your painting could show one of the chores you do at home or an interesting school activity.

Consider using a mixed media technique for this painting. For example, you might use oil pastels for the people and main shapes in your painting, then combine collage elements and tempera. What other combinations are possible? Which ones might be best for your idea?

Max Ernst, *Europe After the Rain*, 1940-1942. The shape of this painting and complex textured areas are an important part of the theme. The "melting" textured areas were created by the technique of decalcomania. Oil on canvas, 21 ⁹/₁₆" x 58 ³/₁₆" (55 x 148 cm). Wadsworth Atheneum, Hartford. The Ella Gallup Sumner and Mary Catlin Sumner Collection.

Fantasy

Dreams and fantasies are another subject you can explore in painting. Paintings of this kind can be pleasant or frightening. They can show things we recognize or include many invented colors and shapes. They can be dark and shadowy or have other exaggerated features. Usually there is a strange or mysterious quality to paintings of this kind.

Surrealistic paintings are very clear in detail, but seem illogical. Max Ernst, a Surrealist artist, was especially interested in finding unusual ideas for paintings. One of his techniques is called decalcomania. To try it out, use two sheets of damp paper and fairly thick tempera or acrylic paint. First mix several colors following a plan (warm, cool, analogous). Apply drops of the colors with a spoon or stick in a random pattern to each sheet. Let the paint form small puddles. Do not brush the colors out completely.

Next, place the painted sides of both sheets face to face. Lightly press and rub several areas, then pull them apart slowly. Study the unusual shapes and colors. Use your brush or other tools to change each painting slightly, but let some of the random shapes and colors remain as part of the final painting.

Try other unusual techniques for beginning an imaginative painting. Dip cardboard into paint and press it down on paper. Try using a sponge or other objects to apply paint. Do these and other techniques suggest ideas for imaginative paintings?

What other methods might you use to create an imaginative painting? Could you combine unrelated ideas (parts of an insect and an airplane)? Could you combine general styles (realism and geometric shapes)?

René Magritte, *The False Mirror*, 1928. Magritte was fascinated with illusions as well as logical and illogical ideas. The pupil of the eye seems to be a mirror for an image in the sky. Does the title of the work help you interpret its meaning? Oil on canvas, 21 ¹/₄" x 31 ⁷/₈" (54 x 81 cm). Collection, The Museum of Modern Art, New York. Purchase.

Painting in Three Dimensions

Artists are breaking down many of the classifications of art forms that experts have used for a long time. Sculptors are creating "paintings" on three-dimensional forms. Some craftsworkers say that their works in fiber, enamels and other media are paintings.

Create an experimental painting with some three-dimensional elements. You might begin by cutting flat shapes of paper. Plan how they can be assembled into a sculpture. They might be slotted, folded, or scored and bent. After you have made this plan, paint each paper and let it dry. Then assemble it according to your plan.

You might prefer to paint an existing three-dimensional form. It could be a tree branch or a cardboard box. What other forms might you paint?

Study your form before you begin. The contours or overall shape might suggest an idea. Use your imagination. Think about the possibilities for subjects and themes. Show that you know how to use the elements and principles of design.

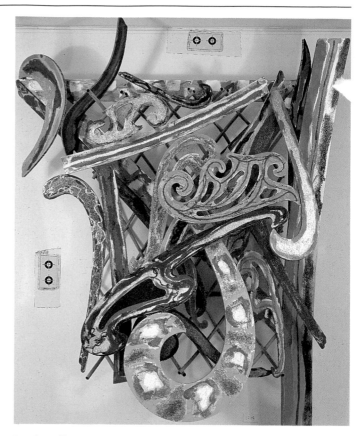

Frank Stella, *Ram-Gangra*, 1978. Mixed media on metal relief, 115 $\frac{1}{2}$" x 90 $\frac{1}{2}$" x 43 $\frac{1}{2}$" (292 x 230 x 110 cm). Collection Leo Castelli Gallery, New York.

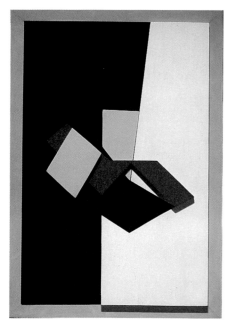

Gertrude Green, *Space Construction*, 1942. Painted composition board and wood, 39 $\frac{1}{2}$" x 27 $\frac{1}{2}$" x 30" (100 x 70 x 80 cm). Collection of Whitney Museum of American Art. Gift Balcomb Greene. Photograph: Robert Mates.

Elizabeth Murray, *Duck Foot*, 1983. Oil on canvas, 129" x 132" (328 x 335 cm). Private collection. Courtesy The Paula Cooper Gallery, New York.

Summary

Artists create paintings for a variety of purposes. They may create realistic or abstract works. Their paintings may be imaginative or express strong feelings. In nonobjective paintings, there is no recognizable subject. The mood is created by the artist's choice of visual elements and use of the principles of design.

Painting involves the selective use of pigments, binders and surfaces. Each painting medium has unique qualities and possibilities. In mixed media paintings, artists may include collage and other materials. Today, most artists try to develop their own individual styles and methods of painting. Their subjects are as varied as life itself.

Using What You Learned

Art History

1 Write a phrase that describes one feature of these kinds of painting.
- *still life*
- *genre*
- *nonobjective*
- *Surrealistic*
- *Pointillism*
- *soft-edged*
- *hard-edged*
- *trompe l'oeil*

2 What are three characteristics of Georgia O'Keeffe's style of painting?

3 What makes a fresco painting different from other forms of painting?

Creating Art

1 What are the steps you should take to mix a tint? What steps should you follow to mix a shade? Why are these steps recommended?

2 What are three points to remember when you create a watercolor painting?

3 Create an original painting on a subject of your choice. Demonstrate your ability to interpret the subject in a personal way. Develop an appropriate design and use your painting medium effectively.

4 How many "mixed-media" paintings by artists can you find in this chapter?

5 What is meant by "atmospheric perspective"?

Aesthetics and Art Criticism

1 Define the following terms.
- *chiaroscuro*
- *painterly style*
- *linear style*
- *monochromatic*
- *complementary*
- *opaque*
- *transparent*

2 Choose one painting from the Gallery in this chapter. Work through the steps in art criticism for that painting. Write your interpretation of the painting. Then compare your interpretation with ones written by your classmates. Explain why interpretations of the same work may sometimes be very similar. Explain why interpretations can sometimes be very different.

3 Select one of your best paintings. Evaluate it using the steps in art criticism introduced in Chapter 4.

M. C. Escher, *Rind*, 1955. Have you ever created a print? How did you get the idea for your print? What seems to have been the inspiration for the form you see in this print? Wood engraving in four colors, 13 ⁵/₈" x 9 ¹/₄" (345 x 235 cm). Collection Haags Gemeentemuseum, The Hague.

Chapter 10
Printmaking

Printing is the process of transferring an inked design from one surface to another. You may have already printed with found objects such as dowels, or you may have carved a design in a sliced potato and then printed with it. Texture rubbing is also a simple form of printmaking.

A fine art print is called a "multiple original" because it is one of a series created from a surface – usually a block or plate – that the artist has prepared. Each print made and signed by the artist is called an *impression*. The total number of prints created from a block or plate is called an edition. Each print must be numbered and signed by the artist in the lower right corner, under the edge of the image.

Reproductions are photographic copies of images produced on machine-driven presses. Because these images are machine-made, they are not considered original prints, even if they are signed and numbered by the artist.

The fine art of printmaking has a long history. In the Renaissance, Rembrandt created etchings with dramatic light and shadow. Albrecht Dürer engraved metal plates to create crisp images of people and animals.

After the Renaissance, printed images became a major way for artists such as William Hogarth, Francisco Goya and Honoré Daumier to express their political beliefs.

Throughout Asia, prints are made from wood or stone blocks. Japanese artists, such as Hokusai and Hiroshige, mastered the art of making multicolored woodcut prints.

In the twentieth century, painters or sculptors have often explored printmaking. Powerful abstract woodcuts were created by German Expressionists such as Karl Schmidt-Rottluff and the Mexican artist José Chavez Morado, among others.

Today, artists are creating prints using a wide variety of methods. Sometimes prints are combined with collage or painting. Prints can also be made on surfaces such as cloth, plastic or metal, then shaped into three-dimensional forms.

After completing this chapter and some of the activities, you will be better able to:

Art History and Creating Art	• appreciate and create prints using traditional and experimental methods.
Aesthetics and Art Criticism	• use correct terms to describe, analyze, interpret, and evaluate your own and others' prints.
Creating Art and Art Criticism	• create and evaluate original prints with attention to their unique expressive, technical, and sensory qualities.

Chapter Vocabulary

impression
relief
intaglio
lithography
serigraphy
stencil
brayer
inking slab
proof
collage
squeegee
monoprint

Gallery

As a fine art, printmaking allows an artist to create many images from one original design. The prints in this Gallery were each created by one of four basic methods.

Relief Prints Wood and linoleum cuts are created by carving the surface of a block with a sharp chisel. The printed lines and shapes from the block often have clean, precise edges.

Carol Summers, *Road to Ketchikan*, 1976. Woodcut. Courtesy of the artist.

Katsushika Hokusai, *South Wind and Fair Weather*, Edo Period. Woodblock print, 10 ¹/₈" x 15" (26 x 38 cm). Copyright 1990 Indianapolis Museum of Art, Carl H. Lieber Memorial Fund.

Lithographic Prints Lithographs combine the qualities of drawing and painting. Look for tonal qualities from the use of greasy pencils or crayons. These can be very soft and subdued or have high contrasts in light and dark areas. Look for painterly qualities from the use of *tusche*, a thin, inky grease applied with a brush.

Henri de Toulouse-Lautrec, *Jane Avril: Jardin de Paris*, 1893. Lithograph, printed in color, 48 ⁷/₈" x 35" (124 x 89 cm). Collection, The Museum of Modern Art, New York. Gift of A. Conger Goodyear.

Edvard Munch, *The Cry*, 1895. Lithograph, 13 ³/₄" x 9 ⁷/₈" (35 x 25 cm). National Gallery of Art, Washington, DC. Rosenwald Collection.

Intaglio Prints Many drypoint etchings have light, airy effects, soft edges or deep, velvety shadows. Engravings usually have strong contrast and crisp details.

Myrna Báez, *The Judge*, 1970. Collagraph on paper, 19 ½" x 22" (50 x 56 cm). Museo de Antropologia, Universidad de Puerto Rico.

Rembrandt, *Portrait of Rembrandt's Mother*. Etching. The Metropolitan Museum of Art. Rogers Fund, 1918.

Rip Woods, *Grass Moon*. Serigraph. Courtesy of the Udinotti Gallery, San Francisco, California, and Scottsdale, Arizona.

Stencil Prints and Serigraphy (Silkscreen) A stencil is a sheet of paper with holes cut in it. The ink is applied through the holes. A serigraph is based on a stencil process, usually with some overlapping of colors. The surface effects can be highly geometric and hard-edged (from cutout film); they can look like crayon or chalk drawings (from crayon); or, they can be quite painterly (from tusche).

Andy Warhol, *Cow Wallpaper*, 1966 (detail). Silkscreen ink on paper, 44" x 30" (112 x 76 cm). Courtesy the Leo Castelli Gallery, New York.

Meet the Artist

Albrecht Dürer

1471-1528

Some experts have called him the greatest artist of the northern Renaissance. Although he was a gifted draftsman and painter, his work as a printmaker helped to establish his international reputation.

Dürer changed the style of engraving and woodcut prints. Before they had been based on lines. Dürer created prints with a range of values similar to those in painting and drawing. Many of his prints are filled with dense, subtle textures never seen before. His prints influenced many other Renaissance artists. He was one of the first artists of his time to express himself mainly through printmaking.

Like many Renaissance artists, Dürer was fascinated with all aspects of nature, especially the details and surface textures in animals, plants and people. His

works often included religious themes as well as legends.

Dürer was also interested in the philosophy and theory of art. He wrote about ideal proportions for the human figure. He produced an album of woodcuts on the Apocalypse, a theme from the Bible.

Albrecht Dürer was born in Nuremburg, Germany. His father, a goldsmith, was his first teacher. As a teenager, he was apprenticed to study with a painter in Nuremburg.

He twice traveled to Venice, Italy, for study and soon became known there for his intelligence and his art. When he returned to Germany, his reputation was well established. In 1515, he was appointed the court painter for Emperor Maximilian I. On a trip to the Netherlands in 1520, Dürer was received as a great artist and intellectual.

More than any other artist of his time, Dürer united in his art the elements of style in northern and southern European art. Dürer is often credited with the invention of the idea of a trademark. Unlike most artists of his time, Dürer dated his work and often signed it with an unusual combination of his initials.

Albrecht Dürer, *Self-portrait*, 1498 . Museo del Prado, Madrid.

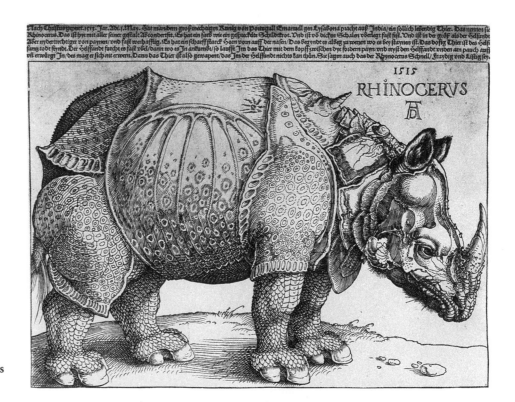

Albrecht Dürer, *The Rhinocerous*, 1515. Woodcut, 8 ¹/₂" x 11 ⁵/₈" (22 x 30 cm). The Metropolitan Museum of Art. Gift of Junius S. Morgan, 1919.

Albrecht Dürer, *Knight, Death and Devil*, 1513. Engraving, 9 ¾" x 7 ⅜" (25 x 19 cm). Los Angeles County Museum of Art, Graphic Arts Council Fund.

He once wrote: "What beauty is, I know not, though it adheres to many things. When we wish to bring it into our work we find it very hard. We must gather it from far and wide.... For from many beautiful things something good may be gathered, even as honey is gathered from many flowers."

Critical Thinking Think of some reasons why Dürer and other artists might prefer to create prints rather than paintings.

Methods of Printing

Printmaking is the exciting process of preparing an image on a surface, then creating a series of artworks from that one carefully prepared surface.

There are four basic processes for creating fine art prints. You have seen some of the effects artists create with these processes. How do they create these effects?

Relief prints are made from a raised surface that receives ink. Some examples are woodcuts, linoleum cuts, prints from found objects – and even fingerprints. In the final print, the carved or low areas are white or the color of the background paper. The raised surface is inked. To transfer ink to the paper, pressure is usually applied with a press, but it can also be applied with something as simple as your hand or a spoon.

Katsushika Hokusai, *South Wind and Fair Weather*, Edo period. A woodcut detail.

For *intaglio* prints, lines are cut or etched into a smooth plate of metal or plastic. Ink is rubbed into the grooves and the surface of the plate is wiped clean. Damp paper is forced into the inked grooves by heavy pressure, usually a printing press. The ink from the grooves is transferred to the paper.

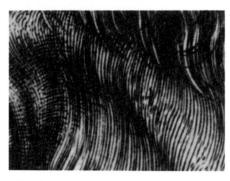

Albrecht Dürer, *Knight, Death, and Devil*, 1513. An engraving detail.

There are several kinds of intaglio. In *drypoint*, the lines are scratched into the plate. If the lines are made by acid, the print is an *etching*. If the lines are gouged out, the print is an *engraving*.

Rembrandt, *Portrait of Rembrandt's Mother*. An etching detail.

Silkscreen prints are called *serigraphs*. The image is made by forcing ink through silk or a similar fabric stretched on a wood frame.

Rip Woods, *Grass Moon* (detail). A serigraph detail.

The design is created by a *stencil* or block-out fluid applied to the silk. The ink design fills up all the areas within the frame except those blocked by the stencil or the fluid.

Eskimo (Oshaweetuk), *Four Musk Oxen*, 1959 (detail). A stencil detail.

Serigraphy (Silk Screen)

Relief

Intaglio

Stencil

In *lithography*, a greasy (oil-based) crayon or ink is applied to a smooth block of limestone or a specially prepared metal plate. Acid is applied to clean and prepare the surface for printing.

Water is sponged on the stone or metal plate. Oil-based ink is rolled over the surface. The oily ink sticks to the greasy drawing, but not to the wet surface. Paper is placed over the stone or plate. A large press is used to apply pressure and transfer the ink to the paper.

Henri de Toulouse-Lautrec, *Jane Avril: Jardin de Paris*, ca. 1893. A lithography detail.

Materials for Printing

Almost all printmaking techniques require some knowledge of the following materials.

Inks You will probably use water-based printing ink. This ink dries in an hour or so. For cleanup, use soap and water.

Tempera paints can be substituted for printing ink. The prints tend to be fuzzier (less well defined). Add a drop or two of glycerin to slow the drying time and make the paint stickier, more like printing ink.

Brayer A brayer is a special roller used to apply ink to a printing block. The ink is first applied to an *inking slab* – a smooth nonabsorbent surface such as plate glass, plastic, sheet metal, Formica or a cookie tray. The inking slab should be wider than the brayer.

Place the ink near the center of the slab. Squeeze the ink tube gently, leaving a trail of ink about 2" long (like toothpaste). Roll out the ink until it is evenly distributed over the roller of the brayer.

Surfaces You can make prints on a variety of papers. You might try printing on bond paper, newsprint, construction paper, colored paper, wallpaper or tissue paper.

You can stain the papers with paint before you print on them. You can print on top of magazine photographs. You can print on top of a print you have made (print a light color first, then a darker color on top). Prints can be made on cloth and many other materials. You might need special waterproof inks for such materials.

Rolling ink onto the brayer. Photograph by Roger Kerkham.

Paper for printing can be colored.

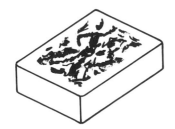

Lithography

Developing Ideas for Prints

Most printmaking techniques require you to complete several steps with the same image. For this reason, you should take the time to choose an interesting subject and interpret it your own original way.

Subjects are unlimited: people, places, things, animals, plants and events. The geometric shape of bottle caps or the rhythmic lines in combs may suggest ideas for prints. Collect small objects and examine them under a magnifying glass or microscope. Use a viewfinder to select, frame and sketch a landscape or still-life composition.

Make imaginative sketches that combine two or three features from unrelated objects – for example, machines that exhibit human behavior, animals that are human-like, plants that can move or fly.

Your hobbies and special interests, heroes and heroines you admire, family events – all may provide ideas for prints.

Prints can be created as artwork to be mounted and displayed. You can also print useful items such as greeting cards or wrapping tissue. Your design might be planned for a report cover, as a cartoon or as an illustration for a poem or story.

You might design a monogram to use for stationery or to label things you own. Prints could be created for a class-produced calendar or a book of illustrated poems or cartoons. You might print notes, invitations, announcements or posters. Remember, if you use any lettering in your design, be sure it is reversed on the block!

William H. Johnson, *Self-Portrait*, ca. 1935. A strong design was developed in this self-portrait. This artist was a leader in the Harlem Renaissance. Woodcut, relief print, 9" x 9" (23 x 23 cm). Hampton University Museum, Hampton, Virginia.

Student art.

206

Designing a Print

Each printmaking technique has special possibilities and limitations for expression. Successful prints come from a good match between your idea and the process you select.

For example, if your subject is a porcupine, etching would let you show fine, spiky quills. In a woodcut or linoleum cut, you would probably suggest spiky quills but with fewer and broader cuts. How could you simplify the porcupine idea for a stencil or silkscreen print?

Woodcuts and linoleum cuts are carved with a knife and with V- or U-shaped chisels. For a linoleum cut or woodcut, interpret your subject boldly as you sketch. Lines should be wide and textures obvious. Strong contrasts are best.

Etchings can contain fine details and textures. In your sketches for etchings, include details, patterns and fine textures. You can suggest values through crosshatching.

Broad, flat areas of color are best for stencils and silkscreen prints. Your sketch might be made from cut or torn paper shapes. Think about your design in relation to simple, flat shapes and large areas of color.

Intaglio, lithography, and silkscreen printing techniques require equipment your school may not have. There are some simple versions of these processes that you might try.

Even with simple tools and materials you can create imaginative and carefully planned prints. On the following pages you will find more information about making prints. You might choose one or several methods to try out. If the method is new to you, try a small sample print first.

Student art.

Edvard Munch, *The Kiss,* 1902. The wood grain in this print has been integrated into the design of the work. Color woodcut, 18 ³/₈" x 18 ⁵/₁₆"(47 x 46 cm). Museum of Modern Art, New York. Gift of Abby Aldrich Rockefeller.

Relief Printing

Review the following steps before you create a print. All of the steps apply to relief printing. Many also apply to other techniques.

PREPARING YOUR DESIGN. Make your preliminary sketches the same size as your printing block. Use thin bond paper and a soft pencil.

Remember that your final print will be like your sketch, but reversed. To study the reversed image, hold the sketch up. You can see it on the back of the thin paper.

Check the spacing of major parts before you carve the block. When you are satisfied with the design, go over it with a soft pencil, using carbon paper to transfer it onto the block.

CUTTING A BLOCK. Practice some cuts on a piece of scrap wood or linoleum. Always hold the block securely and cut away from the hand holding the block. Use caution. Work slowly. If the block is wood, cut with the grain when possible. Shallow cuts often print just as well as deep ones. If you warm the linoleum, it will be softer and easier to cut.

Textures and patterns on the block can be created by lightly tapping objects into the surface with a hammer.

Try bits of gravel, nails or the end of a small pipe. Brush away all loose particles, chips and dust before you print the block.

Safety Note Always hold the block securely and cut away from the hand holding the block. Use caution. Work slowly. Wear safety goggles.

INKING THE BLOCK. Roll the brayer across the inking slab until the ink is evenly distributed. Then roll the brayer across the printing block using a smooth, even stroke.

PLACING THE PRINTING PAPER. Pick up your printing paper at opposite edges or corners. Make sure your hands are clean. Center the paper above the block, then put it straight down on the surface.

APPLYING PRESSURE TO THE PAPER. For most prints, you can apply pressure with your hand or use the bowl part of a large wooden spoon. Rub the whole surface of the paper. Begin at the center and work toward the edges. Your school may have a printing press you can use instead of hand rubbing.

You can also print by placing several layers of newspaper on the floor to serve as a pad. Place the printing paper on the pad, then center the block on top of the paper, face down. Slowly apply pressure by stepping onto

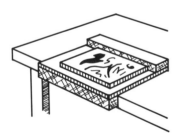

A safety block helps to support your work while you are cutting.

In a relief print, the image you create on the block will be reversed in the print. Student art.

Make sure the ink is evenly distributed on the brayer and on the block.

Student art.

the back of the block. Think of other ways to apply pressure evenly.

PULLING THE PRINT. After the print is made, it is *pulled* (slowly peeled away from the block). To keep your prints clean, make up sets of paper fingers. Paper fingers are short strips of clean paper folded in half. Slip them over the edges of the paper and put your fingers on top of them as you slowly lift the paper. Make sure you have a clean space to place your print until it dries.

EXAMINING YOUR PRINT. Check your print. Is the ink evenly distributed? Too much ink will blur the detail; too little and it won't show. Are the shapes, lines, and other elements as clearly defined as you want them to be? Should you change some areas? If so, wash and dry the block. Before you print again, make sure the block is clear of all loose chips or dust.

Place your paper on the block carefully.

Applying pressure to the paper.

Pulling the print is always exciting. Photographs by Roger Kerkham.

Using a printing press. If you have a printing press, learn and follow all directions for using it safely.

Pulling an impression from a plate.

Use a wooden spoon, baren or smooth rounded stone to burnish paper. Use your hand or smooth surface to rub the back of the paper.

Multicolored Relief Prints

Multicolored prints can be made in several ways. In the most complex method, you cut a separate block for each color. After you make several prints and let them dry, reprint them with a second color. In all multicolored prints, the lighter colors should be printed first.

With only one block, different colored inks can be applied with a brush, one at a time. When you've printed one color, you might cut a stencil and place it over the print. When you ink the block with another color and print over your first color, the stencilled area will be unchanged. You can also add color by pasting shapes of colored tissue paper to the background paper before printing it.

Pablo Picasso, *Head of a Woman*, 1962. Linoleum cut in color, 24 ¼" x 21" (64 x 53 cm). The Harvard Fogg Museum, Harvard Univeristy, Cambridge. Given in memory of Howard Muelnner.

Max Weber, *Rabbi Reading*, 1919. In this print, wide bands were used to separate colors. This makes it easier to register the colors. Woodcut, printed in color, 4 ³/₁₆" x 1 ¹⁵/₁₆" (10 x 6 cm). Collection, The Museum of Modern Art, New York. Gift of Abby Aldrich Rockefeller.

Other Ideas for Relief Prints

Wood-Scrap Prints Find small blocks of soft wood that might be combined to create a print. Look for pieces with unusual shapes: one might be treelike, another might look like part of a house. Carve details into the blocks.

Print each block in a separate color on a single sheet. Try printing one block on top of another (overprinting).

Collage Prints You can make a print from a block prepared like a collage. Use heavy cardboard or some other rigid surface as the block. Glue other materials to this background. Your collage might include shapes cut from cloth, textured paper, Styrofoam or string.

Plants are a rich source of forms for collage prints. Print leaves with distinct veins or shapes. Flattened, dried weeds, flowers or pine needles are among many natural materials you might use for collage prints.

In all collage-based prints, it is wise to seal the completed block with polymer medium before printing. Unsealed fabrics, for example, will absorb too much ink. A sealed surface also lasts longer.

To print the block, roll ink onto the collage and lay the paper over the inked surface. Then use your hand to rub the paper or roll a clean, soft brayer over the paper to make the print.

Paraffin wax Paraffin wax blocks can be carved with a nail or an old ball-point pen. You may need to add a drop of liquid detergent to water-based ink or paint to get a good print with a wax block.

Oil-based clay A smooth slab of oil-based (plasticene) clay can be carved to create a printing block. For this kind of block, it is best to put the paper on top of the inked surface. Then rub the paper with light pressure to make a print.

Cardboard tubes, cans, large dowels These cylindrical forms can be modified to create allover designs. The prepared cylinder is rolled across the inking plate, then across the paper. Create the designs by gluing string, textured papers or cloth on the cylinder.

Charles Smith, *Cocks*, 1939. Separate blocks of wood were used to create the print. Monoprint, 10 ¹/₄" x 8 ¹/₄" (26 x 46 cm). Collection, The Museum of Modern Art, New York. Purchase.

Making a collage relief print. Blocks for relief printing can be made from a variety of materials. Photograph by Roger Kerkham.

Pulling a print from oil-based clay. Photograph by Barbara Caldwell.

Oshaweetuk, *Four Musk Oxen*, 1959. Stencils can be cut from paper and used to create complex prints. Stencil print, 5 ¹/₂" x 17" (14 x 43 cm). Courtesy The Brooklyn Museum, New York.

Stencil Prints

A stencil is made by cutting a shape out of a sheet of paper or thin cardboard. A stencil print is made by placing the stencil on another sheet of paper and applying ink or paint through the opening.

Special stencil paper, lightly waxed, can be purchased at art supply stores. You can also cut a stencil out of stiff paper such as a manila file folder or an index card. A stencil brush, with short stiff bristles, is the traditional way to apply the ink or paint. It is dipped in the ink, then wiped or stippled on newspaper to eliminate any excess. A light stippling motion (up and down) or a light "feathery" stroke is commonly used to apply the ink.

Silkscreen Prints Standard silkscreens are made of fine silk or organdy cloth tightly stretched over a wood frame. The frame is often equipped with special hinges that fit onto a baseboard. This system allows you to raise and lower the screen easily. A kickstand holds the screen at an angle while you put paper on the baseboard. A *squeegee* (a rubber blade inserted in a block) can be used to push ink or paint through the screen.

You can create a simple screen frame. Begin with a shoebox lid. Cut a window in the center with a 1" (2 cm) margin all around. Stretch organdy cloth over the opening on the outside. Staple the cloth tightly to the vertical sides of the cardboard.

Seal the edges around the opening with masking tape, inside and outside. Use pieces of tape about 2" (5 cm) longer than each side. Fold and press the extra tape so the corners of the box are sealed. Allow each piece of tape to overlap the cloth about ¹/₄" (6 mm). Press all edges of the tape together securely.

Cloth, especially organdy, can also be stretched on an embroidery hoop to create a screen. Wax crayon can be used to "block out" areas you don't want to cover with ink or paint. Finger paint can be used for printing on paper.

Plan your design, including numbers or letters, as a normal image (not reversed). This is unlike other printing methods, where you need to reverse the design.

Cut the largest shapes in your design from the center area of bond paper, wax paper or newsprint.

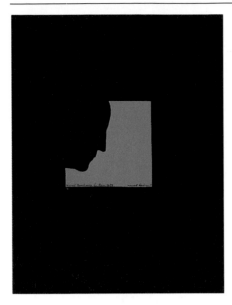

Marcel Duchamp, *Self-Portrait*, 1959.
Serigraph, printed in blue on black paper,
7 7/8" x 7 7/8" (20 x 20 cm). Collection, The
Museum of Modern Art, New York. Gift of
Lang Charities, Inc.

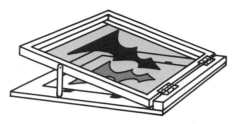

A silkscreen with a hinge and kickstand
makes it easy to create many prints rapidly.

The squeegee held at an angle draws the ink
across the film and forces it through the
open areas onto the paper below, thereby
making a print.

This cutout is your stencil. It will block out part of the screen. Tape the stencil to the bottom of the screen with masking tape. Use library paste, not a permanent white glue, to attach other small shapes to the screen. You might add paper tape to cover any screen space between the edge of the stencil and frame. This prevents ink from getting on the border of your print.

Place the printing paper under the screen. Release the kickstand. Spoon water-based screen ink across the edge of the screen near the hinges.

Standing across from the hinges, hold the squeegee in both hands, slanting toward you. Firmly pull the ink forward. Lift the squeegee and slant it away from you. Push the ink back toward the hinged edge. Lay the squeegee parallel to the hinged edge until you are ready to make the next print. Slowly raise the frame. Set the kickstand and remove the print. Hang the print to dry.

For cleanup, remove extra ink from the frame and return it to the can. Remove the stencil and thoroughly wash the screen. Any dry ink left on the screen will block out color in later prints.

If you are making a multicolor print, put small tabs of masking tape on the baseboard or printing surface. These are called registration marks. The paper and screen for each print can be aligned against them. Try to make all prints in the first color during one session. Allow them to dry before printing each additional color.

For the second color of a multicolor print, begin with a clean screen and new stencil. This stencil may have some openings that overlap the openings in the first one. In these overlapping areas, the two colors of ink will slightly blend. For example, if a red ink is screened over yellow ink, the result is a red-orange.

Intaglio Prints: Drypoint Etching

Drypoint etchings can be made from a smooth sheet of metal, plastic, Plexiglas, Formica, vinyl floor tile, or other hard, smooth materials. The material must be firm enough to allow lines to be scratched (or incised). A sharp-pointed tool called a *stylus* is used to scratch the lines. A long sharp nail can be used as a stylus.

After the design has been scratched into the surface, ink all of the lines thoroughly with a stiff brush. Wipe the smooth surface free of ink. Use cheesecloth or a folded paper towel in a gentle circular motion. The ink should remain only in the incised lines.

Center a piece of damp paper on the plate. Cover the paper with felt. A printing press or an old clothes wringer should be used to apply pressure. If these are not available, cover the paper with felt and rub it hard with the bowl of a spoon. Apply pressure heavily until the ink comes out of the recessed lines onto the paper.

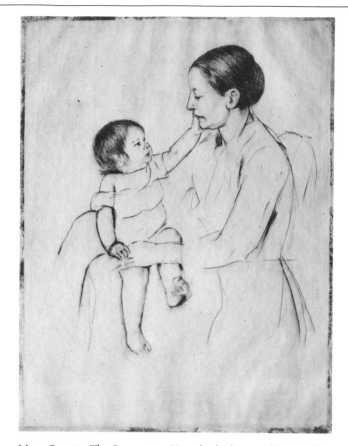

Mary Cassatt, *The Caress*, 1891. How do the line qualities in this etching differ from those in the print by Whistler? Drypoint, 8" x 5 ³/₄" (20 x 15 cm). Courtesy of the Metropolitan Museum of Art, New York. Gift of Arthur Sachs, 1916.

James McNeill Whistler, *Thames Set: Longshoreman.* Whistler's etching has the quality of a sketch. Some areas are crosshatched to create darker values. Etching, 5 ¹¹/₁₆" x 6 ⁷/₈" (14 x 17 cm). Courtesy of the Metropolitan Museum of Art. Dick Fund, 1917.

Monoprinting

"Mono" means one and a monoprint is just that – an edition of only one print. This is because the preparations you make on the plate do not survive after that print is pulled. You can prepare and print your plate in several ways.

METHOD 1. On a smooth, nonabsorbent surface (plastic, Formica, cookie sheet), roll out an even layer of ink. Draw directly into the ink with tools such as a toothpick, a pencil eraser, a cotton swab, a facial tissue, a bristle brush or an old comb. Place paper over the design and rub it evenly but lightly with your hand. Pull the print. Find out what happens if you try to make a second print from the design.

METHOD 2. On a smooth, nonabsorbent surface, paint an image with tempera paint. Make sure that all of the painted areas stay wet. Place paper over the painted image and rub it. Pull your print.

METHOD 3. Roll a thin, even layer of ink on a smooth nonabsorbent surface. Place paper over the inked surface but do not rub it. Draw an image on the paper. When you lift the paper, the side facing the ink will be your monoprint. Try several monoprints using different tools. Find out what happens if you draw and lightly rub your fingers over parts of the paper.

Student art.

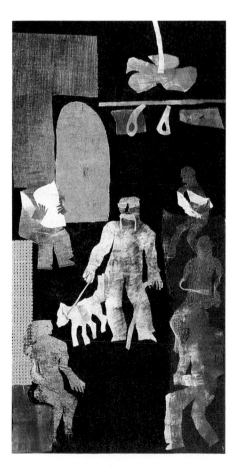

Robert Broner, *Blind Subway Minstrel: Harmonica Player*, 1955. Monoprints are usually made by inking a smooth surface, then wiping through the wet ink with a tool. Monotype, printed in color, 35 ⁵/₈" x 17 ⁵/₈" (91 x 45 cm). Collection, The Museum of Modern Art, New York. Gift of Mr. and Mrs. E. Powis Jones.

Subtracting ink from the surface prior to making a monoprint. Photograph courtesy of Barbara Caldwell.

Printing and Other Art Forms

Contemporary artists often combine several traditional techniques in a single print (relief and silkscreen). Some artists combine printmaking techniques with other media. Others create prints that look like sculpture or become elements for a collage.

Many of the new directions in printmaking also involve new media and technologies. For example, photocopy machines can be used to make color copies of an image. Some printmakers are using photocopiers to create a new kind of monoprint (each image prepared for the photocopy process is unique).

Critical Thinking Imagine you work in an art gallery or art museum. How would you classify the prints by Nevelson and Oldenburg? Do you think of them as relief sculpture or as prints? Give reasons for your answers.

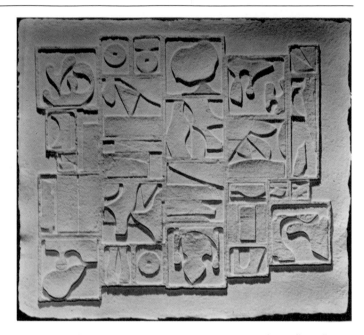

Louise Nevelson, *Dawnscape*, 1975. Cast paper relief, 31 ½" x 34" (80 x 86 cm). Courtesy Pace Editions, Inc., New York.

Claes Oldenburg, *Profile Airflow*. Copyright Gemini G.E.L., Los Angeles, California, 1990.

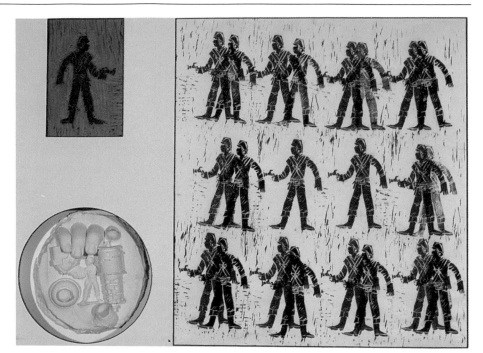

Student art.

Student art.

Student art.

Student art.

217

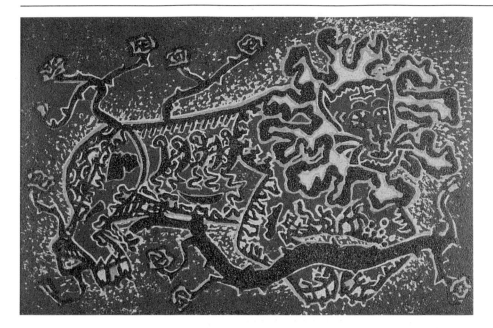

Student art.

Student art.

Student art.

Student art.

Summary

Printing is a process of transferring an inked design from one surface, usually a block or plate, to another surface, such as paper or cloth.

Printmaking processes are divided into four major categories: relief, intaglio, lithography and serigraphy (silkscreen and stencil). Each process has unique possibilities and limitations.

A fine art print is a "multiple original." It is created from a surface the artist has prepared. Each original print is numbered and signed by the artist (in the lower right corner, under the edge of the image).

Reproductions are photographic copies of images produced on machine-driven presses. Because these images are machine-made, they are not considered original prints, even if they are signed by the artist.

The art of printmaking has a long history. It became a major art form during the Renaissance and has continued to appeal to many artists. Asian artists, such as Hokusai and Hiroshige, mastered the art of making multicolored woodcut prints. Today, artists are creating prints using a variety of methods, inks and surfaces, including three-dimensional forms.

Using What You Learned

Art History and Creating Art

1 What are three of Dürer's accomplishments as a printmaker and artist?

2 What are three characteristics of an original fine art print?

3 What is the main difference between a reproduction and a fine art print?

4 For what kind of printmaking are Hokusai and Hiroshige best known?

Aesthetics and Art Criticism

1 Describe the main differences between the following printing processes.
- *relief*
- *intaglio*
- *stencil*

2 Select a fine art print in this chapter that interests you. Describe, analyze and interpret it. Use the appropriate printmaking terms to point out its sensory, technical and expressive qualities.

Creating Art and Art Criticism

1 Select one of your best prints. Apply your knowledge of the steps in art criticism to describe, analyze and interpret it.

2 State at least four criteria that can be used to judge your best print. The criteria might refer to the subject or theme, design, technique or purpose. Evaluate your print, stating reasons why it does or does not fully meet the criteria.

3 Select one of your least effective prints. Identify at least one step you might have taken to improve it.

Bradbury Thompson is known as one of the leaders of graphic design in the twentieth century. This design was used on the cover of a book about his work.

Chapter 11

Graphic Design

Chapter Vocabulary

graphic design
calligraphy
illuminated manuscript
layout
typography
monogram
logo
corporate identity
serif
sans-serif
surface design
motif

When you opened this chapter, what did you see first? Was it the chapter title? Was it this opening paragraph? Or was it the design on the opposite page?

Probably the first thing you looked at was the page to the left. This design by Bradbury Thompson grabs your attention.

The goal of *graphic design* is to catch your eye. It often must compete for your attention with hundreds of other visual images. You can go to a quiet gallery to see sculpture or painting, but you see graphic design in busy environments such as on street corners, highways and on the crowded pages of magazines.

The purpose of graphic design is to communicate a message – often, but not always, with words or letters. Sometimes the entire design is simply well-designed type or beautiful handwriting (called *calligraphy*).

Beautiful examples of lettering are found in *illuminated manuscripts* from medieval times in Europe. Most illuminated manuscripts were handlettered prayer books. Many had pages with intricate painted illustrations. Sometimes these illustrations included gold leaf that reflected light, making them look "illuminated."

Most graphic designs today are printed by high-speed presses. A designer prepares artwork for the printer. A *layout* is a sketch showing the location and size of all the major parts of the design. A layout is usually a combination of type (letter forms), illustrations and other instructions for the printer.

Many graphic designers today also plan three-dimensional forms such as new packages or signs for roads and buildings. Some create graphics for television and motion pictures, using electronic media.

In this chapter, you will learn more about graphic design. After completing the chapter and some of the activities you will be able to:

Aesthetics and Art Criticism	• discuss and evaluate varieties of graphic design, past and present.
Creating Art	• create original graphic designs of several types.
Art History	• understand some historical changes and cultural influences on graphic design.

Gallery

Graphic design came from the need to communicate through visual symbols. The alphabet for most languages in Western culture evolved from pictographs. Pictographs developed thousands of years ago in the region around the Mediterranean Sea (see this page, top).

The forms for letters of the alphabet have changed over time. Many changes came with the invention of the printing press in the 1450's. The printing press reduced the need for handwritten books. It created a demand for alphabets that were simple and easy to read.

With the Industrial Revolution, advertising for consumers grew. The earliest graphic designers were artists who could illustrate products and use eye-catching lettering in their designs.

Professional training in graphic design began in the twentieth century. Today, thousands of graphic designers are employed in advertising, publishing and television. Their main job is to communicate with people using visual symbols.

Critical Thinking Which of the images in this gallery were probably created by professionally trained graphic designers? Which images were probably created by persons trained in a craft or fine art? Give reasons for your answers.

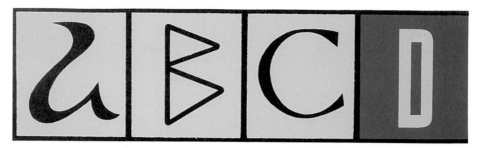

John Cataldo, "Lettering: Symbol evolution."

Lindisfarne Gospels, Folio 29, Late 7th century. The British Museum, London. Courtesy Trustees of the British Museum.

Ivan Chermayeff, *Outdoor Sculpture for 9 West 57th Street, New York City.* Photograph by David Robbins.

Henri de Toulouse-Lautrec, *Moulin Rouge-La Goulue*, 1891. Color lithograph, 66 ¹/₈" x 46 ¹/₄" (168 x 117 cm). Copyright 1990 Indianapolis Museum of Art, Gift of the Gamboliers.

Sears, Roebuck Catalogue, Fall 1897.

Saul Bass, Girl Scout logo, 1978.

Ben Shahn, *Arrangement of Letters,* 1963. Cast silver with gold wash, 3 ¹/₄" x 2" x 1 ⁷/₈" (10 x 5 x 5 cm). Collection, The Museum of Modern Art, New York. Given anonymously.

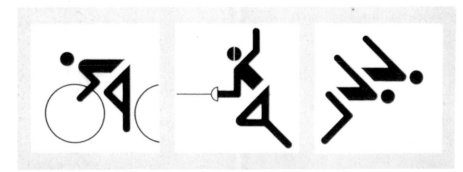

Otl Aicher, Pictograms, Munich Olympics, 1972 and Montreal Olympics.

Beatrix Potter

1866-1943

Beatrix Potter grew up in a well-to-do home in London, but her early life was isolated and lonely. Although she never had a formal education in a school, she had many interests and always found interesting things to do.

Potter was fascinated by both nature and art. She kept rabbits that slept by the fire, bats in birdcages, lizards, toads, even an owl. She painted beautiful watercolors of insects and plants. Her ability to draw animals led her to take art lessons. Her animal illustrations became extremely accurate.

Nothing escaped Potter's curious eye. Once she found an ancient printing press. She cleaned it up, made ink from chimney soot and printed her own woodcuts. She even memorized entire Shakespeare plays!

In her early twenties she sold some drawings to a greeting card publisher. But the work didn't satisfy her. She wanted a personal way to express herself, some way to use her unique vision.

Then she happened to send an illustrated letter to a five-year-old boy who had had a long illness. "My dear Noel," she wrote "I don't know what to write to you, so I shall tell you a story about four little rabbits, whose names are Flopsy, Mopsy, Cottontail and Peter...."

Beatrix Potter, Illustration from "The Tailor of Gloucester."

Beatrix Potter at her farm, Hill Top, ca. 1907.

Beatrix Potter, Illustration from "The Tale of Squirrel Nutkin."

And so her most famous book, *The Tale of Peter Rabbit*, was born. She went on to write and illustrate 30 enchanting tales about animals who have human-like feeling and adventures. She became one of the world's best-known illustrators and writers of books for children. She designed the books herself and had them printed in small, inexpensive editions that a child could easily hold.

Over 65 million copies of *The Tale of Peter Rabbit* have been sold. It has been translated into 15 languages, including Japanese, French, Spanish, Latin and Icelandic. Because *The Tale of Peter Rabbit* has enchanted generation after generation, it is called a classic.

Critical Thinking How does the art of illustrating a book differ from creating images just for personal expression? What illustrations in books from your own childhood do you remember most fondly? What made you remember the illustrations?

> April 6th 96
> 2 Bolton Gardens
>
> My dear Noël,
>
> Thank you for your nice letter, I should like to see you riding the big dog, here is a picture of Tom Thumb on a mouse.
>
> We are going to Swanage next

Beatrix Potter, Illustrated Letter, 1896. Bolton Gardens. Courtesy of the Pierpont Morgan Library, New York.

Sources of Ideas
for Graphic Design

The main purpose of most graphic design is visual communication. This means that you must know what message you want to communicate, to whom and why.

For example, suppose the basic message for an anti-litter campaign (what) in your school is "Stop Littering." The audience (who) is anyone in or around school. One reason for the campaign might be that litter is ugly (why). Other reasons are that some litter is unhealthy or dangerous. Litter also reflects an uncaring attitude.

Now suppose that posters are used to communicate about litter. Some posters might stress that litter is ugly. Others might have a message about the dangers of litter. What other ideas could the posters communicate? Remember that if your graphic design has a definite purpose, always begin by asking: *What* do I want to communicate? To *whom?* and *Why?*

Some of your graphic designs might be created for more personal reasons. You might want to design a banner for your room. The main audience might include yourself, your friends and family. It might include a poem or message you especially enjoy.

Another source of ideas for graphic design is your curiosity about communication with type (lettering) and illustrations. Look through the rest of this chapter. With your teacher's advice, choose ideas to explore.

What is the message of this poster? Why is it important? Who is the audience?

Most posters need to communicate a few basic ideas in a simple, unified composition. Student art.

Designing Graphics

Most graphic designs are created to communicate a message. This means that you will use the elements and principles of design to make sure the message attracts attention and is visually clear.

Attracting attention is important in posters and other graphics that people see while they are moving. When the design is simple, clear and unified, people can see the main message at a distance.

How can you make the design simple? Choose only the most important ideas to illustrate. The elements will be visually clear if they are well spaced and have a strong contrast. For example, light lettering will show up best on a dark background.

Spacing is important at several levels. Leaving some "empty" space around the main elements is often a good idea. Carefully plan the spacing between letters, words and sentences. Careful spacing makes the information easy to read. A block of type can be a narrow column, a wide band or another shape.

To attract attention, your design must be unified and have a clear center of interest. Symmetrical balance might be best for a message about a formal event such as a concert of classical music. What kind of balance might be appropriate for a more active event? Effective graphic design meets its purpose.

Before you begin a final graphic design, always try several layouts. The layout will help you see possible problems with your design.

Evaluate your layout by asking questions: Should I use bright or dull colors in this graphic? Why? Is the spacing between parts effective? Should I use symmetrical or asymmetrical balance? What should I emphasize? It might help to review the elements and principles of design in Chapter 3.

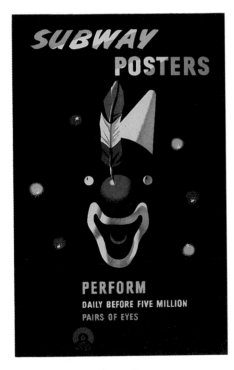

E. McKnight Kauffer, *Subway Posters Perform Daily Before Five Million Pairs of Eyes,* 1947. This poster was created to help potential advertisers understand that many people in New York City might see a subway poster. Offset lithograph, printed in color, 45 3/8" x 29 1/2" (116 x 75 cm). Collection, The Museum of Modern Art, New York. Gift of the designer.

Ed Emberly, 1990. This author likes to illustrate his own books. What media did he use?

Max Ernst, 1924. Letters of the alphabet can take many forms. Typography is the art of designing and creatively using letters of the alphabet.

Joseph Volpicelli, Alphabet. What theme unites each of these creative letters? Courtesy Werner Pfeiffer.

Ideas to Explore

Typography

Typography is the art of designing a typeface – letters in an alphabet. Roman-style letters have thick and thin elements with serifs (tags on each letter). Early letters were chiseled in stone and the serifs at the ends of lines kept the stone from cracking. Later, the thick and thin lines and the serifs were handlettered with a chisel-shaped quill.

Script typefaces resemble handwriting. Old English script lettering is hard to read but popular for diplomas and other documents because it looks formal. It is based on illuminated manuscripts from the Middle Ages. Sans-serif types (those without tags) are called Gothic typefaces.

Today, there are many typefaces available to graphic designers. They are often named for the typographers who designed them. Bodoni, for example, is a Roman style of type designed around 1800 by the Italian Giambattista Bodoni.

You might enjoy designing an alphabet. It could be very precise with each letter carefully planned in a grid. It could be a funny alphabet with letters shaped to resemble fish, flowers, sports equipment or the like.

You might design an alphabet book as a class project. It could be planned as a gift for a kindergarten or pre-school class.

You can also learn about the importance of shapes and styles of letterforms by lettering your name in different styles. You might try designing letters that fit words like *swirling*, *fire*, *ice*, or *gentle*.

A Personal Monogram

Many people enjoy having a personal monogram. A *monogram* is a special design made from your initials. Albrecht Dürer (1471-1528) was the first artist to invent and use a monogram on his artwork.

Today, monograms are often used on clothing as well as stationery, luggage and the like. The same design is often used for all these items.

Many companies also have monogram-like designs often based on their initials. In the business world, the use of initials or a special design for a company name is called a *logo.*

In a *corporate identity* program, a logo is used to identify the products or services of a company. It might be used on office supplies, uniforms, delivery trucks and buildings owned by the company. Most government and public agencies also have logos.

Graphic designers often plan a monogram or logo so the shapes have very clear and interesting positive and negative spaces. They also think about a style of lettering that matches the person or group for whom the logo is designed.

Plan a monogram for your initials. To try many compositions quickly, cut each letter from paper. Cut one set of all capital letters. Cut another set of lowercase letters. Choose a style of lettering that matches your personality or interests.

Arrange the letters in different ways. Trace around the edges of combinations you like. Try overlapping some letters and combining the edges. Think about grouping smaller letters inside a larger one.

When your design has a unique character and very strong positive-negative shapes, complete a drawing of it. Use black ink or another medium.

Monogram printed from an original wood engraving found at the S. George Company in West Virginia.

Sudler, Hennessey & Lubalin logo. Strong positive and negative spaces and graceful curves are seen in this monogram.

Monograms can include images related to the meaning of the initial. What image has been integrated into this letter L?

Babs Glass, *Metaphor/Moon Passages.*

Babs Glass, *Metaphor/Moon Passages.*
Calligraphic lettering has been built up to
form an image. What metaphor inspired
this work and the one to the right?

George Lane, *Ohohohohohohoho/Heya
Heya.* Sound poem, Navajo.

Expressive Lettering

Graphic designers enjoy looking at the shapes and edges
of letters. They notice whether the letters have *serifs*
(tags) or are *sans-serif* (plain). The letters may be bold
(thick), medium or light (thin).

Collect some examples of lettering from old magazines
or newspapers. Compare the lettering. Is every letter the
same thickness or do they combine thick and thin lines?
Are the letters slanted *(italic)* or upright? Are the letters
skinny *(condensed)*, extra wide or average? Are *uppercase*
(capital letters) and *lowercase* (small letters) used or are
there unusual combinations of these?

Graphic designers use this knowledge creatively.
Sometimes they do projects just for the expressive use of
lettering. In expressive lettering, the shapes of letters are
designed to show what they mean. They are arranged on
the page to express an idea, mood or feeling.

For example, the word "rugged" might have letter
forms that look strong (bold, wide) but have jagged
edges. A word like "tree" might be made up of letters
that fit inside a tree-shape. The letters might be placed to
suggest how a tree grows.

Try some creative lettering. Write down two or three
adjectives and two or three nouns. Make some thumb-
nail sketches to explore ideas. Create letter forms that
look like and express the meaning of each word.

Choose your best idea and create a larger finished
version of it. Choose a medium and colors that will add
expressiveness to your design.

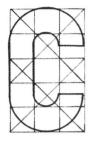
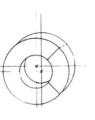

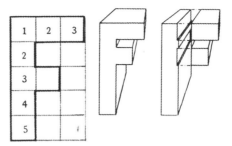

John Cataldo, diagram of block letters in perspective. Perspective lettering can be done by starting with block letters like these or a wide script such as that used in the student artwork below.

Ivan Chermayeff, Poster for the Guggenheim Museum. The type in this poster has been distorted to suggest the contours of the outer walls of the Guggenheim Museum. This kind of work is called pictorial typography. Chermayeff & Geismar Associates, New York for Mobil Oil Corporation.

The vanishing point in this student's work is shown by the dot in the upper right corner. Student art.

Perspective Lettering

You can probably write or letter your name without thinking. In this activity, you will use your name as the basis for a graphic design with block letters. The letters will be drawn in one-point perspective to create the illusion of space and distance.

To begin, lightly letter your first name in the center of a sheet of paper. Use only capital letters in a simple block style. Leave at least ¼" (6 mm) clear between each letter. Make each letter about 2" (5 cm) tall and at least ¼" (6 mm) wide. If your name is short, make each letter ½" (1 cm) wide.

Now set up a vanishing point anywhere near the border of your paper. Draw it as a dot. Align a ruler's edge from this dot to the upper left corner of your first block letter. Hold the ruler firmly and draw a very light line from the vanishing point to that corner.

Repeat this process. Draw a very light line from the vanishing point to the next corner at the top of your letter. Continue across all the top corners, connecting them to the vanishing point with a light line. Soon you will see the perspective effect along the top edges of your letter.

Continue this process across the bottom of your letters. Connect the corners of each letter to the vanishing point.

After your perspective lines are in place, be creative. Draw, redraw or erase lines to make the letters stand out. Color them in. Add shadows or textures. For a challenge, try a variation using your regular handwriting. Perhaps you can do a variation based on two-point perspective.

Posters

The first posters were handpainted announcements on large sheets of paper, called broadsides. Today, most poster designs are planned so that many copies can be printed.

Posters are commonly used to sell products, announce special events or sales, and promote ideas or social causes. Posters can be as large as billboards or as small as handbills (letter-size paper). They can be flat or have three-dimensional elements. Poster-like road signs may have moving parts and bright lights.

Simplicity, clarity and visual impact are important in posters. This is because most posters are first seen at a distance, often while people are moving from place to place.

Posters should make effective use of type and illustrations. Good posters avoid clutter, confusion and visual clichés. A visual cliché is an image used so often that it has become uninteresting.

Select an event or an idea you would like to promote. Explore the theme, design and media possibilities in sketches.

Select your best sketch and enlarge it to check effectiveness. Make adjustments in the enlarged version. Is the design simple, clear and attention-getting? If so, create your final poster in a medium of your choice.

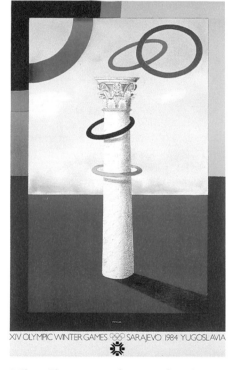

Milton Glaser, Poster for XIV Olympic Winter Games in Sarajevo, 1984. What do the five rings and the column represent in this poster? Courtesy Milton Glaser, Inc., New York.

Joseph Binder, 1951. In addition to the lettering, what visual symbols are used in this poster?

Greeting Card Designs

Today, greeting cards are sold for almost every occasion. They vary in purpose, style, shape and message (humor, sympathy, write-your-own-message).

Some cards have three-dimensional elements. Even perfumes and sound from small computer chips have been added to cards. Some shops sell blank cards and envelopes so you can make your own greeting cards.

Many artists enjoy making their own holiday cards using techniques such as block printing, painting, drawing, or computer drawing programs.

Greeting cards were first used in Germany in the late Renaissance to celebrate New Year's Day. The cards were illustrated with woodcuts. Personal greeting cards for Christmas became popular in England in the 1800's. In the United States, Louis Prang set up the first company to print colored greeting cards in 1856. These early cards had floral designs, landscapes and well-known poems.

Today, the greeting card industry employs thousands of illustrators and graphic designers. Some create designs for invitations, cards, gift wrapping, party utensils and decorations.

Collect some greeting cards. Sort them according to purpose, style, subject and medium. Analyze and interpret the visual messages.

Try your own skill in designing a greeting card. Perhaps you could design a three-dimensional or "pop-up" greeting card.

Three-dimensional elements can be developed for greeting cards.

Greeting cards have become a major form of graphic design and communication in the twentieth century. Why do you think they are so widely used?

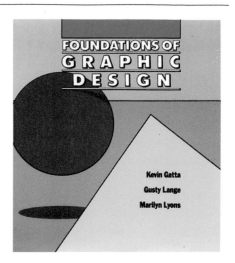

William Morris and Edward Bourne-Jones, *Kelmscott Chaucer*, page.

Selma G. Lanes, *The Art of Maurice Sendak,* Copyright 1980. Abrams.

Kevin Gatta, Cover of "Foundations of Graphic Design." Copyright 1991 Davis Publications.

Book and Record Jacket Design

Many graphic designers enjoy doing jacket designs for books and records. These assignments are interesting because the idea may be suggested by the content of the book or the style of music.

An effective jacket design identifies the content or theme and attracts the attention of the buyer. The jacket may be designed around a photograph, an illustration in pen and ink, or another medium like collage or paint. It might feature lettering more than pictures.

Today, many designs for records are planned so they can be adapted for an audio tape package, or a compact disc. The main artwork and lettering may also be coordinated with a poster and a music video.

You might design an original book cover or record jacket. Think about the general theme of the book or the style of music. Design the cover so it is related to the theme or style. For example, a jacket for classical music should probably be more quiet and reserved than one for jazz or rock music. Remember, your design should be unified and attract the attention of the buyer.

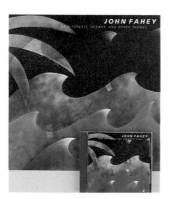

Design and illustration by Susan Marsh.

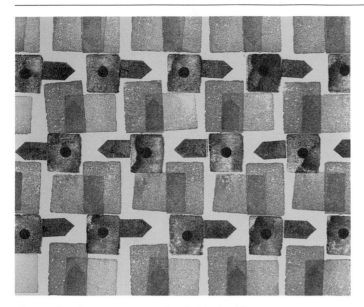

This surface design was printed with inked rubber stamps. Student art.

Candace Wheeler, Daffodil pattern, ca. 1885. Can you find the pattern in this design? Printed cotton velveteen, 32 ¹/₂" x 37" (83 x 94 cm). The Metropolitan Museum of Art. Gift of Mrs. Boudinot Keith, 1928.

Surface Designs: Walls, Fabric, Paper

Surface designs are another area of graphic design. The most familiar examples are wallpaper, fabrics and gift-wrapping paper.

Stamped designs on paper 4,000 years old have been found in Egypt. In Ghana, the Ashanti carve intricate wood stamps to print designs on cloth with dye.

Wallpaper was developed in the Orient for large folding or sliding screens within rooms. Handpainted and handprinted wallpaper designs were developed in Europe in the 1600's. In colonial America, wallpaper designs were made to look like expensive tapestries.

In the 1870's, William Morris led a new design move-ment in England. He created surface and other decora-tive designs that were repeated in an unusual way. He also believed that handcrafted designs should be available for everyone, not just the wealthy.

Today, many surface designs on fabrics and gift paper are printed with a silkscreen process. Textile artists use computers to help them design repeated patterns. They can also test many design ideas quickly.

You might create a surface design on cloth (such as an old shirt) or paper. Begin with a basic *motif* or repeat unit. Use a stencil, found objects or another form of printing. Try different ways of repeating the design.

Try to go beyond a simple straight repeat pattern (side by side). Motifs can be planned to interlock or to form alternating patterns. Some motifs can be diagonally stepped (dropped) to create complex patterns in several directions.

Other Activities

Use a magnifying lens. Examine the patterns of ink in newspaper photographs, stamps, colored magazine advertisements, textbook illustrations, dollar bills or other fine engravings and etchings. Compare the grain and texture of the paper on which the different images are printed.

Find newspaper advertisements for stores that sell inexpensive clothes or appliances. Compare the graphic designs in these ads with similar ads from stores that sell more expensive items.

Pictographs and hieroglyphics were systems of visual communication in ancient China, Japan, Egypt and among early Native North Americans and aboriginal tribes. Invent your own system of pictographs to tell a story.

Cut examples of your initials out of old magazines. Sort the examples into uppercase and lowercase versions. Then sort them further into look-alike groups – serif or sans-serif, italic or standard, bold or thin, stretched out or condensed. Select letters that match your personality and create an imaginative collage based on them.

Cut some cardboard letter forms or use a lettering stencil. Trace around the letters to make a word picture. You might arrange the letter forms in the shape of an animal, a person or an object. The letters might spell out brief poems. Illustrate the poem with pencil, crayon, ink or watercolor.

Save some empty cereal or laundry-soap boxes and bring them to school. Discuss the designer's choices of colors, size and style of letters, images on the box and placement of the logo. Discuss why the appearance of a package is important to the manufacturer as well as to the consumer.

Count the times you see the logo or brand name of a particular soft drink as you go from home to school. Explain the reasons why you see the logo or brand name more often. How many variations in the size or use of the logo did you find?

What similarities do you see in the visual symbols and the names on these packages? What main ideas do the package designs communicate to the consumer? Why?

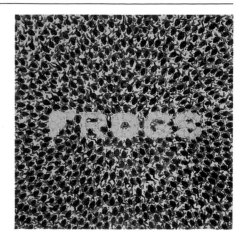

Student art.

Student art.

Student art.

Student art.

Student art.

Student art.

Student art.

Summary

Graphic design is a form of visual communication. It is called graphic because it usually involves words (type, lettering, visual symbols). Among many examples of graphic design are book and album covers, posters, billboards and packages.

Graphic designers prepare a layout – type, illustrations and other details of a design. The final design is then printed by technicians. In a corporate identity program, the designer often develops a logo – a visual symbol – that can be printed on many different company items.

The history of graphic design is as old as systems of writing. This history includes the art of designing styles of alphabets, calligraphy, and illuminated manuscripts from the Middle Ages. Graphic design became a speciality in art with the growth of industry and advertising in the 1800's.

Today, there are many areas of graphic design. These include as graphics for surfaces such as wallpaper, as well as graphics for motion pictures and television. Although we usually think of graphics as two-dimensional, they can also be three-dimensional items such as packages or signs on buildings.

Using What You Learned

Art History

1 What are the main differences between Roman, Script and Gothic typefaces?

2 When and where were greeting cards first created?

3 For what graphic design activities are the following people known?

- *William Morris*
- *Louis Prang*
- *Giambattista Bodoni*
- *Albrecht Dürer*

4 A motif is used in the development of a surface design for wallpaper. What is a motif?

Aesthetics and Art Criticism

1 What are three points to remember when you are designing a visual communication that will be seen at a distance?

2 Briefly define these terms:

- *serif*
- *sans-serif*
- *typography*
- *surface design*
- *motif*
- *monogram*
- *logo*
- *pictograph*
- *illuminated manuscript*
- *calligraphy*
- *layout*

3 Select your most effective example of graphic design. State at least four criteria that should be used in judging the kind of design you have created. Then describe how effectively you have met each criterion.

Creating Art

1 What are three questions you should ask before you begin designing a poster or other form of visual communication?

2 Spacing between letters is important when you are planning a graphic design. Name two other kinds of spacing that you should carefully plan.

3 Demonstrate your knowledge of basic lettering principles and basic styles. On lined paper, letter your name in the following ways.

- *Roman, uppercase and lowercase*
- *Gothic, all uppercase letters*
- *Script, uppercase and lowercase*

4 Graphic design skills take time and practice to develop. Name one of your graphic design skills that has improved. Name one that you still need to practice.

Have you ever visited the studio of a sculptor? This photograph shows the stone-carving studio of Dame Barbara Hepworth, one of England's most honored sculptors. Her studio has been preserved as a historically important site. What features of the studio are familiar to you? Photograph by Michael Duffett.

Chapter 12
Sculpture

Chapter Vocabulary

kinetic
earthworks
assemblage
relief
freestanding
repoussé
theme and variation
modular

Sculpture can be as large as a carved mountain or so small you can wear it. You have probably seen sculpture in museums, parks, plazas or shopping malls. Perhaps there is a sculptured historical monument in your town.

Sculpture is called a three-dimensional art form. This means that it has height, width and depth. A freestanding sculpture is designed so it can be seen from all sides. A relief sculpture is designed to be seen from one direction.

Sculpture has often been linked with architecture. The exterior and interior of buildings can be decorated with sculptural elements. Outdoor sculptures have often taken the form of public monuments such as triumphal columns or arches, equestrian statues (a rider on a horse), or fountains in plazas or gardens.

Among nomadic people, sculptural forms are often small, portable and used for decoration or trade. Examples are coins and medallions as well as miniatures, small shrines or sculptural containers.

Traditional materials for sculpture are wood, ivory, stone, clay and cast metal, especially bronze, which is very durable. Today many sculptors are using modern industrial materials and techniques to create sculpture. With materials such as plastic, wire and welded steel, forms can thrust outward in many directions or be suspended so they move freely in space. *Kinetic* sculptures have parts that are moved by natural forces (air currents or water) or by electricity or magnetic forces. Sound, electrical lighting and mechanical devices can be part of a sculpture.

Some artists create environmental sculptures. *Earthworks* are sculptures created by shaping the land with bulldozers. Earthworks often include walks, bridges or new plants. Performance sculpture is a recent development. In performance sculpture, people are asked to interact with each other, their environment, or other things in a new way.

In this chapter, you will learn more about the materials, processes and expressive possibilities for creating sculpture. After you study the chapter and complete some of the activities, you will be better able to:

Art History • understand and appreciate major types, processes and artistic traditions in sculpture.

Art Criticism • apply your knowledge of sculptural processes to evaluate sculpture.

Aesthetics • use art terms to describe sculptural qualities.

Creating Art • develop ideas, design and create expressive sculpture.

Gallery

There are many kinds of sculpture. A few are shown here. Take time to look at each one. Which do you find the most fascinating? Why? Try to imagine yourself as the artist who created the work. What features of the sculpture would you want people to notice and think about?

Here are some other questions you might answer. Three of the sculptures were first created as symbols for religious beliefs. Can you identify these works?

Critical Thinking Which sculptures have been created in the twentieth century? How do they differ from the sculptures created before the twentieth century?

Nyoirin-Kannon (Bodhisattva), 645-647. Nara Period. This is Kannon, a Bodhisattva, or wise being who represents kindness. Most bronzes are first made in wax. Bronze. Oka-Dera Temple, Nara, Japan.

Egyptian, *Cat*, ca. 665-525 BC. This cat symbolizes Bastet, the Egyptian goddess of joy. What features are unusual? Courtesy of the Trustees of the British Museum.

Red Grooms, *The Woolworth Building from Ruckus Manhattan*, 1976. This is part of a large work about New York City. What are the clues to its humorous intent? Courtesy Marlborough Gallery, New York. Photograph by Richard L. Plaut, Jr.

Barbara Chavous, *Sky Woman*, 1982. Painted wood, 14" x 14' x 8' (36 x 42 x 122 cm). Holden Arboretum, Kirkland, Ohio, Photograph by Ellen Eisenman.

Ida Kohlmeyer, *Semiotic Bush*, 1984. Nylon on wood, 64" x 44" x 44" (163 x 112 x 112 cm). Courtesy of the artist.

Robert Smithson, *Spiral Jetty*, 1970. This earthwork – a sculpture made from earth and natural materials – was created with the help of bulldozers. Natural changes in the color and form were part of the original idea. Black rock, salt crystals, earth and red water (algae) composing a coil, 1500' x 15' (457 x 5 m). Great Salt Lake, Utah. Photograph Gianfranco Gorgoni. Contact Press Images, Inc., New York.

Gregory Curci, *Peacock*. Painted aluminum, 48" x 32" x 18" (122 x 81 x 46 cm). Courtesy David Bernstein Gallery.

Donatello, *Mary Magdalen*, ca. 1455. Experts call this sculpture a masterpiece of Western culture. Why do you think experts have made this judgment? Wood, partially gilded, 74" (188 cm) high. Cathedral Museum, Florence.

Claire Zeisler, *Tri-Color Arch*, 1983-1984. The use of fiber for sculpture was pioneered by this artist. Hemp, synthetic fiber, knotted, wrapped, 74" x 11" (188 x 28 cm); spill 66" x 44" (168 x 112 cm). Courtesy The Rhona Hoffman Gallery.

Michelangelo Buonarroti
1475-1564

Michelangelo is one of the best known sculptors in the history of art. Even though he was also a painter, a master of drawing, an architect and a poet, he always referred to himself as "Michelangelo, sculptor of Rome." His drawings, paintings and work on architecture are known for their sculptural qualities.

He was born in Caprese, Italy. As a child, he could draw very well. At 13 he was apprenticed to the workshop of the painter Domenico Ghirlandaio. One year later, Michelangelo joined the household of Lorenzo de'Medici, a banker and great patron of the arts who supported promising young artists. Lorenzo's house was filled with exciting thinkers and artists and it was the happiest time of Michelangelo's life.

Within three years, Lorenzo was dead and Michelangelo, at 17, was on his own. Throughout his life, Michelangelo traveled to major cities in Italy to create art for wealthy patrons, including six Popes. At the age of twenty-five, he completed one of his first major sculptures, the *Pietà*, shown here. This work established his reputation and lead to many other commissions.

All his life, Michelangelo loved the city of Florence. His great sculpture, *David*, was created as a symbol of civic pride for the people of Florence. In the Old Testament, David slew the giant, Goliath. Michelangelo often combined classical ideas of strength and beauty with a Christian theme.

At the age of 30, Michelangelo began two large projects. One was to be a massive tomb for Pope Julius II, containing 40 sculptures. Of these, only *Moses* was fully completed. The second project was the fresco for the Sistine Chapel ceiling, 118´ x 46´ (36 x 14 m). Large panels interpret major events in the Old Testament. All the frescos appear to be as three-dimensional as sculpture and architecture.

Someone once complained to Michelangelo that his statues of the great Medici family did not look like them. Michelangelo replied, "Who will remember their faces in a thousand years?"

He knew that his art would endure the test of time.

Critical Thinking Michelangelo's art inspired awe among people of his own time. They called him "divine." Four hundred years after his death, almost everyone finds much to admire in Michelangelo's work. What do you most admire? Why?

Michelangelo, *Self-portrait as Nicodemus*, (detail of *Pietà*) ca. 1550-1555. Florence.

Michelangelo, *Moses*, 1513-1516. Marble, 93" (235 cm) high. S. Pietro, Vincoli, Rome.

Michelangelo, *David*, 1501-1504. Marble, 18' (540 cm) high. S. Pietro, Vincoli, Rome.

Michelangelo, *The Pietà*, 1499. *Pietà* is the common title for artworks that portray the Virgin Mary mourning the dead Christ. *The Pietà* beautifully solves the problem of showing a full-length male figure draped across a woman's lap. The composition makes you think that the Virgin supports the weight without effort. Her face and pose capture a calm yet sad mood. The muscular forms of the body of Christ convey a feeling of strength, even in death. The polished marble surface is superbly crafted. Marble, 5' 9" (175 cm). The Vatican, St. Peter's, Rome.

Thinking in Three Dimensions

The ideas you develop for sculpture can come from many sources: nature, people, the environment or your imagination. You might think of a general theme such as events in your everyday life or a feeling such as your greatest hope or fear.

As you explore ideas, think about the design of your work and the sculptural media and processes you will use. The materials you choose may suggest an idea. The design of a sculpture should match your idea and the materials or processes you will use.

Sometimes you need to change your idea or consider a different material to come up with an effective design. For example, it is very difficult to use plaster to carve a figure with delicate arms, legs or other extensions into space. For an "action" figure, you might consider a material such as wire. If you want to use plaster you could think of a pose such as a reclining or seated figure or a bulky form. Before you begin to carve, make some sketches of the pose. Show how the sculpture will look from the side, front, top and bottom.

Design in Sculpture

As you develop a sculpture, remember to think about the elements and principles of design. Some of them have a special meaning when applied to three-dimensional art.

Sculptors often refer to *lines* or contours in their work as either static or active. The *textures* of forms may be smooth or rough.

Color may be a natural part of the material, added on to the surface or created by special lighting. Lighting is especially important for sculpture. The interplay of *values* – light and shadow – reveals the three-dimensional form and texture of a work.

Forms may have smooth transitions or clear angular shifts. Forms may be open or closed. They can be concave or convex. Materials may be transparent or opaque.

Sculptures may be small or large in scale. *Proportions* can be planned so they are normal, ideal or exaggerated. In some works, proportions may be less important than rhythmic intervals, fluid *movement* or *pattern*. Some works can seem to be held by gravity to the base or ground. Other can seem to lift and soar, or turn and twist. Motion may be actual (real) or implied.

Return to these ideas and to Chapter 3 as you design your sculpture.

These diagrams are based on Patricia Renick's sculpture on the next page. The diagrams show the action qualities and the positive and negative shapes in three views.

Sketching in clay is one way to explore design concepts in sculpture. Student art.

Robert Laurent, *Pigeon,* 1936. Cast red limestone, 5 ¹/₂" (14 cm) tall. Vassar College Art Gallery, Poughkeepsie, New York. Purchase.

Lee Bonctecou, *Untitled,* ca. 1965-1966. If Lee Bontecou had tried to carve her thin-legged bird in stone, what problems would she have encountered? In what other ways do the two sculptures of birds differ? Bronze, 4 ¹/₄" x 10 ¹/₄" x 2 ¹/₄" (11 x 26 x 6 cm). Courtesy Leo Castelli Gallery, New York. Photograph by Eric Pollitzer.

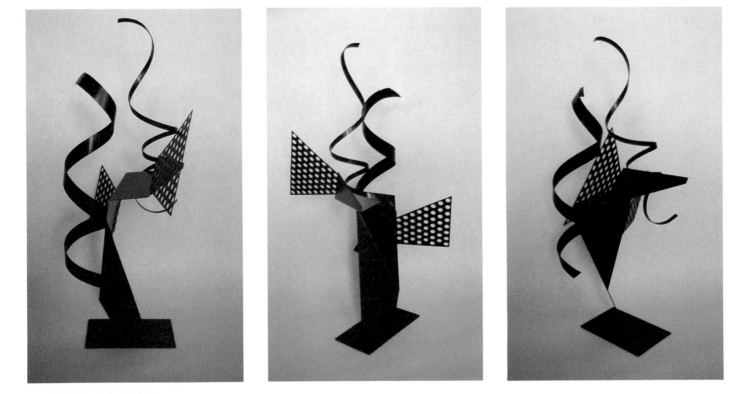

Patricia A. Renick, *Night Dancer,* 1990 (three views). Steel, 24" x 12" (61 x 30 cm). Courtesy the artist.

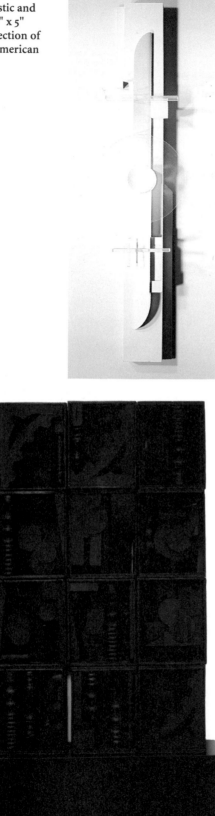

Theodore Roszak, *Vertical Construction*, 1943. Plastic and painted wood, 76" x 30" x 5" (193 x 76 x 13 cm). Collection of Whitney Museum of American Art. Gift of the artist.

Louise Nevelson, *Black Wall*, 1964. Painted wood construction, 64 ³/₄" x 39 ¹/₂" x 10 ¹/₈" (164 x 100 x 26 cm). Hirshhorn Museum and Sculpture Garden, Smithsonian Institution. Gift of Joseph H. Hirshhorn.

Media and Processes

There are four major ways to create a sculpture: carving, constructing, modeling and casting.

Carving is called a *subtractive* process because you cut into and take away materials. Constructing, modeling and casting are called *additive* processes because you join or combine materials. Modeling is the process of shaping and building up forms with clay, wax and other soft materials. Modeling is often the first step in casting. (For a description of casting, see "Casting a Relief Sculpture," page 254.)

In the remainder of this chapter, you will learn more about these processes. Most of the topics and processes can be tried in more than one medium. For example, if you do not have ceramic clay for modeling, you might model oil-based clay or papier-mâché.

Found Object Assemblage: Relief

An *assemblage* is a form of sculpture related to collage. It is sculpture made by combining objects such as boxes, pieces of wood, parts of old machines, and the like. Assemblages, like collages, are usually organized around a definite theme. For example, they can be planned around smooth geometric forms or forms with varied textures and irregular edges.

The two assemblages you see here are relief sculptures. *Relief* sculptures are three-dimensional but are usually designed for a wall or niche. They are seen primarily from the front. In a *low relief* sculpture the surfaces are raised up very slightly from the background. In a *high relief* sculpture, there is greater depth. The forms seem to be arranged on a theater-like stage.

Create a relief sculpture in a shallow box. Choose items to express a definite theme or idea. The theme or idea might be suggested by the materials you collect. You might try to create a nonobjective sculpture with related or contrasting textures, colors or forms.

Found Object Assemblage: Full Round

Most of the sculpture you have seen is called "in the round" or *freestanding* sculpture. It is created so it can be seen from all sides. Many artists construct full round assemblages. Often the shapes of "found" objects are the inspiration for the sculpture. New or used wood can be glued, nailed, screwed or bolted together. Pieces of metal can be welded, bolted or riveted together.

Construct an assemblage that can be seen from all sides. You might use wooden spools, old chair legs and scraps from a lumber yard or cabinet shop. You might collect egg-cartons, bottle caps and small paper or plastic containers to assemble. Often the odd shapes of materials will suggest ideas for a sculpture.

It is usually best to begin with one or two larger pieces and add smaller shapes to these. Try several positions for each shape before you attach it. A sculpture in the round should be planned from all sides, not just the front. Think about the design elements and principles as you work. Turn your work or move around it as you decide where to add new pieces.

Your work should be well crafted. Make sure you wipe away excess glue before it dries. If you use nails, plan the location and angle before using the hammer. If the nails are too large, or are placed too near the end of a piece, it may split.

You might consider staining or painting some pieces with acrylic paint before joining them to the assemblage. You might create textures or patterns on some scraps. The natural color and grain of wood may be so beautiful that no decoration is needed.

Safety Note Use shellac, varnish or oil-based paints only by permission and under the teacher's supervision. These finishes cannot be cleaned up with soap and water. The special solvents required for cleanup can irritate your skin. The vapors can irritate your lungs. Read, understand and follow all safety precautions.

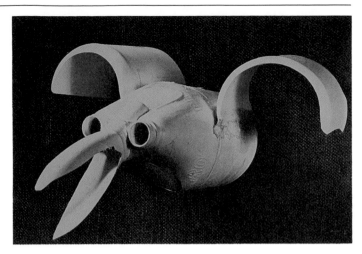

Marie van Orden, *Plastic Bird.*

Georges Vantongerloo, *Construction of Volume Relations,* 1921. Mahogany, 16 ¹/₈" x 5 ⁵/₈" x 5 ³/₄" (41 x 14 x 15 cm). Collection, The Museum of Modern Art, New York. Gift of Silvia Pizitz.

Terra-cotta head from the Han dynasty. British Museum. Photograph by John W. Mills.

Adaline Kent, *Citadel*, 1955. Terra-cotta, 13" (33 cm). Collection of Whitney Museum of American Art, New York. Purchase.

Modeling

Modeling is a process of using your hands and a few simple tools to shape soft materials such as wax, clay, papier-mâché pulp, thin metal or wire. Clay gives you freedom to experiment with forms, spaces and textures. Many artists like to use oil-based clay or wax for "sketches" in three dimensions.

Ceramic clay is often used for modeling when a more permanent sculpture is desired. You will find basic information about this medium in Chapter 13. If you will be modeling ceramic clay, read about the materials and processes before you begin a sculpture.

Approaches

One of the sculptures you see here was formed by direct modeling. In direct modeling, you pinch and pull clay. One of them was made, in part, by assembling clay slabs. Can you see these differences between the sculptures?

You can combine modeling methods by creating several slabs and clay pinch pots, then joining them together for a basic structure. You might begin with one large form like a ball or cylinder and shape it by pinching and pulling the clay.

To join two pieces of moist clay, scratch both surfaces and apply *slip* (watery clay). Then press the parts together and smooth the joints. Between work sessions, cover your sculpture with a moist towel and an airtight plastic bag to keep it from drying out.

Surfaces can be finished in several ways. While the clay is moist, stamp or scratch textures into it or build up patterns with small balls or coils of clay. When the clay is *leather-hard* (almost dry), you can apply underglazes. After the clay is *bisque-fired* (fired once), you can add color with ceramic glazes. The work must be refired to fuse the glaze to the surface. A bisque-fired sculpture can also be decorated with acrylic paint.

Victor Spinski, *Covered Pail*, 1979. Hand-built cast whiteware, 13" x 15" (33 x 38 cm). Courtesy of the artist.

Wendell Castle, *Louis IV Chest with Hat and Scarf*, 1979. 40" x 20" x 32" (102 x 51 x 81 cm). Photograph by George Kanper. Courtesy of the artist.

Sculpting a Familiar Object

Most people think of still-life objects as the subject of drawings, paintings and other two-dimensional art. During the 1960's, some sculptors explored still lifes in three-dimensional media. One group, called Pop artists, used popular objects as a source of ideas. They wanted people to see ordinary things such as hamburgers as sculptural forms and symbols of our culture.

Other sculptors became interested in the forms of natural objects. They created sculptures based on one complete form such as a flower or a pea pod.

Today, sculptures of objects are often called descriptive sculpture. A *descriptive sculpture* is a model of a familiar object but is created in an unexpected size or material.

You could model a descriptive sculpture in ceramic clay and glaze or paint it. You might prefer to model one in papier-mâché. You could even assemble a soft sculpture from fabric.

Choose a natural form or a manufactured object to represent in a sculpture. Keep the proportions as accurate as possible. Your work can be realistic or abstract (simplified). You might use a scale of ½" – 1" (1 ½ cm – 3 cm) for an object that is about 12" (31 cm) long.

After you complete your descriptive sculpture, explain how it differs from the real object.

Carving a Relief Sculpture

Carving is the process of cutting into and removing material such as wood or stone. It is called a *subtractive* process because you take away material. In most materials, you cannot reconnect what you have cut off. Therefore, you must plan and carve your work carefully. If you make mistakes, you may have to change your original plan.

In some media, such as oil-based clay, ceramic clay or paraffin wax, you can combine carving and modeling. Use one of these materials to practice carving and modeling a relief sculpture.

The sculptures shown here are examples of relief sculpture. They were made in a soft material, then cast in a more permanent material. You might try to create a relief sculpture of a face. It could be based on a photograph of yourself or someone you admire. It could be based on a theme that has deep meaning to you.

Begin with a slab of clay or wax about 6" to 8" (15 cm to 20 cm) and 1" (3 cm) thick. Shape the slab into a circle, square or rectangle. Combine carving and modeling to create your relief sculpture. Use your fingers and tools such as a paper clip or tongue depressor. Develop the form and the textures in your work. Think of your work as a much larger version of the relief sculpture you see on a coin.

If you use wax or oil-based clay for your relief sculpture, you might want to create a more permanent version in papier-mâchè. If so, follow these steps:

1. Cover your relief with a thin coat of petroleum jelly.

2. Soak small torn strips of newsprint paper in diluted white glue or wheat paste. Press each piece down on the relief and smooth it carefully. Build up at least five layers.

3. Allow the papier-mâchè to dry completely. Remove the wax or clay.

4. Paint your sculpture with acrylics. For a metallic effect, use only one color of paint. After the color is dry, stain it with diluted black acrylic or shoe polish.

School of Leonardo da Vinci, *Bust of Scipio*. Bas relief, 27" x 15" (69 x 38 cm). The Louvre, Paris.

Roman, Coffer handle, 1st or 2nd century AD. Bronze, relief mold, cast and chased. Courtesy of The Hurst Gallery.

Carving: An Abstract Sculpture

Traditional materials for carving are stone or wood. Probably you will carve a soft material such as white pine wood, plaster, firebrick, soap, lava stone, soapstone or unfired dry clay. Tools for carving include chisels, rasps, files and sandpaper. You should have proper tools for carving and follow safety precautions.

Carve a simple abstract sculpture. Make it a full-round sculpture (one to be seen from all sides). Every view should be interesting and flow into the next one.

Remember, an abstract sculpture is based on a recognizable subject or theme. When you abstract an idea, you simplify the form and show only the important features, without any details.

You might try carving your favorite animal, a vegetable, your hand or a flower. You can rearrange some features to create a pleasing form. Some parts may be longer or shorter than normal. They may be much smoother or much rougher than you would see in the original object.

Simple abstract forms were fascinating to many early twentieth-century sculptors. You can see simple forms in Munyarudzi's *Young Boy* and Smiler's *The Archer*.

Safety Notes Always carve away from your body. Hold the work securely. A safety block or vise will often help to support a sculpture while you carve it. Wear protective goggles. For work in plaster, dust masks are recommended. Follow all directions given by your teacher. To reduce dust and make cleanup easier, keep your work damp and carve your form in a shallow box or tray lined with a damp cloth or damp newspapers. Do not use plaster if you have a skin rash or open sores.

Isa Smiler, *The Archer*, Inukjuak, stone. Courtesy of the Toronto-Dominion Bank, Ontario.

Henry Munyarudzi, *Young Boy.* Courtesy of the African Influence Gallery.

Casting a Relief Sculpture

Many sculptures you see in parks, museums and galleries are made by the process of casting. Casting is a multistep process for creating sculpture in bronze and other materials.

Some casting techniques permit the artist to create several identical sculptures from one mold. Sometimes cast sculptures are made from other materials such as concrete, plaster, or plastic. The usual steps are:

1. A sculpture is first modeled in wax. It can also be modeled in ceramic clay, plaster or another material, then covered with wax.

2. A heat-resistant mold is made. The mold is heated to dry it out and melt the wax. These steps leave an open space in the mold.

3. Molten metal is poured into the open space of the mold. When the metal cools, the mold is removed. The metal sculpture is like the original model but more permanent.

You might try casting a relief sculpture using sand or oil-based clay for a mold. Your final sculpture will be plaster. Find a strong cardboard box about 3" (8 cm) deep. Wrap masking tape around the outside edge to strengthen it. Place about 1" (3 cm) of fine damp sand or oil-based clay in the bottom of the box.

Gather some objects to press into the clay or sand. These objects might be large shells, acorns, or nuts. They could include a pencil, old comb, thick rope, paper clips or thumbtacks. Press these straight down into the sand or clay and lift them straight out again. You are creating the mold or negative design for the sculpture you will cast. Everything you press into the clay will appear raised up in your final sculpture.

When your design is ready, mix and pour the plaster into the box as directed by your teacher. If you want to hang the sculpture on a wall, press a loop of thick string firmly into the wet plaster *before* it begins to set. After the plaster dries, peel away the box. Remove the clay or brush away the sand.

After you have completed your first cast, try others. Push stones, shells, rope or other objects that do not rust down into the sand and pour the plaster over them. When the plaster sets, they will be locked into the sculpture.

Tino Nivola, *Dues*, 1953. Sand and plaster, 64 ³/₄" x 34 ¹/₂" (164 x 88 cm). Collection of Whitney Museum of American Art. Purchase.

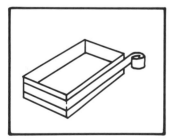

Casting

Tape for strength. Line a box with damp sand or oil-based clay.

Press objects straight down. Vary the depth and textures.

Tie thick string. Place over edge of box. Mix and pour plaster.

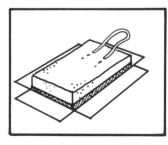

Embed a loop of string for a wall plaque.

Carefully remove cast and remove excess sand or clay.

Creating a Metal Relief Sculpture

Thousands of years ago in Egypt, Syria and northern Europe, people learned to shape thin sheets of metal by pressing on the front and the back. This technique of embossing metal is called *repoussé.*

The artist who created the stag-god repoussé is thought to have been Celtic (people whose descendants are Irish, Scottish or Welsh). The antlers are a symbol for powers of regeneration.

Create a metal repoussé sculpture. Think of an animal with powers you admire. How could you use it as a symbol? You might invent a symbol that stands for your ideals or goals in life. Use one of the methods for repoussé outlined below.

METHOD 1. Use craft-weight aluminum or copper foil (36 gauge). Tape the edges of the foil for safety. Plan on paper a design that will fit the size of the foil. Place the foil on a soft pad of newspaper or an old magazine. Tape the design on top of the foil and trace it with a blunt pencil. Press hard enough to leave clear grooves in the foil.

Remove the paper. With a tongue depressor or other wood tools, press down the background. To make other shapes stand out, turn the foil over and press them from the back. Create contrasting areas of pattern, lines and dots on the front and back.

To finish your relief sculpture, brush waterproof ink over the foil. When it is dry, buff the raised surface with a dry paper towel. Mount your work on wood for display.

METHOD 2. Begin a relief sculpture as though you were making a collage. Collect nearly flat materials such as cardboard, textured paper, fabric, buttons, toothpicks, leaves, weeds or shells. Glue these to cardboard.

After the glue is dry, apply thinned white glue or white library paste to the whole design.

Place a sheet of extra heavy-duty aluminum foil (kitchen type) on top of the design. Work from the center to the edges, gently pressing the foil down. Fold back the extra foil. With a blunt pencil, outline the edges of the shapes you have glued. Add other lines, textures or patterns to flat areas of the foil. Finish as described under Method 1.

Student art.

The Stag-god, Detail of the Gundestrip Cauldron, 1st century BC, Silver, 28" (71 cm) diameter. Nationalmuseet, Copenhagen.

Alexander Calder, *Sow*, 1928. Wire construction, 7 ¹/₂" x 17" x 3" (19 x 43 x 8 cm). Collection, The Museum of Modern Art, New York. Gift of the artist.

Alexander Calder, *Soda Fountain*, 1928. Iron-wire construction, wood base, 1 ⁵/₈" x 5 ¹/₂" x 3 ¹/₂" (4 x 14 x 8 cm). Collection, The Museum of Modern Art, New York. Gift of the artist.

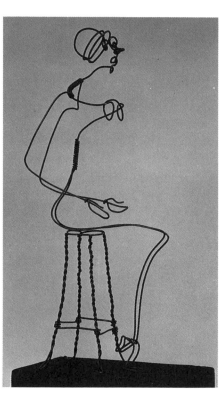

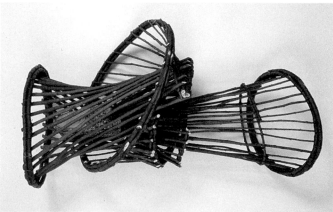

Carol Hepper, *Ventricle*, 1989. Wood and wire, 48" x 29" x 26" (22 x 74 x 66 cm). Courtesy Rosa Esman Gallery, New York.

Other Ideas to Explore

Modeling a Linear Sculpture

In linear sculpture, the voids are as carefully planned as the direction of lines. Voids are the open spaces you see between and around the lines. Sometimes voids are called negative spaces.

Many artists have explored linear forms of sculpture. Some have bent metal rods and welded them together. Others have joined huge steel beams with rivets. Logs have been carved and assembled to create linear sculpture.

Alexander Calder liked the open airy quality of lines in space. He often used one continuous piece of wire to create a freestanding sculpture. A freestanding sculpture does not have a special base or platform.

Creating a linear sculpture with wire is like drawing in space. You bend the wire in many directions to create a three-dimensional form. For this activity, you could use long pipe cleaners, stovepipe wire, floral wire or multicolored telephone wire. You could even use flexible vines called reeds.

Model the wire into a freestanding sculpture. Try to create a form with curving organic forms. It might have some angular geometric bends too. Remember that a sculpture in wire should be three-dimensional, not flat. You might use one of your contour drawings for an idea. Other ideas may come if you experiment.

To start a symmetrical form (such as an animal or person), bend the wire in the center and begin with a loop for the head. Create the main outlines, then add details. If you plan to mount the work on a block of wood, leave some extra wire so it can be firmly attached to the block.

While you are working, study your sculpture from all angles. Try to improve parts that look flat or are not carefully bent. Look at the open negative spaces *between* the wires, not just the wire. If you bend wire in the same place repeatedly, it becomes brittle and may break. After you complete your sculpture, mount or display it.

For variations, use short straws and string, toothpicks, tongue depressors or twigs. These rod-like materials are well-suited to geometric, angular sculpture.

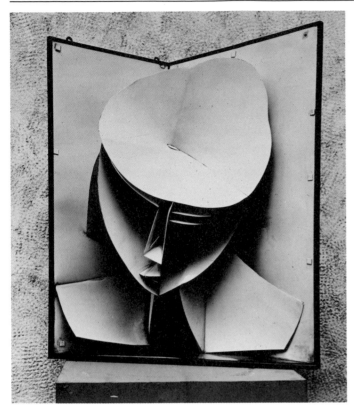

Naum Gabo, *Head of a Woman*, ca. 1917-1920. Construction in celluloid and metal, 24 ½" x 19 ¼" x 14" (62 x 49 x 36 cm). Collection, The Museum of Modern Art, New York. Purchase.

Creating Forms from Shapes

In sculpture, flat shapes are often called planes. The sculptures you see here were created with flat sheet-like materials or narrow slabs. Sculptures like these were developed early in the twentieth century. They are often called by style names such as Cubism or Constructivism.

Try some ideas for sculptures based on planes. Use thin poster board, Bristol board, or unlined index cards. Learn to score paper and fold it into curves. Press long curved lines in thin cardboard with the point of a scissors or an unopened paper clip. You are scoring the cardboard. It will bend easily along the line you scored.

Try some of the other techniques shown below. Then create a sculpture that uses flat surfaces but is well-planned and three-dimensional on all sides. Make sure the separate pieces will fit together before you join them with glue. Use paper clips, pins or tape to hold pieces together while the glue dries.

You might enlarge your first work. The larger version could be made of corrugated cardboard and covered with papier-mâchè or thin cloth dipped in plaster. What other materials could you use for planes?

Ways of shaping paper

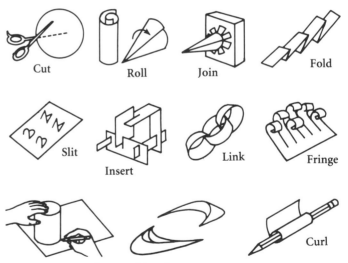

R. Freedman, *Yard without a Swing*, 1982. Oil on wood relief, 9 ½" x 12" (24 x 30 cm).

Henri Matisse, *Heads of Jeanette*, 1910-1913. Bronze, each approximately 20" (51 cm) high. The Los Angeles County Museum of Art. Presented by the Art Museum Council in memory of Penelope Rigby.

Theme and Variation

Many sculptors create a series of related works based on one theme or idea. Each work is called a variation on a theme.

Theme and variation may be familiar to you from music or dance. This idea also applies to visual art. For example, in many cultures, traditional visual symbols are used again and again. The same theme (a visual symbol) may be varied and used in many different art forms.

You can see this approach in the five sculptured heads created by Henri Matisse. Which sculpture is the most realistic? Which is the most abstract? In what other ways did he create variations on his theme?

You can explore this way of thinking about sculpture. Begin by creating in clay three or four identical forms, such as cones or cylinders. Leave one of your forms as the "theme." Then change each of your other forms. You might add or take away parts. You could vary the texture.

You might also begin with four or five small ready-made forms such as paper cups, plastic dinnerware or folded index cards. For a real challenge, try creating at least three small sculptures of one person. Then give each one a different facial expression such as anger, sorrow and joy. Can you think of other ways to create variations?

These forms were created from stiff paper. Can you identify the theme and variation on it? Student art.

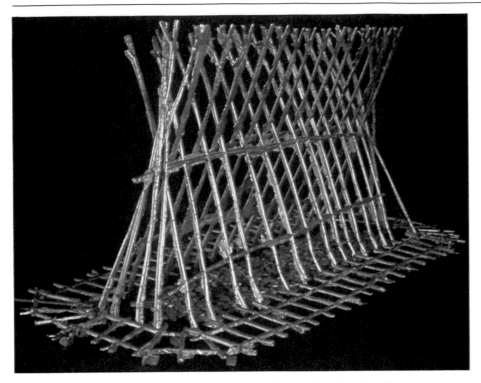

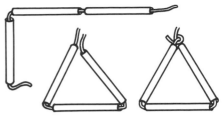

For a modular sculpture you might try different arrangements of straws. Create two or three shapes and then join them together. Be creative! Triangles are very strong when they are joined. This form was made by using two long strings in the bottom triangle.

Clarice A. Dreyer, *Rainbows for Dad*, 1983. Cast aluminum, paint, 5' x 10' x 5' (152 x 305 x 152 cm). Courtesy of the artist.

Modular Sculpture

A *modular* sculpture uses one basic form over and over. A familiar example of a module is a brick; the same form is used over and over to create a rhythmic pattern in a wall.

In sculpture, artists often combine identical or related modules. They consider ways of stacking, linking or combining modules. Sometimes they change the size or color of the module to add interest.

Find or create a set of modular forms. Your modules might be rods or stick-like forms such as toothpicks, drinking straws, or tongue depressors. They could be bulky forms such as pine cones or paper cups.

Arrange your modules to create a definite rhythmic movement through space. Try several compositions before you join the modules together.

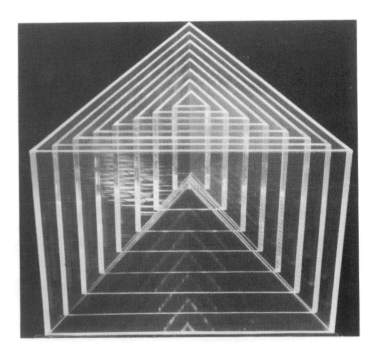

Harriet FeBland, *Mystic*. Plexiglas, 9 ¼" x 12" x 12" (23 x 30 x 30 cm). Private Collection.

Sculpture in Its Setting

Everyone expects to see sculpture in museums. Today, you can see sculpture in parks, plazas and shopping malls as well.

Many sculptors who accept commissions for large works try to plan their work around one of two main purposes. One purpose is to create a sculpture to be a dominant center of interest at the site. A second purpose is to create a work that blends into the architecture in a subtle way.

Look at the two sculptures shown here. Which one seems to have been planned to blend in with its site? Which one is a center of interest at the site? Why do you think so?

Sculptures for public places are often selected by holding a competition. The sponsors of the project choose the location and set up the budget for the sculpture. They publicize the competition and send information so artists can prepare a maquette.

A *maquette* is a small-scale model of a sculpture. The maquettes are submitted to a jury that decides on the best entry. The one chosen is then created in final form.

A maquette can be made of any material that suggests how the final sculpture will look. If the final sculpture will be made from sheets and rods of steel, the maquette might be made from sheets of cardboard and toothpicks or straws. The model for a cast bronze sculpture might be made of wax or clay.

Pretend to hold a sculpture competition. Choose a location and general theme that would be appropriate for the site. Choose one scale that everyone will use to create a maquette. For example, the scale might be ½ inch = 1 foot (1 ½ cm = 3 cm). If the final sculpture is 12' (3.5 m) tall, the maquette would be 6" (15 cm) tall. Create your maquette so it will either be the center of interest at the site or blend into the site.

Pablo Picasso, *Woman.* New York University, New York.

Lin Emery, *Free Enterprise,* 1977. Bronze aquamobile, 16' x 20' (488 x 610 cm). Courtesy Helmerich & Payne, Inc.

Student art.

Student art.

Student art.

Student art.

Student art.

Student art.

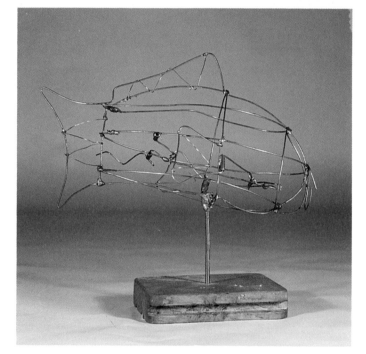

Student art.

Student art.

Student art.

Summary

Sculpture is a major form of three-dimensional art. Freestanding sculptures are designed to be seen from all sides. Relief sculptures are designed to be seen from one main view. Kinetic sculptures move or have moving parts. Earthworks are one of many forms of environmental sculptures that artists have developed in the last several decades.

There is a wide range of sculptural materials available today. They range from the traditional – metal, wood, stone and clay – to the most modern industrial media. The basic processes for creating sculpture are modeling, carving, casting and construction (assembling).

Using What You Learned

Art History

1 Name and describe three well-known sculptures by Michelangelo.

2 Why were members of the de'Medici family and the Popes important to Michelangelo and many other Renaissance artists?

3 Name at least two industrial materials or processes that 20th century artists have used for sculpture.

4 In what regions were early metal repoussé sculpture created? About how old are some of these sculptures?

5 What two style names are sometimes used to describe sculpture with many flat planes?

Aesthetics and Art Criticism

1 Define the following terms as they are used to describe sculpture:
- *freestanding*
- *relief*
- *kinetic*
- *assemblage*
- *repoussé*
- *theme and variation*
- *modular*
- *earthworks*

2 Select a sculpture in this chapter that you especially like. Describe the features – sensory, formal, technical, expressive – that you appreciate.

3 Apply the method of criticism in Chapter 4 to evaluate your most successful sculpture. Be sure to state the criteria you are using for your judgment.

Creating Art

1 Problem-solving is an important part of learning to create art. Briefly describe at least two problems that you solved while you were creating sculpture. State the steps you took to solve each problem.

2 What are the four main methods for creating sculpture?

Computers and Sculpture

Some sculptors are now using computers as a sketching tool to try ideas for sculpture. Software drawing programs for computers make it possible to sketch ideas.

With some programs, the artist can develop a sketch that shows a wire-like "skeleton" frame of a sculptural form. The computer can be given instructions to show the same form filled in with solid planes.

The form can be rotated to show how it will look from any angle, distance, and with lighting from different angles. This kind of software is widely used by industrial designers and film animators.

Critical Thinking What are some qualities of sculpture that no computer can capture?

Sherry Markovitz, *Blue Boy,* 1983. Beads, papiér mâche, oil paint, 34" x 16" x 22" (86 x 41 x 56 cm). Collection of Dr. Diane Stein. Photograph copyright 1987 Eduardo Calderón.

Chapter 13
Crafts

Chapter Vocabulary: Each of the following sections contains its own vocabulary list:

ceramics
mosaics
papier-mâché (maskmaking)
jewelry
weaving
stitchery
macramé
batik and tie dye

Safety Note Many crafts require special safety precautions. Learn and follow all safety instructions given by your teacher. Your teacher may suggest alternative media and techniques.

Handcrafted objects appeal to many people today. Perhaps this appeal comes from the fact that most of the products we use today are mass-produced. Handcrafted objects, however, have a unique design. They are shaped by methods that show the skill and imagination of the artist. An emphasis on fine work is common to all work in crafts.

In some cultures, traditional crafts are practiced in about the same way from one generation to the next. Some Egyptian baskets, for example, are still being made by methods used 4,000 years ago. In other cultures, traditional craft designs have been changed to appeal to tourists and foreign markets. This trend began hundreds of years ago when Marco Polo traveled to the Orient and set up trade routes between the Eastern and Western Hemispheres.

In Western culture, the Industrial Revolution changed the value of handcrafted items. Mass production created a demand for more products. Manufactured goods could be made rapidly and at lower cost than handcrafted items. As factory-made items became more popular, the need for the skills of craftsworkers declined. For a time, crafts became "luxury items" for the very wealthy.

Today, work in handcrafted items is varied. In most communities, people can buy imported crafts and fine or folk crafts. Today's artists explore almost every crafts tradition. You can see this in the sculpture of a deer at the left. This artist has used beadwork to create surface texture and pattern. This kind of work developed into an art form among Native North Americans in the Eastern woodlands and North Central plains.

Some weavers are creating sculptural forms with fibers. Ceramic and glass artists create forms that are both useful and expressive. Mixed media works are also being explored, such as combining metal with fiber or wood with ceramics.

Your teacher will help you decide which craft activities to try. It is best to approach your first project as a way to learn techniques and solve problems. Work with simple design ideas.

After studying the chapter and completing some of the activities, you will be better able to:

Art History • understand some characteristics of traditional and contemporary handcrafts.

Art Criticism and Aesthetics • apply your knowledge of aesthetics and art criticism when you create crafts and study them.

Creating Art • demonstrate your skills in creating well-designed, expressive handcrafts.

Gallery

Traditional crafts are those made in much the same way for a long time. They are usually things created to be used either in everyday life or for special occasions. The craftspeople pass their techniques down from one generation to another. Sometimes the designs are important visual symbols. They are used over and over and give the item its special meaning.

Many modern craftsworkers are experimenting and working like fine artists. They are not concerned with making useful objects. They may paint with yarn or create jewelry similar to small sculpture. They are creating objects as a form of personal, creative expression.

Critical Thinking Which of the artworks in this gallery are probably traditional crafts? Which seem to be more like a new form of art? Why do you think so?

Henri Matisse, *Mimosa*, 1949-1951. Wool rug, 58 ¹/₈" x 36 ³/₈" (148 x 92 cm). The Baltimore Museum of Art. Gift of Mr. and Mrs. Alexander S. Cochran, Baltimore.

Textile, Pre-Columbian, Peru. Courtesy of The Textile Museum, Washington, DC. Photograph by Schwartz, 1983.

Gary DiPasquale, 1989. Stoneware. Courtesy Alianza Contemporary Crafts, Boston.

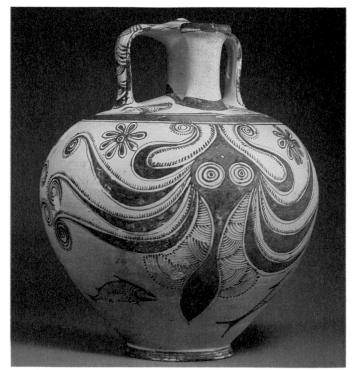

Mycenaean, Stirrup jar, decorated with two octopi and other fish, ca. 1200-1125 BC. Terra-cotta, 10 ¹/₄" x 3 ⁵/₁₆" (26 x 8 cm). The Metropolitan Museum of Art. Louisa Eldridge McBurney Gift Fund.

Henri van de Velde, Gold and tortoiseshell hair comb, made by
Theodor Muller, Weimar, ca. 1902.

Africa, Brass and fiber comb.

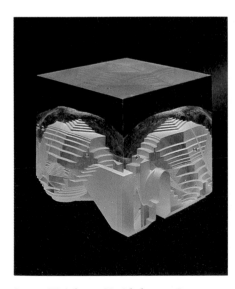

Steven Weinberg, *Untitled*, 1989. Cast
crystal cube, 8 ¹/₂" (22 cm). Courtesy of the
artist. Photograph by Douglas Schaible.

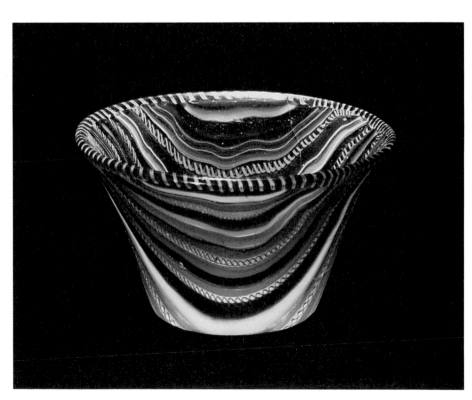

Bowl, early to mid-first century AD Roman Empire. Ribbon glass technique, 2" x 3" (4.8 x 8.7
cm). The Corning Museum of Glass, Corning, New York.

Meet the Artist

María Martínez
about 1881-1980

María Martínez, a Native American, lived in the pueblo of San Ildefonso, New Mexico. She grew up watching her aunt and other women in her pueblo create pottery. Like them, she learned to use the coil method and quickly became very proficient. A major change in her life began while she was attending school in Santa Fe. There she met her future husband, Julian Martínez.

María and her husband were married in 1904. They soon became a team in making pottery. She created the pots and Julian decorated them. Their work was dramatically changed by a chance meeting with Dr. Edgar L. Hewett, an archaeologist who was working at a nearby site. Dr. Hewett knew of María's skill as a potter. He asked her to reconstruct a whole pot that would resemble part of an old broken pot he had found. She was able to do this by using a "black ware" technique.

In the black ware technique, red clay pots are placed in a dung-fueled bonfire to make them hard. When the pots are properly heated, the flames are smothered, leaving the clay a shiny black. The shiny black surface is then gently scraped in areas, creating a matte design.

This black-on-black pottery was soon a major source of income for the Martínezes. Private collectors admired it and museums began to show it. María was asked to give demonstrations at world fairs. In the 1930's she visited the White House at the invitation of President Franklin D. Roosevelt and his wife, Eleanor.

Although María's husband died in 1943, her pottery-making business grew to include four sons, their wives, children and grandchildren. Before she died, María Martínez received many honors, including the American Ceramic Society's highest award, and an honorary doctor's degree from the University of Colorado. Today she is known and honored for reviving the finest traditions of pottery among the Pueblo. Her skills and achievements are being kept alive by her great-grandchildren.

Critical Thinking Suppose that traditions of craftwork were not passed along to future generations. What would a group of people need to do to set up a new tradition of craftwork?

Maria Martinez, Plate. The Indian Art Center of California.

Maria and Julian Martinez, ca. 1920. Photograph by Pedro de Lemos.

Maria Bowl. Collection of Gilbert and Jean Davis.

Maria Martinez, San Ildefonso Blackware Plate.
Private Collection, Texas.

Ideas for Crafts

Ideas for craftwork are usually a blend of thinking about objects to create and the materials or processes you might use.

Ideas for a craft can begin with thinking about the function of the object. For example, your ideas for jewelry you make for yourself or a friend might be different from jewelry you make for others.

Crafts ideas might come from your interests. For example, if you like nature, you might choose a leaf, flower or animal for a design idea. You might need to simplify and abstract the ideas to make them appropriate for your materials.

If you like geometric forms, these might have a place in your craftwork. Imagination and humor may be your special interest. Your ideas might come after you have made small experimental pieces in clay, fiber or another material.

In most crafts, there are procedures you must follow for a well-crafted item. Your creativity is important, too. It will show up in your sensitive use of each medium and your attention to the elements and principles of design.

Designing Your Craftwork

When you create crafts, it is a good idea to plan carefully. Make sketches or models of your ideas. Experiment with materials and processes. These steps will help you plan an effective design. Planning is also important because some craft materials are expensive.

If you are using clay, try several methods of using it before you begin a final work. To plan a large weaving, create a small sample weaving.

Before you begin your final design, review the elements and principles of design in Chapter 3. Use them to think about your choices of colors, textures and other elements. Refer to the principles of design to evaluate how the parts of your design work together.

While you are using a craft material or process, be flexible in your thinking. For example, sometimes a glazed ceramic work will turn out differently than you expect. You may begin a weaving one way but change your mind as you work on it. Always try for a good way to use new ideas or unexpected effects.

Sketches can help you explore design concepts for crafts. Student artwork.

Sarah Nelson, *Unfolding*. Nature is one of many sources of ideas for craftwork. Titanium/copper, photoetched/anodized, 8" x 6" x 6" (20 x 15 x 15 cm). Courtesy of the artist.

Ceramics

Ceramic clay is a wonderful, pliable mixture of earth and water. You can use it to create containers, jewelry, sculpture and other items. Before you work with clay, study the vocabulary, safety rules and concepts in this section.

Ceramic clay has water in it. When a formed piece dries, it is called *greenware*. Greenware is fragile and must be handled with care. When dry clay is baked in a furnace-like oven called a *kiln* (say "KIL"), it becomes hard and strong. This once-fired clay work is called *bisqueware*.

Bisqueware can be made waterproof by adding glaze and refiring the work. In the hot kilns, glazes melt and create a glass-like surface.

Materials and Preparation

You will probably use pre-mixed, moist clay for ceramic work. Other materials include: a workboard, sticks 12" or 18" (30 cm or 46 cm) long and about ¼" to ⅜" (6 mm to 9 mm) thick, a rolling pin or thick dowel, sponges, water containers, an 18" (46 cm) square of cloth, plastic bag (to cover work in progress), slip (liquid clay). Handy tools include a table knife and fork and tools for creating textures (nails, screws, spools, screen wire, shells, a rope).

Air pockets in clay can explode when the work is fired. To remove air pockets you must knead or wedge it. If the clay has cracks, add a little water as you wedge it.

KNEADING. Clay is kneaded like dough. Flatten the clay with your palms. Roll and fold forward about half of the clay nearest to you. Press down on it with your palms to form a new slab. Repeat this process several times.

WEDGING. Form a large ball and cut it in half with wire. Put one half on the wedging board or a strong table covered with cloth. Slam the other half on top of it. Repeat the process until the cut edges have no air pockets and the clay has an even consistency.

Wedging clay. Courtesy of Alice Sprintzen.

Checking the clay for air pockets. Courtesy of Alice Sprintzen.

CERAMICS VOCABULARY

Bisqueware Clay that has been fired once but not glazed.
Engobe A clay slip, white or colored, applied to a leather-hard or bisque-fired work.
Fired Hardened by the high temperature of the kiln.
Glaze A paint-like mixture of finely-ground colored minerals that melt at a high temperature to form a thin, permanent, often glassy surface on clay.
Greenware Dry, unfired clay.
Kiln The furnace-like oven in which the clay is fired.
Kneading Flattening, rolling and folding clay to release air bubbles.
Leather-hard Slightly moist but firm clay that holds its shape.
Sgraffito Italian for "scratched through." A process of scratching through a layer of colored slip so the clay color underneath will show through.
Slip Clay mixed with water to form a thick liquid.
Wedging A process used to release air bubbles from clay by cutting clay in half with a taut wire, then slamming the pieces onto a hard surface.

Mary Barringer, *City Person*, 1988. Stoneware, sgraffito, 11" x 6" x 5" (28 x 15 x 13 cm). Collection of the Berkshire Museum.

A well-crafted pinch pot has even walls.

Rolling out a clay coil. Forming a coil.

Assembling a coil pot. Building a coiled form.

Rolling out a slab.

Joining slabs.

Draping a slab over a mold.

Adding a base to a bowl. Photographs courtesy of Alice Sprintzen.

Handbuilding Techniques

There are several basic ways to shape clay. Try some of the following handbuilding methods.

Pinch Form a fist-sized ball of clay. Insert both thumbs into the ball, pressing down until you have a bottom about ½" (1 cm) thick. Pinch and squeeze the clay to open up the pot. Keep turning the ball in your hands until the bottom and sides are even in thickness. Gently tap the base on the table to flatten it.

How can you decorate the pot? How might you join or combine pinch pots with other clay methods to create a larger work?

Coil Prepare a slab about ½" (1 cm) thick. Cut it into a shape for the base. Roll out coils of clay about ¾" (2 cm) thick. These will be used to build up the sides of the container.

Scratch the edge of the clay slab with a fork. Apply slip on top of the roughened clay. Press the first coil to the base. Blend the coil to the base. Continue building, coil upon coil. Scratch the clay and use slip before you blend the coils together. The coils might become part of the final design.

Slab Place a work-cloth flat on the table. Put the clay on your work-cloth. Place two flat sticks, ¼" to ⅜" (6 mm to 9 mm) thick on each side of the clay. The slab will be as thick as the sticks. Press a rolling pin down on the center of the clay, letting it rest on top of the sticks. Roll it forward then back until the clay is flat.

Your first slab might become a tile. Cut a cardboard pattern. Place it on the clay and cut around it. To cut circles, press the open end of a can straight down into the slab. Create textures or patterns on the tile.

You can assemble several slabs to create cubic forms. Always crosshatch the surface and use slip when you join pieces of clay.

Curved slab An untrimmed slab can be curved in several ways. Always lift and curve the slab by placing your hands under the work-cloth.

Pick up the slab and turn it over onto a mold covered with gauze or damp paper towels. Gently press the slab down. Trim the edges of the wet clay. Allow the slab to dry leather-hard, then lift it off the mold and finish the work.

TECHNIQUE 1. Wrap the untrimmed slab around a paper cylinder to begin a tall vase, bottle or cylinder. Overlap and pinch the edges together. You can also trim the rolled slab for a smooth joint.

TECHNIQUE 2. Find a smooth form (an empty container, an old ball). This will be a mold. Drape a slab of soft clay *over* the mold.

TECHNIQUE 3. Find a shallow bowl, tray or box. Gently press the slab *down* into the mold.

What other clay techniques can you invent? How can you combine and use them in an effective design?

Christine Federighi, *Landscape Chair*. This fanciful slab-based sculpture has a carefully developed landscape created with glaze. Courtesy Esther Saks Gallery, Chicago.

Unknown artist, Hemispherical bowl, mid-fifth millennium BC. The narrow base on this ancient pot means that it was designed to be placed in sand or earth. Notice the variety of incised designs. 7" x 10" (19 x 25 cm). Museum of Art and Archaeology. University of Missouri-Columbia.

Maker unknown, Vase. United States, ca. 1928. Pottery, 5 ³/₄" (15 cm) high. Private collection.

Dorothy Hafner, *Lightning Bolt Punch Bowl*, 1984. Slab tiles with relief and incised elements were assembled for this sculpture. Handbuilt porcelain, underglaze, 8 ¹/₂" x 13" x 13" (22 x 33 x 33 cm).

A variety of objects can be used to create textures. Courtesy of Alice Sprintzen.

Leon Nigrosh, Platter. Wheel-thrown, porcelain, luster, 17" (43 cm) diameter. Courtesy of the artist.

Roman mosaic, 2nd century (detail). The Metropolitan Museum of Art, New York.

Decorating Clay

Clay can be decorated in many ways. You can add small balls or coils of clay to the surface for a relief design. Be sure to score both surfaces and use slip to join the pieces together.

Moist surfaces can be impressed with a variety of tools: a coil of corrugated cardboard, bark, leaves, shells, a comb, a nut, a bolt and the like. Leather-hard clay can be incised or carved.

Your teacher may provide instruction on the use of colored underglaze or *engobe* (colored clay slip). Brush these on or squeeze them from a plastic bottle. Thick engobe leaves a slightly raised line or texture on the surface. In the *sgraffito* method of decoration, you scratch a design into the dry engobe so the color of the clay shows through.

Most glazes can be used only on bisqueware – once-fired clay. You can apply glaze with a large soft brush or dip your clay work into the glaze. You can apply glaze to the whole surface or selected areas. Glazed areas will be waterproof after the clay is refired.

Safety Note Use only lead-free glazes. Avoid breathing dust from clay and dry glaze. Wash your hands thoroughly. If you have a dust allergy, notify your teacher.

Mosaics

Mosaic work is created by adhering small bits of material, called *tesserae,* to a firm support such as wood or Masonite.

Traditional tesserae are glass or small pieces of colored clay tiles. However, tesserae can be almost anything small and sturdy enough to be glued to a support. They might be small pieces of wood, smooth pebbles, flat shells or plastic bottle caps.

After the tesserae are glued down, the spaces around them are usually filled with *grout* – a plaster-like material. Use white glue or a water-resistant (acrylic) adhesive. Read the vocabulary list and understand all safety precautions before you begin.

Fully Planned Design Draw a design on paper the same size as the support. Keep the design simple. Small details are not easily or effectively done in mosaic designs.

Lay out the tesserae on the drawing. Pick up the tesserae one by one and glue them to the support. If your work cannot be completed in one class, slip cardboard under the paper and store the unglued terrerae flat. Cover the unfinished design with wax paper so the wet glue does not stick to another surface.

Roman Mosaic. The subtle shading in this ancient work comes from the careful selection and placement of each tiny piece of colored glass. Reproduced courtesy of The Metropolitan Museum of Art, New York. Gift of J. Pierpont Morgan, 1917.

Nippers are used to cut ceramic tiles into small bits. Nippers must be used with extreme care.

Direct Method This is an excellent way to experiment with mosaic because you can see the design developing as you work. Use a flat-bottomed cardboard container, such as a shoe box lid, at least ¾" (2 cm) deep. Spread glue on the inside of the box. Press the tesserae into the glue, leaving narrow spaces between them. Let the glued tesserae dry overnight.

Mix the grout. Follow all instructions given by your teacher. Gently work the grout down into the cracks with a tongue depressor. Before the grout sets, use a strip of cardboard and a sponge to wipe off the excess grout. Do not try for a perfect cleanup at this time. Let the work stand until the next day. Gently wipe away any residue of grout.

Indirect Method Place a ¼" (6 mm) layer of clean, damp sand in the bottom of a cardboard box at least 1" (3 cm) deep. Press tesserae face down into the sand to a depth of about ⅛" (3 mm).

Mix and slowly pour grout over the tesserae until the grout is at least ¾" (2 cm) thick above them. After the grout sets, peel off the cardboard to expose the front of the mosaic. Brush away the excess sand.

Safety Note If the ceramic tile tesserae must be cut or broken to change their shape, use proper tile nippers and with extreme caution. You must wear safety goggles. It is best to cut the tiles within a box draped with clear plastic cloth. Handle the edges of tile carefully.

Grout is a plaster-like material. It is best to wear rubber gloves. Do not inhale grout dust. Put waste grout inside newspapers and place these in a trashcan. Do not put wet or dry grout in a sink. It will clog pipes.

MOSAIC VOCABULARY

Tesserae Small pieces of material fitted together to form a mosaic design.

Grout A plaster-like filler rubbed into the small spaces between the tesserae.

Support The background on to which you stick the tesserae.

Adhesives Glue, paste, cement or other substances used to stick the tessarae to the support.

Vaquero (Cowboy) Mask. This kind of Mexican mask is used in special dances and festivals for different occupations. This mask honors the work of vaqueros (cowboys) who capture bulls. From "Mexican Masks" by Donald Cordry. Courtesy of the University of Texas at Austin Libraries.

Student art.

Maskmaking

In Western culture, people wear masks for fun at Halloween or for other festive occasions such as the Mardi Gras. However, in many cultures, masks are an important form of art. They are not just a disguise nor always just for fun. Instead, they are used in rituals and ceremonies. Sometimes they are made in secret and worn only by the leaders of special groups. In many cultures, masks are created for traditional plays, dances and festivals. The masks often portray characters in myths or legends.

Spirit masks and costumes are believed to transform the person, giving the wearer special powers. These powers sometimes include the ability to heal people or to give or receive messages from a spirit world.

You might make a "spirit" mask or mask for a story character using papier-mâché. Think of the way a mask helps to disguise and transform the wearer. Your mask might be like a human face but have an exaggerated expression of joy or sorrow. Your mask might be based on the traits of an animal that you admire. Can you think of other ideas for a mask?

There are many ways to begin a mask. You might use a ½" (1 cm) slab of oil-based clay draped over a wad of newspaper. Build up the features and carve into the clay form. Rub a light coat of petroleum jelly over the completed clay. Then cover the clay with at least five layers of papier-mâché. When the papier-mâché is dry, remove the clay and paint the mask with acrylic. Add details with yarn, raffia or other materials.

You might find or make a large cardboard cylinder or box and build up parts with papier-mâché. An inflated balloon can also be an *armature* (support). Other ideas are shown on page 277.

Safety Note Use only wheat paste certified for crafts. Wheat paste made for hanging wallpaper usually contains a pesticide. A safe alternative is white glue diluted with water.

PAPIER-MÂCHÉ VOCABULARY
Armature A support for any sculptural medium.
Papier-mâché A medium of paper and paste. Can be a pulp for modeling or layered strips.
Wheat paste A paste made from wheat flour and water.
Polymer medium A clear plastic suspended in water; it dries to give a water-resistant surface.

Nahua Devil Mask. From "Mexican Masks" by Donald Cordry. Courtesy of the University of Texas at Austin General Libraries.

Papier-mâché Techniques

Wheat paste + water + newsprint or paper towels (mix a "soupy" paste)

1. Apply paste to paper. Roll paper up. Bend and join it. A wire inside the roll is helpful.

2. Tape cartons together. Then cover entire surface with paste-soaked strips of paper.

3. Blow up a balloon. Cover it with papier-mâché. When it dries, remove balloon.

4. Wad up some newspaper. Use oil-based clay on top. Cover it with papier-mâché. When the papier-mâché dries, remove the clay.

5. Soak bits of paper in water overnight. Mix with wheat paste. Model the pulp like clay.

June Linowitz, *Flight of Fancy*, 1985. Mixed Media, 22¼" x 33¼" x 6" (57 x 84 x 15 cm). Courtesy the artist. Photograph by Stacy Duncan.

Jewelry

Jewelry-making is the creation of objects to adorn the body. In many cultures, jewelry is made of gold, silver and precious stones.

In cultures where people live closely with nature, jewelry may include shells, beads, feather, clay or animal bones. Folk jewelry is often made from papier-mâché or found objects such as buttons, wood beads, nuts, bolts, washers and the like.

Types of jewelry include pendants, necklaces, bracelets, earrings, cufflinks and headbands. Other forms of jewelry are fancy buttons, pins, zipper pulls, ornaments for keyrings and other small items.

Approaches to Design

There are two basic ways of thinking about jewelry design. The first is to choose or gather materials, then decide on a type of jewelry, such as a ring or pendant, that fits the materials. The second method is to decide on the kind of jewelry to create, such as a bracelet, then explore design ideas and materials for creating it.

In either approach, you will need to create an effective design. An effective design will be practical (the jewelry can be worn or used) and it will fit the personality of the person for whom it is made.

You may want to experiment with ideas and media. Detailed plans are important if the materials you are using are costly. Here are some ideas to consider.

Media and Processes

WIRE. You can use many kinds of wire: floral, thin insulated telephone wire, stovepipe, copper, aluminum, or nickel silver wire. (Nickel silver can regularly be worn next to the skin; copper and aluminum cannot). Try bending the wire, wrapping it around colorful stones, coiling it around a dowel and cutting the coil into links.

METAL FOIL AND FOUND OBJECTS. Make shapes from thick cardboard and cover them with heavy-duty aluminum foil. Stain the foil with India ink. Combine the shapes with wire or string links.

Collect aluminum pull-off tabs from cans or other ready-made metal shapes (washers, bolts, bottlecaps). Smooth the edges with files or emery paper. Sort the units so they contrast or are graduated in size or shape. Link or string them together.

WOOD. With simple hand tools – a drill, files, coping saw – shape pieces of wood into jewelry. Find or cut related shapes for bracelets, belts or necklaces. File or drill patterns into the surface of each piece. Try combining wood with ceramic or metal forms.

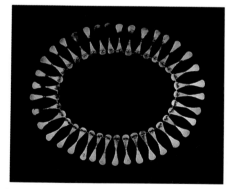

Alexander Calder, *Necklace*, 1941. Hammered silver, inner circumference 26" (66 cm), outer circumference 34" (86 cm). Collection, Museum of Modern Art, new York. James Thrall Soby Fund.

What qualities of shape make this an effective design? Student art.

Nadia Farag Radwan, *Scarab*. Egyptian paste is a form of clay with glaze in it. A scarab is a form of beetle regarded as sacred in ancient Egypt. Scarabs are used in rings, pendants and other forms of jewelry. Egyptian paste; carved, $^3/_4$" x $1^1/_2$" x 1" (1.9 x 3.1 x 2.5 cm). Photograph by J. Russell.

CERAMIC CLAY OR EGYPTIAN PASTE. Egyptian paste is a special ceramic clay mixed with colorful glaze. It is fired once to bring out the color of the clay and glaze. After the ceramic clay is fired, you can stain it with acrylic. You might glaze and refire it. You could also use self-hardening and oven-bake clays (from craft shops). Paint these with acrylic.

Create small clay tiles, beads or other shapes for pendants, earrings or necklaces. Develop the design by carving or pressing into the surface. Make sure any holes for thread or wire are made before the work is fired.

PAPER. Papier-mâché, paper pulp and laminated (layered) paper can be used for jewelry. For papier-mâché, you might begin with cardboard shapes. Soak string or small strips of paper towels in diluted white glue and build up areas. Cover the built-up areas with papier-mâché.

Paper pulp can be shaped into beads, cubes or other forms. Before the pulp dries, press holes through the pieces with a toothpick. Allow the beads to dry on wax paper, then decorate them.

For laminated paper, cut flat circles, triangles or other shapes. Colorful pictures in old magazines can be used. Cover one side with white glue and roll them tightly around a soda straw or toothpick. Remove the straw or toothpick. String the dry pieces together.

You might decorate paper jewelry with paint or colored tissue and diluted white glue. Seal the whole surface with polymer medium.

CLAY PRESS MOLDS. A press mold is used to create small, identical forms in clay. These can be used for jewelry or buttons. You can also decorate clay pots with the small clay pieces.

Use a shallow cardboard box about 2" (6 cm) deep. A cut-down milk carton is excellent. Create a relief design in oil-based clay that fits flat in the center of the box. Avoid having undercuts in your clay design. An *undercut* is a ledge with space under it.

Mix and pour plaster into the box so your design is covered by at least 1" (3 cm) of plaster. When the plaster sets, remove the oil-based clay. Let the mold dry for a day or two.

Press soft ceramic clay into the mold. Allow the clay to stiffen slightly before removing it. Twist a wet toothpick into the clay pieces so they can be used for jewelry.

JEWELRY VOCABULARY
Jewelry Objects created to adorn the body.
Graduated Changing gradually.
Coping saw A C-shaped saw that holds a thin steel sawblade.
Egyptian paste Ceramic clay mixed with glaze.

(Above) Disk-like forms were created and arranged to create a rhythmic design for a necklace. (Below) The fruit and vegetables on this necklace are made from papier-mâché.

Didi Suydam, Squid, Tetra, Swordtail Brooches. Courtesy the artist.

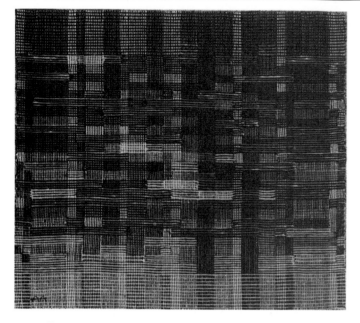

Anni Albers, *Tapestry*, 1948. Albers is known as one of the pioneers of weaving as a fine art. Subtle colors and textures are featured in this work. Handwoven, linen and cotton, 16 ½" x 18 ¾" (42 x 48 cm). Collection, The Museum of Modern Art, New York. Edgar Kaufman, Jr. Purchase Fund.

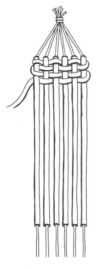

A straw loom.

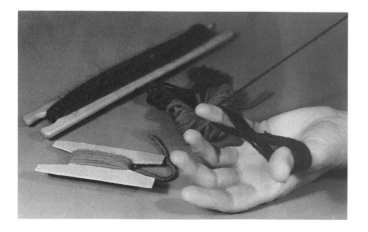

Yarn is wound in a figure eight around the thumb and pinkie. When tied, this bundle can be woven without getting tangled. Weft can be wrapped around a shuttle.

Fiber Arts

Fiber arts are made from cloth and other materials that are thin, long and flexible. Weaving, quilting, stitchery and appliqué are among many fiber arts. Embroidery, knitting and braiding are other examples. A sample of fiber arts is presented here: weaving, stitchery, macrame, batik and tie dye.

Weaving

Weaving is usually considered a practical craft – made to serve a purpose. It can also be a form of expression similar to a painting or sculpture.

All weaving is a process of interlocking yarn or thread-like materials. The supporting yarns are called the *warp*. The *weft* yarns are woven across the warp in a pattern.

Because there are so many approaches and materials, you might want to try some small experimental pieces first. Use your experiments to explore line, space, color, texture and other aspects of design. Try unravelling or pulling out some of the threads in coarsely woven materials such as burlap. Create open patterns. Group and tie together some of the remaining warp or weft threads. Add some stitched elements, feathers and other attractive items to the design.

Straw Loom Cut six pieces of yarn longer than the length of the final band by about one-half. For a band 12" (30 cm) long, cut pieces 18" (46 cm) long. Cut three soda straws in half. Thread the yarn through the straws.

Knot all the yarns together firmly at one end. Press the straws tightly against the knot. Weave over and under the straws. Press the rows of weft threads down tightly.

When the straws are half-covered, push the woven part up and pull the straws down. Continue weaving. To change colors of the weft, tie the new yarn to the piece you are weaving. Try weaving two colors of weft at the same time.

When the weaving is finished, remove the straws and tie the loose ends together. You might use two round metal key rings for a buckle. Tie both rings to the same end.

Cardboard Loom Try a small weaving about 8" x 10" (20 cm x 25 cm) as a practice piece. Cut an odd number of notches about ¼" (6 mm) apart and ¼" (6 mm) deep along the top and bottom of stiff cardboard. Use a single long warp thread. Tape about 4" (10 cm) of the warp to the back of the cardboard.

String the warp through the upper left notch. Pull the warp down to the bottom left notch and across to the second notch at the bottom. Go back to the second notch at the top, across to the third notch, then down. Your warp threads should be parallel. Continue this process across the loom. Tie the two ends of the warp together on the back of the cardboard.

Make a simple *shuttle* (a holder for the weft thread) from stiff cardboard. Notch each end and wrap about 6' (2 m) of weft around it. To keep a straight *selvedge* (edge of fabric), leave a ⅛" (3 cm) loop of weft at the left and right margins as you weave.

To weave a pouch or purse, warp the loom on both sides. Weave continuously around both edges of the cardboard. You can also weave on a cardboard circle, cylinder or shoe box.

Wood Loom Use an old picture frame, canvas stretchers or build a wood frame. Hammer an odd number of nails at ¼" (6 mm) intervals across the top and bottom. Make sure they are in a straight row.

Tie one end of the warp to the first nail, leaving about 6" (15 cm) of extra yarn at one end of the knot. Pull the warp back and forth around the nails so the yarn is parallel. Tie the yarn to the last nail. As you weave, pack the weft down.

A wooden box, open on one or both sides, can also be used as a loom. Instead of using nails, you can saw grooves into the wood as guides for the warp threads.

WEAVING VOCABULARY

Loom Supporting framework for the warp.
Selvedge Edge of fabric where the weft is turned to weave to the opposite edge.
Shuttle Holder for the weft thread; it leads the weft through the warp.
Warp Threads that support the weft.
Weft Thread or other material that goes over and under the warp from side to side.
Shed A separation of warp threads that permits you to rapidly place a weft thread across the warp threads.

Wood frame loom. This box loom has grooves that support the weft.

Types of weaves. Courtesy of Alice Sprintzen.

Twining

Soumak

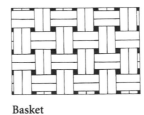

Basket

Rya

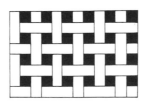

Plain

Seminole, Woven Sash, 1860. The Seminole people of Florida have a long tradition of creating elaborately woven sashes for ceremonial attire. Wool. Museum of the American Indian. Heye Foundation.

A hoop is the loom for this textural free-form weaving. Found object looms can be used as part of the final work. Student art.

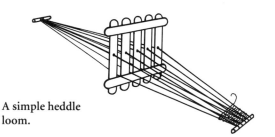

A simple heddle loom.

A Simple Heddle Loom A heddle loom will allow you to lift up or push down alternating threads. The up or down motion of the heddle creates a shed – a separation between sets of threads. The shed lets you place weft threads across the warp threads in one stroke.

Make a simple heddle loom from eight tongue depressors. Drill a ⅛" (6 mm) hole in the center of six of them. Use the other two to join the six pieces at the top and bottom with white glue. Leave ⅛" (6 mm) of space between the sticks.

Cut eleven warp threads twice as long as you want the finished piece to be. Thread the warp threads through the drilled holes in the heddle and the ⅛" (3 mm) spaces between the sticks. Gather the last 4" (10 cm) of the warp threads and tie them together in a large knot.

Anchor the knot at one end to a stationery object. Hook the other knot to a belt or rope around your waist. Lean back to make the warp threads taut.

Lift the heddle and place a strip of paper in the shed. Press the heddle down and place a second paper strip in the shed. The paper helps to straighten the warp threads. Begin weaving.

End the weaving with two paper strips. To finish the work, remove the paper and tie each warp thread to the next one. Can you invent a heddle for other looms?

Found Object Looms You can weave yarns and fibers through the open mesh of vegetable sacks, wire mesh or other coarsely woven materials. Tree limbs at least ½" (1 cm) thick can be trimmed to create a loom. Try weaving across a tree branch that has two or three connected branches.

Chris Roberts-Antieau, *Rabbit on a Bike*. Selecting fabrics for an appliqué is an important step in developing an effective design. 27" x 30" (69 x 76 cm). Courtesy Ferrin Gallery, Northampton, Massachusetts.

Palestinian Embroidery. This embroidered wall hanging has a variety of patterned areas, textural effects and qualities of line.

Types of stitches

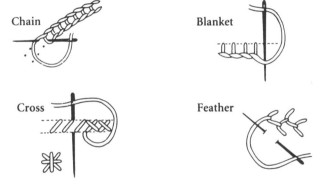

Running
Plain

Satin

Chain

Blanket

Threaded

Outline

Cross

Feather

Stitchery

Stitchery is created with a needle and thread, yarn or related materials. Stitching can be used to create banners, wall hangings and pillows. You can also customize clothing such as a vest, hat or purse. Decorations such as beads, buttons, old jewelry or fringe can be added.

A *quilt* is two layers of cloth stitched together, with padding between the layers. An *appliqué* is like a collage: pieces of fabric are stitched to a background.

A background of burlap or other loosely woven fabric is best for most work. For appliqué, collect a variety of scraps of cloth. Have on hand large-eye tapestry needles as well as yarns and threads in a variety of colors, textures and weights.

Practice some of the stitches shown above. Plan your design. Then sketch the main shapes on burlap as simple guidelines (not stitch-by-stitch plans).

Try ideas with stitchery just as you would in any other art medium. Try a variety of yarns – different colors, sizes, textures – and background fabrics.

Try using stitches to make lines or outlines of shapes, like a linear drawing. Try a painterly approach by placing yarn in patterns and stitching them down.

Try a sculptural approach to fabric work by using quilting. For padding, use cotton or soft fabric scraps. Use thick yarns or cloth appliqué to fill solid areas.

STITCHERY VOCABULARY

Appliqué Artwork created by stitching pieces of cloth to a background.
Quilting Artwork created by stitching two layers of cloth with padding between the layers.
Tapestry needle A needle with a large eye, usually with a blunt point.

Macramé

Macramé is a form of weaving based on knotting cords, thick yarn, jute or rope. It came from the craft of making fishnets. During the late nineteenth century it became popular as a fringe on fabrics.

The cords are tied to an *armature* – a supporting dowel, stick, ring or holding cord. Cut the cords three to four times longer than your finished work will be.

It is helpful to have straight pins and a workboard of ³/₄" (2 cm) styrofoam covered with cloth. For a practice piece, cut 12 or 18 lengths of cord about 8' (3 m) long. The number of cords determines the width of your design.

Fasten the armature to the top of your workboard. Find the middle of one knotting cord and loop it around the armature. Pull the two ends through the loop and tighten the knots. Repeat this with each cord.

Pin each knot to the board and begin tying other knots. Always hold the knot-bearing cord taut.

Create patterns by changing the type of knots, grouping the cords into sections, or knotting two or more cords at a time (as though they were one cord). You might leave open (unknotted) spaces or add beads, feathers or shells to your work.

MACRAMÉ VOCABULARY

Armature A supporting rod, cord or similar device to hold knotting cords.
Lark's head knot The knot commonly attached to the armature.
Knot-bearing cord Similar to a warp thread; the cord held tight when you tie a knot.

Batik

Batik is a method of decorating cloth developed in Indonesia. It is a resist process of creating designs on fabric using dyes and wax (paraffin and beeswax). Melted wax is applied to cloth with a brush, found objects or a tjanting tool.

The partially waxed cloth is placed in dye. The dye soaks into the unwaxed areas of the cloth. These steps can be repeated with dyes of different colors. Dyes are applied in a light to dark order (yellow, then red, then blue).

The final design typically has a fine linear crackle. The crackle is caused when dye seeps into tiny cracks in the wax.

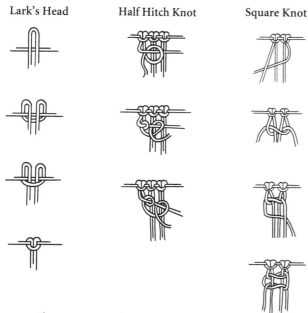

Lark's Head   Half Hitch Knot   Square Knot

Alternate Rows of Square Knots

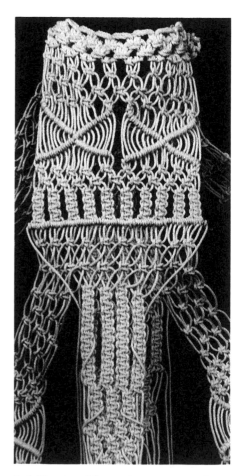

Jack Dunston, Macramé overgarment. A circular armature was used to begin this macramé sculpture. Notice the planned use of open areas. Saratoga, California.

Wax crayon method Tape the cloth to stiff cardboard covered with newspaper. Place unwrapped broken crayons of the same color in each section of a muffin tin. Put the muffin tin in a pan of water on a hot plate set on the lowest temperature.

As the water heats, the crayons will melt. Apply each color with a different brush. Leave some areas unpainted. Remove the cloth. Fold or ball it up to create fine cracks in the wax. Dye, then rinse the cloth and let it dry.

Place the dry cloth between newsprint paper, with a pad of newspapers underneath. Press it with a warm iron. The paper will absorb the wax. Repeat this step with fresh paper. Do not launder batik with other clothing. The dye may not be permanent.

Safety Note Wax batik. Never heat wax directly over a fire or heat source. It might cause a fire. Always heat wax in a container placed in water. Do not allow water to drop into a container of hot wax. The hot wax might splatter. Some dyes are harmful. Use only liquid household dye in a stainless steel bowl or plastic bucket large enough to hold the fabric. Wear rubber gloves or stir the cloth with a stick. Always rest an iron upright on the heel.

Bleach-batik method Use a solid-colored cotton cloth. Draw on the cloth with wax crayons. Use a heavy pressure. Place the cloth between newsprint paper. Press it with a warm iron until the wax penetrates the cloth. Dip the cloth in a half-and-half solution of water and liquid bleach. Areas of the cloth not protected by the wax will whiten.

BATIK AND TIE-DYE VOCABULARY

Resist process Any process in which one material does not fully blend with another.

Dye A chemical that penetrates into a material (instead of staying on the surface).

Wax A water-resistant substance made by bees or as a petroleum by-product.

Crackle An irregular network of fine crack-like lines.

Tjanting tool Tool with a small bowl and spout for pouring hot wax.

Student art.

Sarong (border details). This detail of a fabric design shows the highly developed design qualities in traditional Javanese batiks. Batik on cotton from Java, 20th century.

Tie-Dye

Tie-dye is an ancient technique of decorating cloth, developed into an art form in Indonesia and Africa. The cloth is folded into sections. The sections are tightly tied with string. Smooth stones or sticks may be tied inside the sections. The dye soaks into the untied sections.

After the cloth dries, the string is removed. The design combines accidental and planned effects.

Try some experiments first on plain cotton fabric. Use only liquid household dyes. Follow safety precautions. Perhaps you can tie-dye an old blouse, sheet, apron or pillowcase. You might tie-dye an old sheet, then cut and sew it into a vest, blouse or bookbag.

Tie-bleach is a variation on tie-dye. You begin with cotton cloth of a solid color. Tie the cloth and dip it in a half-and-half solution of bleach and water.

Safety Note Bleach batik and tie-dye. Fumes from bleach can irritate your eyes, lungs and open sores. Be sure the area is well ventilated. Wear rubber gloves or use tongs. Wear an apron to protect your clothes.

Can you identify some of the tie-dyed effects in this work? Courtesy of Victoria Hughes.

A tightly-pulled running stitch can be used to gather material for tie-dyeing. Courtesy of Alice Sprintzen.

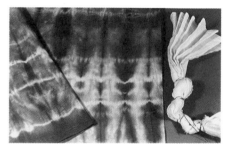

A pleated fabric can be bound tightly for tie-dyeing. Courtesy of Alice Sprintzen.

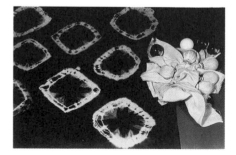

Small water proof objects can be tightly tied into fabric sections for tie-dyeing. Student art.

Student art.

Student art.

Student art.

Student art.

287

Student art.

Student art.

Student art.

Student art.

Summary

The crafts are often called the oldest forms of art. They are handmade objects made from clay, fiber, metal, wood and related materials. They were originally developed as useful items. They can also be expressive art.

In some cultures today, handcrafts are practiced just as they were hundreds of years ago. In other cultures, the traditional designs in the crafts have been altered by trade and international travel.

The Industrial Revolution changed the status of the crafts. Many people preferred to own low-cost factory-made things. There was less demand for handcrafted objects. For a time, the crafts became "luxury items" created for wealthy people.

Today, the crafts are appreciated by many people. Unlike mass-produced items, the crafts are made by hand. They often have unique designs and always display the skill of the craftsworker.

Crafts media and processes are being explored by many contemporary artists. Traditional crafts are being revitalized in many cultures. Many people enjoy the range of craftwork being produced today.

Using What You Learned

Art History

1 Explain two ways the Industrial Revolution affected how people valued the crafts.

2 Give two reasons cultural groups might have modified their traditional crafts designs or processes.

3 For what kind of craftwork is María Martínez known?

4 How does a spirit mask differ from a mask made and worn just for fun?

5 In what country is batik a traditional and highly developed craft?

Aesthetics and Criticism

1 Most crafts use many technical terms. Select one of the crafts in which you have worked. List the main technical terms and use each one correctly in a sentence.

2 Select one work of art in this chapter. Describe how it might have been made. Use appropriate technical terms in your description.

3 In your own words, explain why a knowledge of technical terms for crafts can be useful to you now and in the future.

Creating Art and Art Criticism

1 Select one of your most effective works in a craft. State at least three criteria you have used in judging it. Describe the specific qualities in your work (sensory, design, technical, expressive) that fit your criteria.

2 The *process* of creating in a craft medium can be as satisfying as the final *product*. Which craft medium did you find most satisfying to use? Why?

3 Problem-solving is an important part of almost all work in crafts. Describe at least one problem you encountered and solved while working in a craft medium.

Glossary

abstract An abstract artwork is usually based on a subject you can identify. The artist leaves out details, simplifies, or rearranges some elements so that you may not recognize them. Abstract work based on a subject which you may not be able to recognize is called *nonobjective* art.

academic A general term for artworks that seem to be based on rules set up by some person or group other than the artist. Artists created academic artwork by following rigid rules made by leaders of European art schools or academies in the 1700s and 1800s.

acrylic (a-CRILL-ik) A paint which uses liquid acrylic plastic to hold the color or pigments together. It is similar to oil paint but acrylic can dissolve in water before it dries.

active Expressing movement. Opposite of static.

actual Anything you can perceive through the senses. Lines, shapes, textures or other elements you can sense. (See *implied*.)

adhesive (add-HEE-siv) Glue or other sticky substance used to join materials together.

advertising Communications meant to convince an audience to do or buy something.

aesthetic judgment (es-THET-ik JUDGE-ment) An opinion about art based on whether or not the art produces an aesthetic response. (See *aesthetic perception*.)

aesthetic perception (es-THET-ik per-SEP-shun) A response to art or the environment involving positive thoughts, sensations and feelings.

afterimage A sensation in the eye and brain created by looking at a color for a long period of time. Afterimages appear as complementary colors. If you stare at something red, the afterimage is green.

allover A pattern that covers an entire surface, from one border to another.

alternating A form of visual rhythm created in an artwork by repeating two or more different artistic elements, one beside or near the other.

American Scene Painters 1910-1950. An art history term for artists who portrayed American life in a direct, simple manner.

analogous (an-AL-o-gus) Colors that are closely related because they have one hue in common. For example, blue, blue-violet, and violet all contain the color blue. Analogous colors appear next to one another on the color wheel.

appliqué (ah-plee-KAY) A process of stitching and/or gluing cloth to a background, similar to collage.

architect A person who has been trained to design buildings or communities.

architecture The art of designing and planning the construction of buildings, cities and bridges.

armature (ARM-a-chur) A skeleton-like framework used to support other materials.

art criticism The process and the result of thinking carefully about art. Art criticism involves the description, analysis and interpretation of art. It does not always include a stated judgment of worth or value.

Art Nouveau (art new-VOH) 1900-1915. Means "New Art." A style of art based on the use of curved, plant-like forms. Artists working in this style especially liked the linear qualities of vines.

artisan A person skilled in creating handmade objects.

Ashcan School 1908-1914. American artists who painted pictures of city life, especially alleys, old apartment buildings and people living in slums. The group's original name was "The Eight."

assemblage A three-dimensional work of art consisting of many pieces joined together. Art made by combining a collection of three-dimensional objects into a whole.

asymmetrical A type of visual balance in which the two sides of a composition are different yet balanced. The two sides are equal without being just the same. Also called *informal balance*.

background Parts of artwork that appear to be in the distance or behind the objects in the foreground or front.

balance A principle of design that describes the arrangement of parts of an artwork. An artwork that is balanced seems to have equal visual weight or interest in all areas. It seems stable.

Baroque (bah-ROKE) 1600-1700. Baroque is an art history term for a style marked by swirling curves, many ornate elements and dramatic contrasts of light and shade. Artists used these effects to express energy and strong emotions.

bas-relief (bah ree-LEEF) Also called *low relief*. A form of sculpture in which portions of the design stand out slightly from a flat background.

batik (bah-TEEK) A method of dyeing cloth that involves the use of wax to prevent dye from coloring certain areas of material. Wax is brushed on parts of the design where the color of a dye is not wanted.

Bauhaus (BOW-house) 1918-1933. A German art school that stressed the need, in an industrial time, to join science, technology, fine art and craft.

Benin Kingdom (ben-een KING-dom) A former kingdom of western Africa whose artists achieved a high level of quality, especially in bronze casting.

bisque (bisk) Ceramic that has been fired once but not glazed.

block In printmaking, a piece of flat material such as wood, linoleum or metal used to make a print. In sculpture, any solid material that can be used for carving.

block printing The process of making prints by creating a raised design on a flat surface. The design is inked or covered with color and stamped on a surface such as paper or cloth.

brayer A small, hand-held rubber roller used to spread printing ink evenly on a surface before printing.

brushstroke A line, shape or texture created by putting paint on a surface with a paint brush.

burnish To smooth a surface by rubbing it with a tool that has a hard, smooth surface.

Byzantine (BIZ-ann-teen) 300-1500. An art history term for a style that blended Roman, Greek and Oriental influences. It developed in the Eastern Roman Empire (called Byzantium). It includes rich color (especially gold), flat, stiff figures, and religious themes. An example is Hagia Sophia in Constantinople, now called Istanbul, Turkey.

calligraphy (cah-LIH-grah-fee) Flowing lines made with brushstrokes similar to Oriental writing. It is also the art of using a pen or brushes to write beautiful letters and words.

caricature A picture in which a person's or an animal's features, such as nose, ears or mouth, are different, bigger or smaller than they really are. Caricatures can be funny or critical and are often used in political cartoons.

cartoon A full-sized drawing used as a plan for a painting, especially for a mural. A cartoon can also be a funny drawing that tells a story.

cast The process of reproducing an object, such as sculpture or jewelry, by creating a mold into which liquid plaster, concrete or metal is poured. A cast is also the object produced by this process.

center of interest The part of an artwork which attracts the viewer's eye. Usually the most important part of a work of art.

ceramics (sir-A-miks) The art of making objects from clay, glass or other minerals by baking or firing them at high temperatures in an oven known as a kiln. Ceramics are also the products made in this way.

charcoal A soft drawing material made from charred wood or vines.

chiaroscuro (key-AH-ro-SKUH-ro) An Italian word meaning light and shadow. In two-dimensional art, chiaroscuro is the gradual or sharp contrasts in value that make something look three-dimensional. Chiaroscuro is also called *modeling* and *shading*.

chroma (CROW-mah) The intensity of a color—the brightness of a hue.

cityscape An artwork that uses elements of the city (buildings, streets, shops) as subject matter.

classical An art history term for any art inspired or influenced by ancient Greek or Roman art. Classical works usually have perfect form and proportion. They show little emotion, and seem ideal rather than real.

collage (coh-LAZH) A work of art created by gluing bits of paper, fabric, scraps, photographs or other materials to a flat surface.

collagraph A print made from a surface that has been built up like a collage.

color See *hue*.

color scheme A plan for selecting or organizing colors. Common color schemes include: warm, cool, neutral, monochromatic, analogous, complementary, split-complementary and triad.

color spectrum A band of colors produced when white light shines through a prism. The prism separates the light into different wavelengths. Visible colors are always seen in the same order, from longest wavelength to shortest: red, orange, yellow, green, blue, violet. A rainbow displays the color spectrum which we can see. A color wheel shows the spectrum arranged in a circle.

color wheel A circular chart of colors of the visible spectrum. It is commonly used to remember color relationships when working with pigments.

combine painting Artwork created by mixing together or combining flat, painted surfaces with three-dimensional objects.

complementary Colors that are directly opposite each other on the color wheel, such as red and green, blue and orange, and violet and yellow. When complements are mixed together, they make a neutral brown or gray. When they are used next to each other in a work of art, they create strong contrasts.

composition To create, form or design something by arranging separate parts to create a whole.

computer drawing program Software used to create drawings on the computer.

concave A form that has a hollow area like the inside of a bowl.

conceptual art Artwork in which the concept or idea is more important than the technique or material used to create it.

Constructivism 1917-1920. A style of three-dimensional art that uses industrial materials such as metal, glass and plastic to create abstract art.

contour A line which shows or describes the edges, ridges or outline of a shape or form

contour drawing A drawing which uses only contour lines.

contrast A large difference between two things: for example, rough and smooth, yellow and purple, and light and shadow. Contrasts usually add excitement, drama and interest to artworks.

converging lines Actual or implied lines that seem to point toward a central place in space. A technique related to linear perspective.

convex A form with a raised surface, like the outside of a bowl or hill.

cool colors Colors often connected with cool places, things or feelings. The family of colors ranging from the greens through the blues and violets.

corporate identity program In graphic design, the design of visual elements, including a logo, used consistently to identify the products and services of a company.

crackle Fine lines formed in a surface, usually while using a specific material and technique.

crafts Works of art, decorative or useful, that are skillfully made by hand.

craftsworker A person highly skilled in creating useful or decorative artwork by hand. An artist who designs and creates useful objects such as textiles, ceramics and jewelry.

crayon etching A technique in which crayon is applied heavily to a surface then covered with more crayon or an opaque ink or paint. Designs are scratched (etched) through the covering material to show the crayon below.

crayon resist A drawing made with wax crayon and covered with a thin coat of paint. Since water does not stick to wax, the paint will not cover the crayoned part.

criteria for judging art Standards for art that you can state to others. The standards are not strong personal opinions or vague preferences.

Cubism 1907-1914. An art history term for a style developed by the artists Picasso and Braque. In cubism, the subject matter is broken up into geometric shapes and forms. The forms are analyzed and then put back together into an abstract composition. Often, three-dimensional objects seem to be shown from many different points of view at the same time.

Dada (DAH-dah) 1915-1923. An art movement in which artists created work based on chance. These artists often used ready-made objects to create new art forms. They are also known for having criticized contemporary culture. Many artists involved in the Dada movement became leaders of Surrealism and other new styles of art.

De Stijl (day SHTEEL) 1917-1932. Dutch for "the style." A style developed by Piet Mondrian and other artists. They believed that pure abstract art should be based only on vertical (up and down) and horizontal (side to side) flat areas, and the three primary colors with black, white, gray.

decalcomania (dee-CAL-co-may-nee-ah) A technique of creating random texture patterns. Thick paint is applied to the front of two papers or canvases. The painted surfaces are pressed together and then pulled apart, leaving a textured pattern.

deckle The upper frame of a mold used in hand-forming a sheet of paper. The deckle determines the shape of the paper.

Der Blaue Reiter (dehr BLAH-way RIGHT-er) 1911-1914. German for "the Blue Rider." This name was adopted by a group of European artists who explored the spiritual and expressive meanings of color in painting. The artist Kandinsky used this name for the title of a painting.

design The plan, organization or arrangement of elements in a work of art.

diagonal A direction that a line can have. Diagonal lines may be used to show motion.

Die Brücke (dee BROOK-eh) 1905-1913. German for "the bridge." This group of artists developed a bold, expressionistic style of art, often borrowing design ideas from art created by children or self-taught adults.

dimension A term used in art for actual measurements of length, width and depth. These measurements are used to distinguish between flat or two-dimensional art (such as drawing or painting) and three-dimensional art (such as sculpture and architecture).

docent (DOE-sent) A teacher-guide who leads people through a museum.

dominant The part of an artwork that is most important, powerful or has the most influence on the viewer.

dry media Pencil, chalk, crayon and other media that are not wet and do not require the use of a liquid.

drypoint A method of intaglio printing in which the image is scratched into the surface of the printing plate with a steel needle. The print is also called a drypoint. The lines and tones in the printed image often look very soft.

dye A colored liquid that soaks into a material and stains it.

dye-bath In batik, a container filled with enough dye to stain a fabric soaked in it.

Early Christian art 31-400 AD. Art created by the first Christians, especially in the area around Rome.

Earth/Land Art Sculpture in which land and earth are important as ideas or used as a media for expression.

earthenware A coarse pottery which tends to absorb moisture. Earthenware is usually buff or reddish, and has been fired at a low temperature.

earthwork Any work of art in which land and earth are important media.

eclectic (ek-leck-tik) Art that combines elements from different styles.

edition In printmaking, the total number of impressions or prints made at one time and in the same way from the same block or plate.

elements of art/design The visual "tools" artists use to create art. The elements (categories) include color, value, line, shape, form, texture and space.

Emotionalism A theory of art which values communication of moods, feelings and ideas.

emphasis Area in a work of art that catches and holds the viewer's attention. This area usually has contrasting sizes, shapes, colors or other distinctive features.

engobe (en-GO-bee) A colored clay slip put on leather-hard or bisque-fired ceramics as a form of decoration.

engraving The process of using a sharp tool to cut a design into a material, usually metal. Engraving is also an intaglio printmaking process based on cutting grooves into a metal or wood surface.

environment The surrounding area in which we live. The environment includes the natural world and all of the elements that people have constructed, changed or added.

etching An intaglio printmaking process. The image is made by coating the surface of a metal plate, scratching through the coating, then placing the plate in acid. The acid burns through the scratched lines, making grooves in the metal that can hold ink.

exhibit A temporary show or display of a group of artworks.

expressionism A style of art in which the main idea is to show a definite or strong mood or feeling. If written with a capital E, Expressionism is a definite style of art which was created mostly in Germany, from about 1890 to 1920.

expressive qualities The feelings, moods and ideas communicated to the viewer through a work of art.

Fantasy art Artwork that is meant to look unreal, strange or dream-like.

Fauves (fohv) 1905-1907. French for "wild beasts." A group of painters who used brilliant colors and bold distortions in a surprising way. Henri Matisse was the leading artist of the Fauves.

fiber artists Artists who use long, thin, thread-like materials to create artwork.

figure A general term for any shape or form that we see as separate from a background. A figure is also a human form in a work of art.

fine art Art that is valued for its design, its ideas and the kind of feeling it creates in viewers.

firing In ceramics, the process of placing a clay object in high heat in order to harden it permanently. This process usually happens in an oven called a kiln.

fixative A thin liquid applied to a surface to prevent the smearing, flaking or fading of a medium, or to give a permanent finish.

focal point An area of an artwork that attracts the viewer's attention.

folk art Traditional art made by people who have not had art training in a school. Folk artists may use art styles and techniques that artists have taught each other for many years.

foreground In a scene or artwork, the part that seems closest to you.

form Any three-dimensional object. A form can be measured from top to bottom (height), side to side (width) and front to back (depth). Form is also a general term that means the structure or design of a work. (See *form follows function.*)

form follows function A summary of this idea: The design of a useful artwork should come from (and express) the practical use of the work.

formal balance Artwork in which the parts are arranged in about the same way on both sides, like a mirror image. Formal balance is also called *symmetrical* design.

formal order A theory of art developed by Clive Bell and Roger Fry in the early twentieth-century. Formal order is also known as formalism. In this theory, the visual design of an artwork is more important than its subject matter.

formal qualities The structural qualities of an artwork, usually described using the principles of design.

free-form A term for irregular and uneven shapes or forms. Something that is free-form may be difficult to describe in simple shapes or measurements.

freehand A drawing done without tracing paper or drawing tools such as a ruler or compass.

freestanding A sculpture that does not need a special base or platform to support it.

fresco (FRES-coh) A technique of painting in which pigments are applied to a thin layer of wet plaster. The plaster absorbs the pigments and the painting becomes part of the wall.

frottage (froh-TAZH) A method of reproducing textures by rubbing crayon over paper placed on a textured surface. In painting, textures are made by scraping a freshly painted canvas that has been placed over a textured surface.

Futurism 1909-1914. A style named by Italian artists to describe their interest in the future. Futurists were especially interested in the force of motion at high speed (dynamism) and rapid changes in technology in the twentieth-century.

gauge (gage) A system for measuring the thickness of metal. A higher number means a thinner metal.

genre (ZHA-nra) Subjects and scenes from everyday life.

geometric Mechanical-looking shapes or forms. Something that is geometric may also be described using mathematical formulas. Geometric shapes include circles, squares, rectangles, triangles and ellipses. Geometric forms include cones, cubes, cylinders, slabs, pyramids and spheres.

gesture drawing A quick drawing to show movement.

glaze In painting, a thin layer of transparent paint. In ceramics, a thin coating of minerals fused to clay by firing. Glaze creates a permanent, glassy surface on clay.

Golden Section or **Mean** A ratio (relationship of parts) discovered by Euclid, a Greek Philosopher. When this ratio was rediscovered in the early 1500s it was named the Divine Proportion. Many organic objects have a form described by the ratio.

Gothic Art 1100-1400. A period of change in art in Europe during the late Middle Ages. People began to develop cities and trade with each other. The cities were often built near a large cathedral.

gouache (gwash) An opaque watercolor made from pigments ground in water and mixed with a binder. Gouache looks like school tempera or poster paint.

gradation A gradual, smooth change, as in from light to dark, from rough to smooth, or from one color to another.

graphic design A general term for artwork in which letter forms (writing, typography) are important and carefully placed visual elements.

graphic designer An artist whose knowledge of letter forms (writing, typography) is an important part of the artwork.

Greek Revival A style of art, especially in architecture and sculpture, in which there are elements of ancient Greek art.

greenware Dry, unfired clay artwork or pottery.

grog Ground or crushed fired clay that is added to unfired clay. Grog is used for texture, strength, and often to reduce shrinking and bending.

grottage (grow-TAZH) The technique of scratching into wet ink or paint to create different textures. A variety of tools can be used, including forks and combs.

ground The background of an artwork. A ground is also the surface on which two-dimensional artwork is done, such as paper, canvas or cardboard.

grout A fine cement or plaster used to fill the space between tesserae in a mosaic.

happening A form of performance or event, developed by Allan Kaprow and others during the 1960s. In a happening, there is a plan for unexpected events, or for people to be involved in a natural, unthinking way.

Hard-Edged Painting A style of twentieth-century painting with sharp, definite edges. The values and colors are usually even and flat.

harmony The placement of elements of a composition in a way that is pleasing to the eye. It is similar to a pleasing harmony in music.

Heritage-Based Art A general term for art strongly influenced by the artist's way of life and beliefs, given him or her by a parent, family member or community.

hieroglyphics (hi-row-GLIPH-icks) Picture writing, especially that used by ancient Egyptians.

high relief Sculpture in which areas project far out from a flat surface.

High Tech Art A general term for artwork inspired by technology and using new technologies as art media.

high-key painting A painting using many tints of a single color.

highlight The area on any surface that reflects the most light.

horizon line A level line where water or land seem to end and the sky begins. It is usually on the eye level of the observer. If the horizon cannot be seen, its location must be imagined.

horizontal A line or shape that is parallel to the top and bottom edges of a surface.

hue The common name of a color in or related to the color spectrum, such as yellow, yellow-orange, blue-violet, green. Hue is another word for *color*.

idealized More perfect than you would ordinarily find in life.

illuminated manuscript A decorated or illustrated manuscript in which the pages are often painted with silver, gold and other rich colors. They were popular during the Medieval period.

illustrator An artist who creates pictures to explain a point; to show an important part of a story; or to add decoration to a book, magazine or other printed work.

imagination The ability to picture things in the mind, often things that are not seen in the real world.

imitationalism A theory of art in which a work of art is thought to be successful if it looks like and reminds the viewer of something seen in the real world.

impasto (im-POSS-toe) A very thick textured layer of paint.

implied A series of separate points or edges of shapes that the viewer tends to see as connected.

impression Any mark or imprint made by pressure. In printmaking, an impression is a print made by pressing an inked surface against a paper surface.

Impressionism 1875-1900. A style of painting that began in France. It emphasizes views of subjects at a particular moment and the effects of sunlight on color.

incising (in-SIZE-ing) Cutting or carving thin lines on the surface of a material.

industrial designers Artists who design the visual appearance of cars, dishes, toys and other products that are usually mass-produced.

informal balance See *asymmetrical design.*

ink slab A smooth, non-absorbent surface on which printing ink is rolled out with a brayer.

intaglio (in-TAHL-ee-oh) A print-making process in which the image is carved into the surface. The lines hold the ink.

intensity The brightness or dullness of a hue. A pure hue is called a high-intensity color. A dulled hue (a color mixed with its complement) is called a low-intensity color.

intermediate color A color made by mixing a secondary color with a primary color. Blue-green, yellow-green, yellow-orange, red-orange, red-violet and blue-violet are intermediate colors.

International Style 1930-1970. A style of architecture with machine-like, geometric forms and little decoration.

invented texture A visual sensation of texture created by repeating lines and shapes in a pattern.

jazzy A form of visual rhythm or movement that is complex. It is similar to the rhythms in jazz music.

kiln (kill) An oven similar to a furnace. Kilns are used for firing ceramic objects or for fusing glass or enamels to metal.

kinetic sculpture A sculpture that moves or has moving parts. The motion may be caused by many different forces, including air, gravity and electricity.

knot-bearing cord The cord you hold tightly when tying a macramé knot.

landscape An artwork that shows natural scenery such as mountains, valleys, trees, rivers and lakes.

landscape architect A person who designs natural settings, such as parks, for people to use and enjoy.

layout The arrangement of type and illustrations for a graphic design.

leather-hard Slightly moist clay that is firm and holds its shape.

Light Art Any kind of artwork in which lighting sources and tools are used as media.

line A mark with length and direction, created by a point that moves across a surface. A line can vary in length, width, direction, curvature and color. Line can be two-dimensional (a pencil line on paper), three-dimensional (wire) or implied.

linear perspective A system of drawing or painting used to give a flat surface a look of depth. The lines of buildings and other objects in a picture are usually slanted inward, making them look like they move back in space. If you make these lines longer, they will cross at a point on an imaginary line representing the eye level (sometimes called the *horizon line*). The point at which the lines meet is called a *vanishing point.*

linear style A painting technique in which contours or outlines are most important.

linoleum cut (lih-NO-lee-um cut) A relief print made from a piece of linoleum.

lithography A method of printing from a prepared flat stone or metal plate. Lithography is based on the idea that grease and water do not mix together. A drawing is made on the stone or plate with a greasy drawing material and then washed with water. When greasy ink is applied, it sticks to the greasy drawing but runs off the wet surface. This allows a print to be made of the drawing.

logo A visual symbol that identifies a business, club or other group. Logos are often made of a few artistically drawn letters or shapes.

loom A frame or related base for weaving cloth. Some threads are held by the loom (*warp* threads) while other threads are woven through them (*weft* threads).

low key painting A painting with many dark values.

low relief See *bas-relief.*

macramé (MACK-rah-may) Artwork based on knotting cords.

Magic/Poetic Realism 1920-Present. A style of painting that combines realism with slightly mysterious and strange elements to create the sensation of a moment or experience.

Mannerism 1525-1600. A European artistic style with very emotional scenes and distorted figures. This style was a contrast to the calm balance of the High Renaissance.

maquette (mah-KET) A small model of a larger sculpture.

matte (mat) Having a dull texture. Not glossy or shiny.

media Plural of medium. The materials used by an artist and the special techniques that make their use expressive.

medium The material and technique used by an artist to create a work of art. It may also mean the liquid that is mixed with powdered pigments to make paint.

Mexican Muralists 1910-1940. Mexican artists who brought back the art of fresco mural painting.

mezzotint (MEZZ-oh-tint) An intaglio printing process in which the surface of a metal plate is textured with a tool with fine metal spikes called a rocker. The ink remains in the small cuts made by the rocker. The print is also called a mezzotint.

middle ground Parts of an artwork that appear to be between objects in the foreground and the background.

miniature Very small compared to the size of the human figure.

Minimal Art A style of late twentieth-century painting and sculpture that stressed the idea of using the minimum number of colors, values, shapes, lines and textures.

mixed media Any artwork that is made with more than one medium.

mobile (MOH-beel) A hanging sculpture with parts that can be moved, especially by the flow of air.

model To form clay or another soft material with the hands. A model can be a person or thing an artist looks at in order to create a work of art. It is also a small copy or image that represents a larger object.

modeling A sculpture technique in which a three-dimensional form is shaped in a soft material such as clay. In drawing, modeling is the use of light and shadow to make something look three-dimensional.

module (MAH-jool) A three-dimensional motif or design. A visual unit that is usually repeated to create a larger design.

mold A hollow shape used to make one or many copies of an object. A mold is filled with a material such as plaster or metal. It is removed when the material hardens into the shape of the mold.

monochromatic (mah-no-crow-MAT-ik) Made of only a single color or hue and its tints and shades.

monoprint A printing process that usually involves creating one print instead of many.

montage (mahn-TAZH) A special kind of collage, made from pieces of photographs or other pictures.

monumental Large or extremely large compared to the size of a human.

mosaic (mo-ZAY-ik) Artwork made by fitting together tiny pieces of colored glass or tiles, stones, paper or other materials. These small materials are called *tesserae*.

motif (moh-TEEF) A single or repeated design or part of a design or decoration that appears over and over again.

movement A way of combining visual elements to produce a sense of action. This combination of elements helps the viewer's eye to sweep over the work in a definite manner.

mural A large painting or artwork, usually designed for and created on the wall or ceiling of a public building.

museum A place where works of art are displayed, studied and cared for.

Native North American A term used to describe the art and cultural traditions of people who lived in North America before the continent was settled by Europeans and their descendants.

Near Eastern Art 3500-331 BC. An art historical term used to describe the ancient art of many cultures in the geographic region between India and Greece.

negative shape/space The empty space surrounding shapes or solid forms in a work of art.

Neo-Classicism 1750-1875. A style of art based on interest in the ideals of ancient Greek and Roman art. These ideals were used to express ideas about beauty, courage, sacrifice and love of country.

neutral color A color not associated with a hue—such as black, white, or a gray. Architects and designers call slight changes in black, white, brown and gray neutral because many other hues can be combined with them in pleasing color schemes.

nonobjective art 1917-1932. A style of art that does not have a recognizable subject matter. The subject is the composition of the artwork. It is also known as non-representational art. Nonobjective is often used as a general term for art that contains no recognizable subjects.

oil paint A relatively slow-drying paint made from pigments mixed with an oil base. When the oil dries, it becomes a hard film, protecting the brilliance of the colors.

Op Art 1950-present. A style based on optical (visual) illusions of many types. They are meant to confuse, raise or expand visual sensations, especially sensations of movement.

opaque (oh-PAYK) Not allowing light to go through. You cannot see through an object or a material that is opaque. It is the opposite of *transparent*.

optical color Color seen by the viewer due to the effect of atmosphere or unusual light on the actual color.

organic Having a quality that resembles living things.

Oriental art A general term for art created in Japan, China and other countries in the Eastern Hemisphere.

outline A line that shows or creates the outer edges of a shape or form. It may also be called a *contour*.

painterly style A general painting style in which patches of color and visible brushstrokes show. A painterly style allows the viewer to see the movements the artist made in putting on paint.

palette (PAL-let) A tray or board on which colors of paint are mixed.

Palladian (pah-LAY-dee-en) An architectural style or detail based on an Italian house designed by the Renaissance architect, Andrea Palladio.

papier-mâché (PAY-per mah-SHAY) French for "chewed" or "mashed paper." Papier-mâché pulp is a modeling material made by mixing small bits of paper in water and liquid paste. It is quite strong when it dries.

passive Any element of art that seems to be quiet, at rest or not moving.

paste-up A detailed layout of a printed page. A paste-up is prepared so it can be photographed and made into a plate for printing.

pastel A chalk-like crayon made of finely ground color. A pastel is a picture made with pastel crayons. It is also a term for *tints* of colors.

path of movement Any element of art that seems to lead the eye from one part to another.

pattern A choice of lines, colors or shapes, repeated over and over in a planned way. A pattern is also a model or guide for making something.

Performance Art A form of visual art closely related to theater, but created by persons who have experience in the visual arts.

perspective Techniques for creating a look of depth on a two-dimensional surface.

philosophy of art A general system of ideas for thinking about all parts of art, especially in Western culture. It is also called a theory of art.

Photo-Realism 1970-present. A style of painting in which the distortions and special effects of photography are shown or used for ideas.

photograph A picture made using a camera and light-sensitive film.

pictograph Simple visual symbols representing things, ideas or stories.

picture plane The surface of a two-dimensional artwork.

pigment Any coloring matter, usually a fine powder, mixed with a liquid or binder to make paint, ink, dyes or crayons.

pinch method A method of hand-building pottery or sculpture by pressing, pulling and pinching clay or other soft materials.

plane Any surface that is flat. Most three-dimensional surfaces are made up of many tiny planes that join to form larger angular or curved surfaces.

point of view The angle from which the viewer sees an object or a scene.

Pointillism (POYN-till-iz-im) 1880-1900. A style of painting developed by Seurat in which small dots of color are placed side by side. When viewed from a distance, the eye tends to see the colors as mixed.

Pop Art 1950-Present. A style of art based on subject matter from popular culture (mass media, commercial art, comic strips, advertising).

portfolio A sample of an artist's works (or photographs of them) put together in a book for others to review.

portrait Any form of art expression that features a specific person or animal.

positive space/shape The objects in a work of art, not the background or the space around them.

Post-Impressionism 1880-1900. An art history term for a period of painting immediately following Impressionism in France. Various styles were explored, especially by Cézanne (basic structures), van Gogh (emotionally strong brush-work), and Gauguin (intense color and unusual themes).

Post-modern Architecture 1970-present. A style of architecture which mixes some styles from the past with more decoration than was typical of the International Style.

potter's wheel A flat, spinning disc on which soft clay is placed and shaped by hand.

Pre-Columbian Art 7000 BC to about 1500 AD. An art history term for art created in North and South America before the time of the Spanish conquests.

Precisionism 1920-1940. A style name for paintings with definite or precise edges.

primary color One of three basic colors (red, yellow and blue) that cannot be made by mixing colors. Primary colors are used for mixing other colors.

principles of art/design Guide-lines that help artists to create designs and control how viewers are likely to react to images. Balance, contrast, proportion, pattern, rhythm, emphasis, unity and variety are examples of principles of design.

print A shape or mark made from a printing block or or other object. The block is covered with wet ink and then pressed on a flat surface, such as paper or cloth. Most prints can be repeated over and over again by re-inking the printing block.

progressive pattern or **rhythm** A pattern or rhythm that develops step by step - for example, from smaller to larger or brighter to duller.

proof A trial or practice print.

proportion The relation of one object to another in size, amount, number or degree.

proximity The position of one element compared to others. A chair may be in a distant or close proximity to a table.

pulp Mashed up material known as cellulose mixed with water. Pulp is used to make paper.

quilting A process of stitching together two layers of cloth with padding between the layers.

radial A kind of balance in which lines or shapes spread out from a center point.

ratio (RAY-shee-oh) The relation-ship between two or more things in size or quantity. For example, the ratio in height of an object two feet tall to an object one foot tall is 2 to 1.

Realism 1850-1900. A style of art that shows places, events, people or objects as the eye sees them. It was developed in the mid-nineteenth-century by artists who did not use the formulas of Neoclassicism and the drama of Romanticism.

realistic Art that shows a recogniz-able subject with lifelike colors, textures, shadows and proportions.

recycled paper Paper made from the pulp of other paper.

regular rhythm A visual rhythm of equally spaced and repeated motifs.

relief A three-dimensional form, meant to be seen from one side, in which surfaces project from a background. In high relief, the forms stand far out from the back-ground. In low relief, also known as *bas-relief,* they are shallow.

relief print A print created using a printing process in which ink is placed on the raised portions of the block or plate.

Renaissance (ren-eh-SAHNSS) 1400-1600. French for "rebirth." A period that began in Italy after the Middle Ages. The period was marked by a renewed interest in ancient Greek and Roman culture, science and philosophy, and the study of human beings and their environment. Important Renais-sance artists are Leonardo da Vinci, Michelangelo and Raphael.

repeated pattern A design with parts that are used over and over again in a regular or planned way, usually to create a visual rhythm or harmony.

representational Similar to the way an object or scene looks.

reproduction A copy of an image or a work of art, usually by a photo-graphic or printing process.

resist A process in which materials such as oil or wax are used because they will not mix with water. The resist material is used to block out certain areas of a surface that the artist does not want to be affected by dye, paint, varnish, acid or another substance.

rhythm A type of visual or actual movement in an artwork. Rhythm is a principle of design. It is created by repeating visual elements. Rhythms are often described as regular, alternating, flowing, progressive or jazzy.

Rococo (roh-COH-coh) 1700-1800. A style of eighteenth-century art that began in the luxurious homes of the French nobility and spread to the rest of Europe. It included delicate colors, delicate lines, and graceful movement. Favorite subjects included romance and the carefree life of the aristocracy. Watteau is one of the best-known Rococo painters.

Romanesque 1000-1200. A style of architecture and sculpture influenced by Roman art, that developed in western Europe during the Middle Ages. Cathedrals had heavy walls, rounded arches and sculptural decorations.

Romanticism 1815-1875. A style of art that developed as a reaction against Neoclassicism. Themes focused on dramatic action, exotic settings, adventures, imaginary events, faraway places and strong feelings.

rubbing A technique used to transfer the textural quality of a surface to paper. Paper is placed over the surface. The top of the paper is rubbed with crayon, chalk or pencil.

sans-serif (sann SEH-riff) Simple type and handlettering without decorative tags.

scale The size relationship between two sets of dimensions. For example, if a picture is drawn to scale, all its parts are equally smaller or larger than the parts in the original.

School of Paris 1918-1937. An art history term for artists who worked in Paris between World War I and II. They created work in many styles.

score To press a pointed instrument into but not through paper or thin cardboard. Scoring creates a line where the paper will bend easily. In clay work, artists score grooves or make scratches into surfaces of clay that will be joined together.

sculpture A work of art with three-dimensions: height, width and depth. Such a work may be carved, modeled, constructed or cast.

seascape Artwork that shows a scene of the sea, ocean, an area near a coast or a large lake.

secondary color A color made by mixing equal amounts of two primary colors. Green, orange and violet are the secondary colors. Green is made by mixing blue and yellow. Orange is made by mixing red and yellow. Violet is made by mixing red and blue.

self-portrait Any work of art in which an artist shows himself or herself.

selvedge (SELL-vidge) The uncut edge of a woven fabric.

serif (SEH-riff) Type and handlettering with tags.

serigraphy (sehr-IG-raff-ee) A print, also known as a silkscreen print, made by squeezing ink through a stencil and silk-covered frame to paper below.

shade Any dark value of a color, usually made by adding black.

shading A gradual change from light to dark. Shading is a way of making a picture appear more realistic and three-dimensional.

shape A flat figure created when actual or implied lines meet to surround a space. A change in color or shading can define a shape. Shapes can be divided into several types: geometric (square, triangle, circle) and organic (irregular in outline).

shed The opening in the warp through which the weft is passed. A shed is formed when certain warp threads are raised or lowered, usually using a heddle.

shuttle In weaving, a tool that holds the weft thread so that it can be easily put through the warp.

silhouette (sill-ooh-ETTE) An outline of a solid shape filled in completely, like a shadow. In a silhouette you cannot see inside details.

silkscreen See *serigraphy*.

silverpoint A drawing made with a thin silver wire. The silver darkens or tarnishes to create a dark line.

simplicity The practice of using similar elements or a small number of different elements in an artwork.

simulated texture The use of a pattern to create the look of a three-dimensional texture on a two-dimensional surface.

sketch A drawing done quickly to show the important parts of a subject. A sketch may be used to try out an idea or to plan another work.

slab A form that is solid, flat and thick. It is also a thick, even slice of clay, stone, wood or other material.

slip Clay, combined with water or vinegar, to form a thick liquid. Slip is used on scored areas to join pieces of clay together.

slogan A short, attention-getting phrase used in advertising.

slurry A fiber-based pulp mixed with water in order to make paper.

Social commentary art Art of any time period or culture that has a strong political or social message.

soft sculpture Sculpture made with fabric and stuffed with soft material.

soft-edge In two-dimensional art, shapes with fuzzy, blurred outlines that have a soft quality.

space The empty or open area between, around, above, below or within objects. Space is an element of art. Shapes and forms are made by the space around and within them. Space is often called *three-dimensional* or *two-dimensional*. Positive space is filled by a shape or form. Negative space surrounds a shape or form.

special effects A term used in theater, film and video work for any technique that creates illusions.

sphere A round, three-dimensional geometric form, such as a ball or globe.

split complement A color scheme based on one hue and the hues on each side of its complement on the color wheel. Orange, blue-violet, and blue-green are split complementary colors.

squeegee (SKWEE-jee) A tool for pushing ink through a silkscreen. It has a rubber blade and a handle.

stained glass Pieces of brightly colored glass held together by strips of lead to form a picture or design. Stained glass was first used in Romanesque churches and became a major part of Gothic cathedrals.

statue (STAH-choo) A sculpture, especially of a person or animal, that stands up by itself.

stencil (STEN-sill) A paper or other flat material with a cut-out design that is used for printing. Ink or paint prints through the cut-out design onto the surface below.

still life Art based on an arrangement of objects that are not alive and cannot move, such as fruit, flowers or bottles. The items are often symbols for abstract ideas. A book, for example, may be a symbol for knowledge. A still life is usually shown in an indoor setting.

stitchery A general term for artwork created with needles, thread or yarn, and cloth. A stitch is one in-and-out movement of a threaded needle.

straight A line or edge that goes in one direction without bending.

studio The place where an artist or designer works.

style The result of an artist's means of expression – the use of materials, design qualities, methods of work, and choice of subject matter. In most cases, these choices show the unique qualities of an individual, culture or time period. The style of an artwork helps you to know how it is different from other artworks.

subject A topic or idea shown in an artwork, especially anything recognizable such as a landscape or animals.

subtractive method A technique of making sculpture in which a form is created by cutting, carving away, or otherwise removing material.

Super Realism 1970-present. A style of drawing and painting that tries to look as real as a photograph, and includes the distortions of color, scale and detail found in photographs. It is also called *Photo-Realism.*

support The background to which other materials are attached.

Surrealism 1924-1940. A style of art in which dreams, fantasy and the human mind were sources of ideas for artists. Surrealist works can be representational or abstract. Unrelated objects and situations are often set in unnatural surroundings.

symbol Something that stands for something else; especially a letter, figure or sign that represents a real object or idea. A red heart shape is a common symbol for love.

symmetrical A type of balance in which both sides of a center line are exactly or nearly the same, like a mirror image. For example, the wings of a butterfly are symmetrical. It is also known as *formal balance.*

tactile (TAK-tile) The qualities and feelings experienced from the sense of touch.

technical qualities The visual features and effects created by an artist's special way of using a medium.

technique (tek-NEEK) An artist's way of using art materials to create a desired artwork. A technique can be an artist's own way to create artwork (a special kind of brushstroke) or a step-by-step procedure (how to create a crayon-resist).

tempera A slightly chalky, opaque paint that thins in water. The paint is made by mixing pigments with a glue, egg yolk (egg tempera) or another binder. School poster paint is a type of tempera. Egg tempera was popular before the invention of oil painting.

tesserae (TESS-er-ah) Small pieces of glass, tile, stone, paper or other materials used to make a *mosaic.*

textile Artworks made from cloth or fibers such as yarn. These may include weaving, tapestry, stitchery, appliqué, quilting and printed fabrics.

texture The way a surface feels (actual texture) or how it may look (simulated texture). Texture can be sensed by touch and sight. Textures are described by words such as rough, silky, pebbly.

theme The subject or topic of a work of art. For example, a landscape can have a theme of the desire to save nature, or to destroy nature. A theme such as love, power or respect can be shown through a variety of subjects. The phrase "theme and variations" usually means several ways of showing one idea.

three-dimensional Artwork that can be measured three ways: height, width, depth or thickness. Three-dimensional artwork is not flat. Any object that has depth, height and width is three-dimensional.

thumb-nail sketch A small sketch. Several are usually made on one page.

tie-dye A textile technique in which the design is created by tightly tying or binding the cloth and dipping it in dye. The tied or bound areas do not soak up the colored dye.

tint A light value of a pure color, usually made by adding white. For example, pink is a tint of red.

tjanting tool (CHAN-ting tool) A tool used in batik. It holds hot wax and has a small spout that allows the wax to flow onto the fabric.

traditional art Artwork created in almost the same way year after year because it is part of a culture, custom or belief.

translucent (tranz-LOO-sent) Allowing light to pass through so that the exact colors and details of objects behind the surface cannot be clearly seen.

transparent Allowing light to pass through so that objects behind the surface can be clearly seen. Transparent is the opposite of *opaque.* Window glass, cellophane and watercolors are transparent.

trompe l'oeil (trump l'oy) French for "fool the eye" or "trick of the eye." A term for paintings in which objects look so three-dimensional that the viewer may wonder if the image is a painting or real objects.

two-dimensional Artwork that is flat or measured in only two major ways: height and width.

typography The art of designing and artistically using alphabet forms.

unity A feeling that all parts of a design are working together as a team.

value An element of art that means the darkness or lightness of a surface. Value depends on how much light a surface reflects. Tints are light values of pure colors. Shades are dark values of pure colors. Value can also be an important element in works of art in which there is little or no color (drawings, prints, photographs, most sculpture and architecture).

vanishing point In a perspective drawing, one or more points on the horizon where parallel lines that go back in space seem to meet.

variation, variety A change in form, shape, detail or appearance that makes an object different from others. As a principle of design, variation is the use of different lines, shapes, textures, colors and other elements of design to create interest in a work of art.

vertical A line that runs straight up and down from a level surface. Vertical lines are at right angles to the bottom edge of a paper or canvas. They are parallel to the side of the paper or canvas.

video art Non-commercial artwork created by or using television technology.

viewfinder A small window in a camera (or a rectangle cut into a piece of paper) that an observer looks through in order to see or plan the composition of a picture.

viewpoints The sides and angles from which an object can be seen. If you put a cup and saucer on a table you can move around the table to have different viewpoints of the cup and saucer.

visible color spectrum
Lightwaves of color that the human
eye can see. It is made up of the
primary and secondary hues, which
are often arranged in a circle on a
"color wheel."

visual environment Every visible
thing that surrounds you, usually
divided into two groups: the natural
environment (trees, flowers, water,
sky, rocks) and the human-made or
built environment (buildings, roads,
bridges, automobiles).

visual texture The illusion of a
three-dimensional textured surface.
Something that looks like it has a
textured surface but is actually
smooth.

void An empty space.

warm colors Warm colors are so-
called because they often are associated with fire and the sun and
remind people of warm places,
things and feelings. Warm colors
range from the reds through the
oranges and yellows.

warp A series of tight threads
stretching lengthwise on a loom,
through which the weft is woven.

wash A very thin coat of paint. It is
also a color that has been thinned
with water (or turpentine, if the
paint is oil). When it is brushed on
paper, canvas or board, the surface
beneath can still be seen.

watercolor A transparent paint
made by mixing powdered colors
with a binder and water. The term
also means an artwork done with
this paint.

weaving The process of interlocking threads or fiber-like materials to
create a fabric. These threads are
usually held at right angles to one
another on a loom.

wedging A process used to get air
bubbles out of clay. Wedging can be
done by kneading clay or by cutting
clay in half with a wire, then slamming the pieces onto a hard surface.

weft In weaving, thread or other
fiber-like materials that are woven
across the warp from side to side.

wet media Drawing and painting
materials which have a fluid or
liquid ingredient.

woodcut A type of relief printing
in which areas of the wood block are
carved away; ink is put on the raised
surface and it is printed onto paper
when pressure is applied.

workboard In macrame, a surface
on which you can place macramé
cords while knotting them.

Bibliography

Aesthetics and Appreciation

Belves, Pierre, and François Mathey. *Enjoying the World of Art.* New York: Lion Books, 1966.

—, *How Artists Work: An Introduction to Techniques of Art.* New York: Lion Books, 1968.

Borreson, Mary Jo, *Let's Go To An Art Museum.* New York: G.P. Putman, 1960.

Browner, Richard, *Look Again.* New York: Atheneum, 1962.

Brommer, Gerald F., *Discovering Art History.* Worcester, MA: Davis Publications, Inc., 1988.

—, *Drawing: Ideas, Materials and Techniques.* Worcester, MA: Davis Publications, Inc., 1972.

Campbell, Ann. *Paintings: How to Look at Great Art.* New York: Franklin Watts, 1970.

Chase, Alice Elizabeth, *Looking at Art.* New York: Thomas Y. Crowell, 1966.

Feldman, Edmund B., *Thinking About Art.* Englewood Cliffs, NJ: Prentice-Hall, 1985.

Franc, Helen M., *An Invitation to See: 125 Paintings from The Museum of Modern Art.* New York: Museum of Modern Art, 1973.

Fraser, Kathleen, *Stilts, Somersaults, and Headstands: Game Poems Based on a Painting by Pieter Bruegel.* New York: Atheneum, 1968.

Holme, Bryan, ed., *Drawings to Live With.* New York: Viking Press, 1966.

—, *Pictures to Live With.* New York: Viking Press, 1960.

Levy, Virginia K., *Let's Go To The Art Museum.* New York: Harry N. Abrams, Inc., 1988.

MacAgy, Douglas, and Elizabeth MacAgy, *Going for a Walk with a Line: A Step into the World of Modern Art.* New York: Doubleday, 1959.

Moore, Jane Gaylor, *The First Book of Paintings.* New York: Franklin Watts, 1960.

—, *The Many Ways of Seeing: An Introduction to the Pleasures of Art.* New York: Franklin Watts, 1961.

Munro, Eleanor C., *The Golden Encyclopedia of Art.* New York: McGraw-Hill, 1967.

Paul, L., *The Way Art Happens.* New York: Ives Washburn, 1963.

Art History

Ayer, Margaret, *Made in Thailand.* New York: Alfred A. Knopf, 1964.

Baldwin, Gordon C., *Strange People and Stranger Customs.* New York: Norton, 1967.

Batterberry, Michael, *Chinese and Oriental Art, Discovering Art Series.* New York: McGraw-Hill, 1968.

Baumann, Hans, *The Caves of the Great Hunters.* New York: Pantheon, 1962.

Broder, Patricia J., *American Painting and Sculpture.* New York: Abbeville, 1981.

Chase, Judith, *Afro-American Art and Crafts.* New York: Van Nostrand Reinhold, 1971.

Dockstader, Frederick, *Indian Art of the Americas.* New York: Museum of the American Indian, 1973.

Fine, Elsa H., *The Afro-American Artist.* Miami, FL: Brown Book, 1973.

Glubok, Shirley, *Art and Archaeology Series: The Art of Ancient Egypt, The Art of Ancient Greece, The Art of Ancient Rome, The Art of the Etruscans, The Art of the New American Nation, The Art of the North American Indian, The Art of the Southeastern Indian, The Art of the Spanish in the United States and Puerto Rico.* New York: Harper & Row Junior Books.

—, *The Art of Lands in the Bible.* New York: Atheneum, 1963.

—, *The Art of the Eskimo.* New York: Harper & Row, 1964.

Golden, Grace, *Made in Iceland.* New York: Alfred A. Knopf, 1958.

Helfman, Elizabeth S., *Celebrating Nature: Rites and Ceremonies Around the World.* New York: The Seabury Press, 1969.

Hunt, Kari, and Bernice W. Carlson, *Masks and Mask Makers.* New York: Abingdon Press, 1961.

Janson, Horst W., and Dora J. Janson, *The Story of Painting for Young People.* New York: Harry N. Abrams, Inc., 1962.

Kahane, P.P., *Ancient and Classical Art.* New York: Dell Publishing Co., 1969.

La Farge, Oliver, *The American Indian.* Special Edition for Young Readers. New York: Golden Press, 1973.

Lewis, Samella S. and Rugh G. Waddy, *Black Artists on Art,* 2 vols. Los Angeles, CA: Hancraft, 1969-1971.

Madian, Jon, *Beautiful Junk: A Story of the Watts Towers.* Boston, MA: Little, Brown, 1968.

Marshall, Anthony D., *Africa's Living Arts.* New York: Franklin Watts, 1970.

Quirarte, Jacinto, *Mexican American Artists.* Austin, TX: University of Texas, 1973.

Ruskin, Ariane, *Story of Art for Young People.* New York: Pantheon, 1964.

Sayer, Chloe, *Crafts of Mexico.* New York: Doubleday, 1977.

Smith, Bradley, *Mexico: A History in Art.* Garden City, NY: Doubleday, 1971.

Spencer, Cornelia, *How Art and Music Speak to Us.* New York: John Day, 1968.

—, *Made in China.* New York: Alfred A. Knopf, 1952.

—, *Made in India.* New York: Alfred A. Knopf, 1953.

—, *Made in Japan.* New York: Alfred A. Knopf, 1963.

—, *Made in the Renaissance.* New York: E.P. Dutton, 1963.

Stribling, Mary Lou, *Crafts From North American Indian Art: Techniques, Designs and Contemporary Applications*. New York: Crown Publishing, 1975.

Taylor, Barbara H., *Mexico: Her Daily and Festive Breads*. Claremont, CA: Creative Press, 1969.

Toor, Frances, *Made in Italy*. New York: Alfred A. Knopf, 1957.

Torwell, Margaret and Hans Nevermann, *African and Oceanic Art*. New York: Harry N. Abrams, Inc., 1968.

Willett, Frank, *African Art*. London: Thames and Hudson, 1985.

Individual Artists

Adams, Ansel, *The Portfolios of Ansel Adams*. Boston, MA: Bulfinch Press, 1981.

Aitchison, Dorothy, *Great Artists*. Series (*Rubens, Rembrandt, Vermeer, Leonardo, Raphael, Michelangelo* and others). Loughborough, England: Wells and Hepworth.

Bruzeau, Maurice, *Alexander Calder*. New York: Harry N. Abrams, Inc., 1979.

Freedgood, Lillian, *Great Artists of America*. New York: Thomas Y. Crowell, 1963.

Goldstein, Ernest, *Let's Get Lost in a Painting*. Series (*Winslow Homer, Edward Hicks, Grant Wood* and others). Dallas, TX: Garrard Publications, 1982.

Hollmann, Clide, *Five Artists of the Old West*. New York: Hastings House, 1965.

Lisle, Laurie, *Portrait of an Artist: A Biography of Georgia O'Keeffe*. New York: Seaview Books, 1980.

Locher, J.C., ed., *The World of M.C. Escher*. New York: New American Library, 1972.

Peare, Catherine O., *Rosa Bonheur: Her Life*. New York: Henry Holt, 1956.

Ripley, Elizabeth, *Botticelli: A Biography*. New York: Lippencott, 1960.

—, *Dürer*. New York: Lippencott, 1958.

—, *Goya*. New York: Walck, 1956.

—, *Leonardo da Vinci*. New York: Walck, 1952.

—, *Rembrandt*. New York: Walck, 1955.

—, *Rubens*. New York: Walck, 1957.

Rockwell, Norman, *Norman Rockwell: My Adventures As An Illustrator*. New York: Harry N. Abrams, Inc., 1988.

Willard, Charlotte, *Famous Modern Artists from Cézanne to Pop Art*. New York: Platt & Munk, 1971.

Subjects and Themes in Art

Coen, Rena N., *Kings and Queens in Art*. Minneapolis, MN: Lerner Publications, 1965.

Cornelius, Sue, and Chase Cornelius, *The City in Art*. Minneapolis, MN: Lerner Publications, 1966.

Downer, Marion, *Children in the World's Art*. New York: Lothrop, Lee & Shepard, 1970.

Forte, Nancy, *The Warrior in Art*. Minneapolis, MN: Lerner Publications, 1966.

Gracza, Margaret Young, *The Bird in Art*. Minneapolis, MN: Lerner Publications, 1966.

—, *The Ship and the Sea in Art*. Minneapolis, MN: Lerner Publications, 1965.

Harkonen, Helen B., *Circuses and Fairs in Art*. Minneapolis, MN: Lerner Publications, 1965.

—, *Farms and Farmers in Art*. Minneapolis, MN: Lerner Publications, 1965.

Kainz, Luise C., and Olive L. Riley, *Understanding Art: Portraits, Personalities, and Ideas*. New York: Harry N. Abrams, Inc., 1967.

Medlin, Faith, *Centuries of Owls in Art and the Written Word*. Norwalk, CT: Silvermine, 1967.

Shay, Rieger, *Gargoyles, Monsters, and Other Beasts*. New York: Lothrop, Lee & Shepard, 1972.

Shissler, Barbara, *Sports and Games in Art*. Minneapolis, MN: Lerner Publications, 1966.

Zuelke, Ruth, *The Horse in Art*. Minneapolis, MN: Lerner Publications, 1965.

Careers in Art

Brommer, Gerald F., and Joseph Gatto, *Careers in Art: An Illustrated Guide*. Worcester, MA: Davis Publications, Inc., 1984.

Fixman, Adeline, *Your Future in Creative Careers*. New York: Richard Rosen Press, 1978.

Holden, Donald, *Art Career Guide*. New York: Watson-Guptill Publications, 1983.

Elements and Principles of Design

Brommer, Gerald F., ed., *Concepts of Design*. Series: Books on elements of design (*Line, Color and Value, Shape and Form, Space, Texture*) and principles of design (*Balance and Unity, Contrast, Emphasis, Movement and Rhythm, Pattern*). Worcester, MA: Davis Publications, Inc., 1975.

Collier, Graham, *Form, Space and Vision: An Introduction to Drawing and Design*. Englewood Cliffs, NJ: Prentice-Hall, 1985.

Grillo, Paul, *Form, Function and Design*. New York: Dover Publications, 1975.

Hart, Tony, *The Young Designer*. New York: Frederick Wayne, 1968.

Helfman, Elizabeth S., *Signs and Symbols of the Sun*. New York: Houghton Mifflin, 1974.

Keisler, Leonard, *The Worm, The Bird, and You*. New York: William R. Scott, 1961.

—, *What's in a Line*. New York: William R. Scott, 1962.

Kirn, Ann, *Full of Wonder*. Cleveland, OH: World, 1959.

Kohn, Bernice, *Everything Has a Shape and Everything Has a Size*. Englewood Cliffs, NJ: Prentice-Hall, Inc. 1966.

Landa, Robin, *An Introduction to Design: Basic Ideas & Applications for Painting on the Printed Page*. Englewood Cliffs, NJ: Prentice-Hall, 1983.

Lauer, David A., *Design Basics*. New York: Holt, Rinehart and Winston, 1985.

Malcolm, Dorothea C., *Design: Elements and Principles*. Worcester, MA: Davis Publications, Inc., 1972.

Meilach, Dona Z., Jay Hinz and Bill Hinz, *How to Create Your Own Designs: An Introduction to Color, Form and Composition*. New York: Doubleday, 1975.

Ocvirk, Otto, et al., *Art Fundamentals Theory and Practice*. Dubuque, IA: William C. Brown, 1985.

O'Neill, Mary, *Hailstones and Halibut Bones*. Garden City, NY: Doubleday, 1973.

Strache, Wolf, *Forms and Patterns in Nature*. New York: Pantheon, 1973.

Wolff, Janet, and Bernard Owett. *Let's Imagine Colors*. New York: E.P. Dutton, 1963.

Specific Art Forms

Architecture/Design in Everyday Life

Bardi, P.M., *Architecture: The World We Build*. New York: Franklin Watts, 1972.

Brustlein, Daniel, *The Magic Stones*. New York: McGraw-Hill, 1957.

Crouch, Dora P., *History of Architecture: Stonehenge to Skyscrapers*. New York: McGraw-Hill, 1985.

Hiller, Carl E., *Caves to Cathedrals: Architecture of the Worlds' Religions*. Boston, MA: Little, Brown, 1974.

—, *From Tepees to Towers: A Photographic History of American Architecture*. Boston, MA: Little, Brown, 1974.

Kahn, Ely J., *A Building Goes Up*. New York: Simon & Schuster, 1969.

McAlester, Virginia, and Lee McAlester, *A Field Guide to American Houses*. New York: Alfred A. Knopf, 1984.

Paine, Roberta M., *Looking at Architecture*. New York: Lothrop, Lee & Shepard, 1974.

Pile, John F., *Interior Design*. New York: Harry N. Abrams, Inc., 1988.

Camera/Electronic Arts

Bolognese, Don *Mastering the Computer for Design and Illustration*. New York: Watson-Guptill Publications, 1988.

Bruandet, Pierre, *Photograms*. New York: Watson-Guptill Publications, 1973.

Cooke, Robert, *Designing with Light On Paper and Film*. Worcester, MA: Davis Publications, Inc., 1969.

Eastman Kodak Co., *Movies and Slides without a Camera*. Rochester, NY: 1972.

Editors of Time-Life Books, *Computer Images*. Alexandria, VA: Time-Life Books, 1986.

Halas, John, *The Technique of Film Animation*. Woburn, MA: Focal Press, 1976.

Holter, Patra, *Photography Without A Camera*. New York: Van Nostrand Reinhold, 1972.

Kinsey, Anthony, *How To Make Animated Movies*. New York: Viking, 1970.

Laybourne, Kit, *The Animation Book: A Complete Guide to Animated FilmMaking – From Flip-Books to Sound Cartoons*. New York: Crown Publishing, 1979.

Lewell, John, *Computer Graphics: A Survey of Current Techniques and Applications*. New York: Van Nostrand Reinhold, 1985.

Linder, Carl, *Film Making: A Practical Guide*. Englewood Cliffs, NJ: Prentice-Hall, 1971.

O'Brien, Michael F., and Norman Sibley, *The Photographic Eye: Learning to See with a Camera*. Worcester, MA: Davis Publications, Inc., 1988.

Piper, James, *Personal Film Making*. Englewood Cliffs, NJ: Prentice-Hall, 1975.

Sandler, Martin W., *The Story of American Photography: An Illustrated History for Young People*. Boston, MA: Little, Brown, 1975.

Wilson, Mark, *Drawing with Computers: The Artist's Guide to Computer Graphics*. New York: The Putnam Publishing Group, 1985.

Computer Software

Adobe Illustrator. Mountain View, CA: Adobe Systems.

Cricket Draw. Malvern, PA: Cricket Software.

Fontographer (computer fonts). Plano, TX: Altsys Corp.

Pixel Paint. San Diego, CA: Silicon Beach Software.

Thunderscan (optical scanner and software). Orinda, CA: Thunderware.

Video Works (animation software). Chicago, IL: MicroMind.

Crafts

Ceramics

Nelson, Glenn C., *Ceramics: A Potter's Handbook*. New York: Holt, Rinehart and Winston, 1984.

Nigrosh, Leon I., *Claywork: Form and Idea in Ceramic Design*. Worcester, MA: Davis Publications, Inc., 1986.

Sapiro, Maurice, *Clay: Handbuilding*. Worcester, MA: Davis Publications, Inc., 1983.

—, *Clay: The Potter's Wheel*. Worcester, MA: Davis, 1978.

Sprintzen, Alice, *Crafts: Contemporary Design and Technique*. Worcester, MA: Davis Publications, Inc., 1986.

Fibers

Beinecke, Mary Ann, *Basic Needlery Stitches on Mesh Fabrics*. New York: Dover Publications, 1973.

Belfer, Nancy, *Designing in Batik and Tie Dye*. Worcester, MA: Davis Publications, Inc., 1972.

Brown, Rachel, *The Weaving, Spinning, and Dying Book*. New York: Alfred A. Knopf, 1984.

Guild, Vera P., *Good Housekeeping New Complete Book of Needlecraft*. New York: Hearst Books, 1971.

Held, Shirley E., *Weaving: A Handbook of the Fiber Arts*. New York: Holt, Rinehart and Winston, 1978.

Leeming, Joseph, *Fun with String*. New York: Dover Publications, 1974.

Meilach, Dona Z., *Contemporary Batik and Tie-Dye: Methods, Inspiration, Dyes*. New York: Crown Publishing, 1973.

Rainey, Sarita R., *Weaving without a Loom*. Worcester, MA: Davis Publications, Inc., 1966.

Termini, Maria, *Silkscreening*. Englewood Cliffs, NJ: Prentice-Hall, 1978.

Jewelry

Ferre, R. Duane, *How to Make Wire Jewelry*. Radnor, PA: Chilton, 1980.

Howell-Koehler, Nancy, *Soft Jewelry, Design, Techniques and Materials*. Englewood Cliffs, NJ: Prentice-Hall, 1977.

Meilach, Dona Z., *Ethnic Jewelry: Design and Inspiration for Collectors and Craftsmen*. New York: Crown Publishing, 1981.

Other Crafts

Betts, Victoria, *Exploring Papier-Mâché*. Worcester, MA: Davis Publications, Inc., 1966.

Flower, Cedric, and Alan Fortney, *Puppets: Methods and Materials*. Worcester, MA: Davis Publications, Inc., 1983.

Johnson, Pauline, *Creating with Paper.* Seattle, WA: University of Washington Press, 1966.

Rothenberg, Polly, *Creative Stained Glass.* New York: Crown Publishing, 1973.

Toale, Bernard, *The Art of Papermaking.* Worcester, MA: Davis Publications, Inc., 1983.

Drawing

Brommer, Gerald F., *Discovering Art History.* Worcester, MA: Davis Publications, Inc., 1988.

—, *Drawing: Ideas, Materials and Techniques.* Worcester, MA: Davis, Publications, Inc., 1972.

—, *Exploring Drawing.* Worcester, MA: Davis Publications, Inc., 1988.

Gatto, Joseph, *Drawing Media and Techniques.* Worcester, MA: Davis Publications, Inc., 1987.

Hogarth, Paul, *Creative Pencil Drawing.* New York: Watson-Guptill Publications, 1981.

Kaupelis, Robert, *Learning to Draw.* New York: Watson-Guptill Publications, 1966.

James, Jane H., *Perspective Drawing: A Point of View.* Englewood Cliffs, NJ: Prentice Hall, 1988.

—, *Perspective Drawing.* Englewood Cliffs, NJ: Prentice-Hall, 1981.

Mittler, Gene, and James Howze, *Creating and Understanding Drawings.* Emporia, IL: Bennett Knight, 1988.

Probyn, Peter, ed., *The Complete Drawing Book.* New York: Watson-Guptill Publications, 1970.

Sarnoff, Bolo, *Cartoons and Comics.* Worcester, MA: Davis Publications, Inc., 1988.

Sheaks, Barclay, *Drawing Figures and Faces.* Worcester, MA: Davis Publications, Inc., 1987.

Watson, Ernest W., *The Art of Pencil Drawing.* New York: Watson-Guptill Publications, 1985.

Graphic Design

Barnicoat, John, *A Concise History of Posters 1870-1970.* New York: Oxford University Press, 1972.

Cataldo, John W., *Lettering.* Worcester, MA: Davis Publications, Inc., 1983.

Gatta, Kevin, G. Lange and M. Lyons, *Foundations of Graphic Design.* Worcester, MA: Davis Publications, Inc., 1990.

Gluck, Felix, ed., *Modern Publicity.* New York: MacMillan, 1979.

Herdeg, Walter, ed., *Graphis Posters Eighty-Six: The International Annual of Poster Art.* New York: Watson-Guptill Publications, published annually in October.

Horn, George F., *Cartooning.* Worcester, MA: Davis Publications, Inc., 1965.

—, *Contemporary Posters: Design and Techniques.* Worcester, MA: Davis Publications, Inc., 1976.

—, *Posters: Designing, Making, Reproducing.* Worcester, MA: Davis Publications, Inc., 1964.

Painting and Collage

Ashurst, Elizabeth, *Collage.* London: Marshall Cavendish Publication, 1976.

Brommer, Gerald F., *Transparent Watercolor: Ideas and Techniques.* Worcester, MA: Davis Publications, Inc., 1973.

Lassiter, Barbara Babcock, *American Wilderness: The Hudson River School of Painting.* New York: Doubleday, 1980.

Masterfield, Maxine, *Painting the Spirit of Nature.* New York: Watson-Guptill Publications, 1984.

Porter, Albert W., *Expressive Watercolor Techniques.* Worcester, MA: Davis Publications, Inc., 1982.

Sheaks, Barclay, *Drawing and Painting the Natural Environment.* Worcester, MA: Davis Publications, Inc., 1974.

—, *Painting with Acrylics: From Start to Finish.* Worcester, MA: Davis Publications, Inc., 1972.

Szabo, Zoltan, *Creative Watercolor Techniques.* New York: Watson-Guptill Publications, 1974.

Printmaking

Andrews, Michael F., *Creative Printmaking.* Englewood Cliffs, NJ: Prentice-Hall, 1963.

Brommer, Gerald F., *Relief Printmaking.* Worcester, MA: Davis Publications, Inc., 1970.

Gorbaty, Norman, *Printmaking with a Spoon.* New York: Van Nostrand Reinhold, 1960.

Ross, John, and Clare Romano, *The Complete Relief Print.* New York: Free Press, 1974.

Stoltenberg, Donald, *Collograph Printmaking.* Worcester, MA: Davis Publications, Inc., 1975.

Sculpture

Brommer, Gerald F., *Wire Sculpture and Other Three-Dimensional Construction.* Worcester, MA: Davis Publications, Inc., 1968.

Gendusa, Sam, *Building Playground Sculpture and Homes.* Grand Rapids, MI: Masters Press, 1974.

Hall, Carolyn Vosburg, *Soft Sculpture.* Worcester, MA: Davis Publications, Inc., 1981.

Johnston, Mary G., *Paper Sculpture.* Worcester, MA: Davis Publications, Inc., 1965.

Meilach, Dona Z., *Contemporary Art with Wood: Creative Techniques and Appreciation.* New York: Crown Publishing, 1968.

—, *Soft Sculpture and Other Soft Art Forms.* New York: Crown Publishing, 1974.

Meilach, Dona Z., and Melvin Meilach, *Box Art: Assemblage and Construction.* New York: Crown Publishing, 1975.

Morris, John, *Creative Metal Sculpture: A Step-By-Step Approach.* Encino, CA: Glencoe Publishing, 1971.

Paine, J., *Looking at Sculpture.* New York: Lothrop, Lee & Shepard, 1968.

Reed, Carl, and Joseph Orze, *Art From Scrap.* Worcester, MA: Davis Publications, Inc., 1973.

Rogers, L.R., *Relief Sculpture.* New York: Oxford University Press, 1974.

Zelanski, Paul, *Shaping Space.* New York: Holt, Rinehart and Winston, 1987.

Index

Acknowledgements

Many individuals have helped in developing this book. I am particularly in debt to Davis Publications, Inc. for the able, kind and multi-faceted assistance provided by everyone. In addition, many teachers, students, artists and arts institutions have contributed ideas or images.

I would like to thank the Seven Hills Photo Club, Roger Kerkham and Barbara Caldwell for being particularly helpful in providing photographs for use in this book. I am also grateful to Leon Nigrosh, Alice Sprintzen, Bernard Toale and John Lidstone, who provided additional photographs from their books.

I am especially grateful to Chuck Wentzell and Kathi Prisco for their help in providing images of student artwork. I would also like to thank the students involved for creating such exellent examples to use.

My sincere appreciation to the following people and institutions for permission to reproduce works of art from their collections: Helen Ronan of Sandak; Anita Duquette of the Whitney Museum of Art; Tom Grischkowsky of the Museum of Modern Art; Bernice Steinbaum Gallery; Knoedler Gallery; and countless others, all of whom were essential in producing this book.

Alinari/Art Resource: p.75 (top), p.93 (bottom left); Art Resource: p.85 (middle left), p.92 (bottom), p.98 (top); London/Art Resource: p.101 (top right); Scala/Art Resource: p.52 (top), p.83, p.86 (bottom), p.87 (bottom right and top right), p.88 (top), p.90 (top left, top right and bottom left), p.91 (bottom right and bottom left), p.92 (bottom); Vanni/Art Resource: p.90 (top right).

Special thanks to the following schools for providing student artwork:

Academy of the Holy Names, Tampa, FL; Alamaniu School, Honolulu, HI; Archie R. Cole School, East Greenwich, RI; Avon School, Avon, OH; Bancroft School, Worcester, MA; Bandera School, Bandera, TX; Bellevue School, Bellevue, OH; Binictican ES; Blue Earth School, Blue Earth, MN; Bolton School, Arlington, TN; Boylan Central Catholic School, Rockford, IL; Brady School, Pepper Pike, OH; Bryan School, Omaha, NE; Cambridge School, Weston, MA; Chagrin Falls School, Chagrin Falls, OH; Clay School, Carmel, IN; Clinton School, Clinton, MS; Columbus North School, Columbus, IN; Columbus School for Girls, Columbus, OH; Commack School, Commack, NY; Craig School, Janesville, WI; Dater School, Cincinnati, OH; Delta School, Munci, IN; Dennison Fundamental School, Lakewood, CO; DuPont Manual School, Louisville, KY; Edgren School, Japan; F.A. Day School, Newtonville, MA; Fuquay-Varina School, Fuquay-Varina, NC; Gaither School, Tampa, FL; Glasgow School, Alexandria, VA; Greensboro Day School, Greensboro, NC; Guy B. Phillips School, Chapel Hill, NC; Hamilton Southeastern School; Harrison School, Great Bend, KS; Haynes Bridge School, Alpharetta, GA; Heathwood Hall, Columbia, SC; Highlands School, Fort Thomas, KY; Hillside School; Honors Art Program, Saint Louis, MO; Horning School, Waukesha, WI; J. P. Taravella School, Coral Springs, FL; Jefferson School, Oak Ridge, TN; John D. Pierce School, Drayton Plains, MI; John Sevier School, Kingsport, TN; Kinnick School; Kiser School, Greensboro, NC; Kiski School, Saltsburg, PA; Kubasaki School, Okinawa; Kuemper Catholic School, Carroll, IA; L.B. Johnson School, Melbourne, FL; Lake Zurich School, Lake Zurich, IL; Langley School, McLean, VA; Lewis and Clark School, Omaha, NE; Lexington School, Lexington, MA; Logan School, Circleville, OH; Lowville Academy, Lowville, NY; Marblehead School, Marblehead, MA; McKinley School, Honolulu, HI; Middlesex School, Darien, CT; Milton Hershey School, Hershey, PA; Nanakuli School, Waianae, HI; Old Trail School, Bath, OH; Pembroke Hill School, Kansas City, MO; Pike School, Indianapolis, IN; Pioneer Trail School, Olathe, KS; Portia School; Rabun Gap-Nacoochee School, Rabun Gap, GA; Russelville School, Russelville, KY; Sacred Heart School, Kingston, MA; Seoul American School, Seoul, Korea; Shaker Heights School, Shaker Heights, OH; Shaker School, Latham, NY; South School, Cleveland, OH; South Miami School, Miami, FL; St. Agnes Academy; St. Andrew's Episcopal School, Jackson, MS; St. Joseph School, Avon Lake, OH; St. Xavier School, Cincinnati, OH; Suitland Center for the Arts, Forestville, MD; The Baldwin School, Bryn Mawr, PA; Volney Rogers School, Youngstown, OH; Warren Abbott School, West Bloomfield, MI; Webster School, Webster, NY; West Bend School, West Bend, IN; West Bloomfield School, West Bloomfield, MI; Winthrop School, Winthrop, MA; Woonsocket School, Woonsocket, RI; Yorktown School, Yorktown, IN.